Dickens Centennial Essays

Dickens Centennial Essays

EDITED BY
ADA NISBET AND BLAKE NEVIUS

UNIVERSITY OF CALIFORNIA PRESS
Berkeley   *Los Angeles*   *London*
1971

University of California Press

Berkeley and Los Angeles, California

University of California Press, Ltd.

London, England

Copyright © 1971 by The Regents of the University of California

ISBN: 0–520–01874–5

Library of Congress Catalog Card Number: 77–142047

Printed in the United States of America

Preface

"Charles Dickens died at 6:10 a.m. on June 9, 1870, and was buried privately in Poet's Corner, Westminster Abbey, in the early morning of June 14. In his will he enjoined his friends to erect no monument in his honour, and directed his name and dates only to be inscribed in plain English letters on his tomb, adding this proud provision:—'I rest my claim to the remembrance of my country upon my printed works.' " So begins the brief London *Times* notice in 1920 on the occasion of the fiftieth anniversary of Dickens's death. As is well known, the 1920s were the nadir of that remembrance—at least among those Samuel Butler invariably referred to as "the superior people," those blasted twenty years later by Edmund Wilson as they had never ceased to be blasted by those strange-bedfellow critics Shaw and Chesterton. Of course Dickens was still being read by inferior people, among whom young men were known to have broken off their engagement to girls who misquoted him.

The notice in the *Times* says all the right things on such an occasion, but carefully avoids anything like unseemly panegyric while it zigs from mild praise of Dickens's artlessness to reservations about his "epileptic" history, and zags from comment on faults which "are colossal as those of giants mostly are" to patronizing regrets at his aiming "at national success" which led to his being read "with the sand-blindness that made 'Lady Audley's Secret' and 'East Lynne' so garishly popular." After all this facing both ways, the anonymous leader-writer nods across the channel where, it seems, admiration for Dickens was not epileptic and quotes Anatole France that "everybody in France" reads Dickens even though "in England it is the fashion to neglect the best English author." A more favorable notice in the *Athenaeum*, one of the few journals that took any notice of the event at all, after observing that "Dickens has for many years been in disrepute among the highbrows," praises him as a colossus who "created a world and peopled it," a point emphasized by Chesterton in his "Dickens

94632

50 Years After" in the *Observer*. Chesterton goes on to remon-
strate against those who berate Dickens for not creating a "real"
world and writes, "The trouble is not that his world is not like
our world; it is that our world is a great deal too like his world.
If we differ at all, so to speak, it is by being the same, only more
so."

The story of the shift in the critical estimate of Charles Dickens
in the past fifty years is as melodramatic, irrational, and comic as
any of the author's inventions; one has only to read the many
books and articles that have been published in the 1960s and
compare them with the generally feeble "defenses" of Dickens
published in the 1920s to realize that the mid-twentieth-century
rebirth of Dickens is as much a phenomenon as his leap to fame
with the publication of *Pickwick*. Although the midwives of this
rebirth have been the critics led, significantly, by the anti-academic
Edmund Wilson, those of us engaged in university teaching know
that it is the students who are making it impossible for us to repeat the old clichés. It is they who are reading Dickens with such
close attention that we have been forced to blow the dust off our
old volumes and our old views.

Chesterton was right. The twentieth century is more like
Dickens's world than the nineteenth; it is just that his ear was so
close to the Victorian heart that he heard its beat and diagnosed
its "illth" (as Ruskin called it) in its early stages. He heard its
death rattle in the chaos, exploitation, indifference, and inhu-
manity that were engulfing mankind like the mists over Chesney
Wold. It was a world that could not be encompassed in a well-
made "mimetic" novel that followed familiar patterns and rules,
any more than Shakespeare could encompass his world within the
narrow limits of the three unities. And so Dickens, like Shakespeare, broke the rules. His "baggy monsters" recorded not what
Saul Bellow has called "the penny psychology of private worlds,"
but the undisciplined complexity of worlds within worlds—and
he invented a language and a polyphonic technique that brought
visual and oral and poetic elements together in a rich thematic
montage that left his readers fascinated but often nonplussed as
to its more oblique and profound meaning.

But the university students of the sixties are not nonplussed.
Dickens is on their wave length, speaks their language, sits in the
same room with them. They share, as did Blake before him, his

distrust of Reason weaving its satanic web of spiritual destruction, as they share his distrust of the Establishment. Unlike their great-grandfathers whose uptightness about class and sex and respectability made them ill at ease with Dickens's sentimentality and comic vulgarity, these young readers are at home with both, recognizing them as evidences of Dickens's understanding of human needs and responses at their deepest level, in the face of otherwise unbearable pain. If Dickens's social philosophy is naive, so is theirs, and like him they question all systems whether proposed by politicians or academic theorists. What they admire most in Dickens is his recognition of such monstrous evils as man's (in the singular or plural sense) use of another man or woman or child for his own selfish ends and the brilliant subtlety of the dramatic, poetic, and linguistic techniques he assembles to carry such awareness into the nerve system of his readers—being tuned into such techniques through the experimental films they admire and the poetry and music they listen to. The modern students' response is instantaneous to the things Dickens is saying about his—and their— "hedgehog and porcupine" world: his attacks on the cash nexus, on man's passion for possession of things and people, on the shocking immensity of the gulf between rich and poor, on corruption at high levels and low, on the social hypocrites and the self-swindlers, and the Damoclean monster hanging over all—the bloodless and fleshless Machine. Who, reading the following passages from Dickens's letters, would not think they were written last week?

The absorption . . . in the war is to me, a melancholy thing. Every other subject of popular solicitude and sympathy goes down before it. I fear I clearly see that for years to come domestic reforms are shaken to the root; every miserable red-tapist flourishes war over the head of every protester against his humbug. [On the Crimean War]

Look at the exhausted treasury, the paralyzed government, the uncouth representatives of a free people; the desperate contests between the North and the South; the iron curb and brazen muzzle fastened upon every man who speaks his mind. [On the United States in 1842]

Or these from *Our Mutual Friend*, his last and angriest completed novel?

For when we have got things to the pass that with an enormous treasure at disposal to relieve the poor, the best of the poor detest our mercies, hide their heads from us, and shame us by starving to death in the midst of us, it is a pass impossible of prosperity, impossible of continuance.

It was a foggy day in London, and the fog was heavy and dark. Animate London, with smarting eyes and irritated lungs, was blinking, wheezing, and choking; inanimate London was a sooty spectre, divided in purpose between being visible and invisible and so being wholly neither.

"I must decline to pursue this painful discussion. It is not pleasant to my feelings. It is repugnant to my feelings. I have said that I do not admit these things. I have also said that if they do occur (not that I admit it), the fault lies with the sufferers themselves. It is not for me"— Mr. Podsnap pointed "me" forcibly, as adding by implication though it may be all very well for you—"it is not for me to impugn the workings of providence. I know better than that, I trust."

"Relevance" is a much-abused word these days, but it is the only word relevant here, as we listen to Dickens's megalosaurus slouching through the mud and mists toward a twentieth-century Bethlehem. Dickens was right to rest his claim to remembrance of his printed works. It may be that those works will speak less pertinently (let us hope so) to his bicentenary readers in 2070, but it is impossible to believe that they can ever again be as misunderstood and underestimated—even by intellectuals—as they were in 1920.

NOTE: Professor Miller's paper was delivered in part at a Dickens–Cruikshank Seminar held at the William Andrews Clark Memorial Library, University of California, Los Angeles, on May 9, 1970, and published in full by the William Andrews Clark Library which has generously given permission for its inclusion in this volume. The other eight essays appeared originally in the special Dickens issue of *Nineteenth-Century Fiction*.

ADA NISBET

Notes
on Contributors

DENIS DONOGHUE is Professor of Modern English and American Literature, University College, Dublin, and the author of *The Third Voice, Connoisseurs of Chaos, The Ordinary Universe*, and *Jonathan Swift*.

K. J. FIELDING is Saintsbury Professor of English Literature, University of Edinburgh, author of *Charles Dickens (Writers and Their Work), Charles Dickens: A Critical Introduction*, and editor of *The Speeches of Charles Dickens*. ANNE SMITH, of the University of Edinburgh, is working on the social novel.

GEORGE H. FORD is Professor of English and chairman of the department, University of Rochester, Rochester, N.Y., author of *Keats and the Victorians, Dickens and His Readers: Aspects of Novel Criticism since 1836*, and a study of D. H. Lawrence's novels, *Double Measure*, and editor (with Lauriat Lane, Jr.) of *The Dickens Critics*.

BARBARA HARDY is Professor of English Language and Literature, Birkbeck College, University of London, and author of *The Novels of George Eliot: A Study in Form, The Appropriate Form: an Essay on the Novel, Dickens: the Later Novels (Writers and Their Work)*, and *The Moral Art of Dickens*.

J. HILLIS MILLER is Professor of English, Johns Hopkins University, and author of *Charles Dickens: The World of His Novels, The Disappearance of God: Five Nineteenth Century Writers, Poets of Reality, The Form of Victorian Fiction*, and *Thomas Hardy: Distance and Desire*.

IAN MILNER is Associate Professor of English Literature, Charles University, Prague, and author of *The Structure of Values in George Eliot*.

SYLVÈRE MONOD is Professor of English Contemporary Literature and Civilization at the Sorbonne, and author of *Dickens romancier* (tr. *Dickens the Novelist), Charles Dickens*, and editor of the Dickens Centenary Number of *Études anglaises*.

MICHAEL SLATER is Lecturer, English Language and Literature, Birkbeck College, University of London, and editor of *The Dickensian* (London), *Dickens and Fame 1870–1970*, and *Dickens 1970*.

HARRY STONE is Professor of English, San Fernando Valley State College, and editor of *Charles Dickens' Uncollected Writings from "Household Words" (1830–1859)*.

Contents

The English Dickens and *Dombey and Son*

DENIS DONOGHUE

IT IS WIDELY AGREED that the account of Dickens which Edmund Wilson gave in *The Wound and the Bow* (1941) has had remarkable success with academic readers. It is hardly too much to say that we think of Dickens very largely in Wilson's terms. Santayana's Dickens in *Soliloquies in England* is an engaging figure, the novelist as man's best friend: we are to admire Dickens's "vast sympathetic participation in the daily life of mankind"; but it now seems a picture from a gone time. It would be foolish to disengage ourselves entirely from Santayana's Dickens or from Henry James's Dickens in the *Autobiography* ("the great actuality of the current imagination"), but these figures do not speak to us, it appears, with particular authority. *The Wound and the Bow* presents Dickens as a victim, a man of obsession, and for that very reason as a poet, an artist of modern fears and divisions. We are to think of his fiction in association with the novels of Dostoevsky and Kafka. We do not hope to find him in our Christmas stocking; it is no longer common to speak of his novels in association with good cheer.

The first effect of this interpretation is that Dickens is no longer received in the first instance as a voluble presence, a large arrival (in James's phrase), an entertainer, or a comedian; he is of the modern dispensation now, a tragic hero. If this means that he is taken seriously as a major artist, companion of Shakespeare, George Eliot, James, Dostoevsky, and Tolstoy, perhaps it makes a happy conclusion. But it is hard to avoid the impression that there is still something askew in our sense of Dickens's art. We seem to have run from one extreme position to another. If an instance is required, there is our failure with the comedy. We do not know what to make of it, now that we have moved the center of our interest away from the famous comic scenes. We cannot relate the

[1]

comedy, with any ease, to the main picture, we are almost in the miserable position of thinking the comedy an embarrassment. We have put aside Dickens's sentiment too; we share James's distaste for "the Little Nells, the Smikes, the Paul Dombeys." It is clear that we take Dickens not as we find him but as we improve him. To give ourselves more freedom, we detach him from the English tradition, forgetting that it was largely this tradition which made him what he became; we make him over now as a great European. I think we have gone too far. The similarities between Dickens and Kafka, for instance, are marginal, not central. For one thing Dickens is not a fabulist, he does not insist upon the claims of the imagination over and against every claim of fact or time, he is not intransigent. I would maintain that Dickens is great as Wordsworth is great, not as Kafka is great. In the relation between imagination and reality he does not think of imagination as the senior or the greater term.

Dombey and Son begins with father and infant son in the darkened room. The scene is composed around them, as if their force were already institutional and statutory. Mrs. Dombey's presence in the room is almost accidental; she is in a neglected corner of the picture. Florence is not in the picture at all. Dickens is relying upon the reader to receive these first pages with a sense of the perturbation in the given relationships. The image of this family is presented, set off against another image which is not yet given in fact: that of a properly operative family. The figure of the operative family is still merely virtual, indeed abstract; it is present merely by being denied in the particular case: that of the Dombeys. We hold the given picture poised against another which is not given. The first picture is actual: Dombey, the infant Paul, then the dying mother, and beyond these, Florence. The second image is not yet drawn; it is traditional and categorical, recalled now and present in our outraged sense of its absence. What is unnatural in the given case animates our sense of the natural in other cases; thus a writer knows what he does not need to put in: the other cases—they are there as shadows already. A few pages later Dickens defines the second image, making it actual in the Toodle family. The enforced relation between Dombey and the Toodles, a trading affair, is the first major juxtaposition in the novel; it makes public and overt what is given implicitly in the first picture, the scene in the darkened room.

Dombey is already linked with trade. "The earth was made for Dombey and Son to trade in, and the sun and moon were made to give them light" (2).[1] Trade and money: Florence was "merely a piece of base coin that couldn't be invested—a bad Boy—nothing more" (3). Dombey is "one of those close-shaved close-cut moneyed gentlemen who are glossy and crisp like new bank-notes" (17). He teaches Paul that money "can do anything" (92) or at least that "it could do all that could be done" (93). The lesson is turned to account when Paul is put in the position of giving Walter Gay the money he "begs for" at Brighton. Trade, money, pride, power—in Dombey's world a man is defined by his possessions. If Dombey's wife should die, "he would find a something gone from among his plate and furniture, and other household possessions, which was well worth the having" (5). He thinks Polly Toodle "a deserving object" (16). "You know he has bought me," Edith Granger says to her mother later in the novel: "or that he will, to-morrow. He has considered of his bargain; he has shown it to his friend; he is even rather proud of it; he thinks that it will suit him, and may be had sufficiently cheap; and he will buy to-morrow" (393–94).

On a bleak autumnal day Dombey is "as hard and cold as the weather"; his house has "black, cold rooms" (52). The Toodles, on the other hand, are a genuine family. Toodle is illiterate but sensitive, warm-hearted, and—above all—independent. When Miss Tox says that Polly in her mourning garb will be "so smart that your husband won't know you," Toodle answers briskly: "I should know her anyhows and anywheres" (19). Dombey imposes upon Polly the name "Mrs. Richards" when he hires her milk to save the infant's life. If Toodle is a good man, Dickens says, Polly has a further merit: "She was a good plain sample of a nature that is ever, in the mass, better, truer, higher, nobler, quicker to feel, and much more constant to retain, all tenderness and pity, self-denial and devotion, than the nature of men" (27). When she tells Florence a tale of death, the child speaks of "the cold ground," but Polly says, "No! The warm ground, where the ugly little seeds turn into beautiful flowers, and into grass, and corn, and I don't know what all besides" (24). Polly knows by instinct and nature

---

[1] Page references to *Dombey and Son* in my text are to the New Oxford Illus. Dickens ed. (London, 1950).

what Dombey learns only by a lifetime of error, defeat, and angelic ministry.

Dickens wants this first contrast between Dombey and the Toodles to reverberate throughout the domestic and the public worlds of the novel. The domestic contrast is the difference between two ways of life in terms of intimate relationships. The public equivalent is given as the first radical severance in the novel, the division of rich and poor. In chapter 5 of *Hard Times* Stephen Blackpool speaks to Bounderby of the "black unpassable world betwixt yo," that is, between masters and men, the owners and the "hands." In chapter 8 of *Bleak House* Esther Summerson and Ada Clare reflect upon the "iron barrier" which separates them from such people as the brickmaker whose house they enter. The subtitle of Disraeli's novel *Sybil* is *The Two Nations,* a striking phrase glossed in book 1, chapter 5, when Stephen Gerard says that "there is no community in England; there is aggregation, but aggregation under circumstances which make it rather a dissociating than a uniting principle." "Two nations," he continues, "the rich and the poor; between whom there is no intercourse and no sympathy; who are as ignorant of each other's habits, thoughts, and feelings, as if they were dwellers in different zones, or inhabitants of different planets."

It may appear that in the first juxtaposition of Dombey and Toodle Dickens is already taking sides, sponsoring the poor against the rich; but his attitude is not as simple as that account implies. Toodle is a good man, a worthy husband and parent, but he is clearly limited; he cannot be invoked to mark the range of human possibilities. His vitality is indisputable, his independence impressive, but there are crucial areas of human experience which he cannot think of encompassing. As for Dombey, hard and bleak as he is, he must not be destroyed; he is neither vicious nor deceitful. Indeed, he is a man of honor. Mention of Bounderby is enough to make the point that among Dickens's trading people there are moral distinctions to be drawn. Dombey is not Veneering. So it is not a case of Dickens as Robin Hood, robbing rich Dombey to pay poor Toodle. Dickens is not sentimental on this point, even though there are letters and speeches in which his vote for a "popular" England is clear. His account of Staggs's Gardens is the real evidence.

The Toodles live in the Gardens, and presumably they feel the

traditional English loyalty toward one's own place. Their house is
lively, vivid, full of children. Those who live in the Gardens think
of the place as "a sacred grove not to be withered by railroads"
(64). We are not meant to smile too broadly at the ironic phrase;
the Gardens are indeed a sacred grove to those who live there.
Dickens registers this English sentiment and responds to its
vitality, but he is convinced, nevertheless, that the human advantages of the new railway are worth their cost: "In short, the yet
unfinished and unopened Railroad was in progress; and, from the
very core of all this dire disorder, trailed smoothly away, upon its
mighty course of civilisation and improvement" (63). The tone in
the last phrase is not ironic. Staggs's Gardens are destroyed, but the
railway is a boon; the human cost is high but not, in the long term,
exorbitant. I put the case too bluntly; chapter 15 is entirely given
to the development of the question. To put it more bluntly still,
Dickens is letting the dead bury their dead. At one point he emits
a preservationist's lament: "Oh woe the day when 'not a rood of
English ground'—laid out in Staggs's Gardens—is secure!" (219)
But he continues:

There was no such place as Staggs's Gardens. It had vanished from the
earth. Where the old rotten summer-houses once had stood, palaces
now reared their heads, and granite columns of gigantic girth opened a
vista to the railway world beyond. The miserable waste ground, where
the refuse-matter had been heaped of yore, was swallowed up and gone;
and in its frowsy stead were tiers of warehouses, crammed with rich
goods and costly merchandise.   (217–18)

Up to this point the sentiment could be interpreted, with some
difficulty, as nostalgic on the whole, the narrator a Southern
Agrarian, an English Fugitive. But the passage proceeds:

The old by-streets now swarmed with passengers and vehicles of every
kind: the new streets that had stopped disheartened in the mud and
waggon-ruts, formed towns within themselves, originating wholesome
comforts and conveniences belonging to themselves, and never tried
nor thought of until they sprung into existence. Bridges that had led
to nothing, led to villas, gardens, churches, healthy public walks.   (218)

Dickens is coaxing his own feelings in the direction of that last
sentence. He is persuading himself that all shall be well. Persuasion
is necessary, since his devotion to the old England persists. The

entire passage and the paragraphs which follow are designed to enable him to give the new railway his blessing. He speaks of the trains as containing "the secret knowledge of great powers yet unsuspected in them, and strong purposes not yet achieved" (219). In one sentence, when he has now persuaded himself, he relates the new engines to the fundamental rhythm of human life: "To and from the heart of this great change, all day and night, throbbing currents rushed and returned incessantly like its life's blood" (218). The railway is endorsed because it brings more life into play, it enriches the country by movement and action, it brings people together. Dickens is ready to conceive of the potentialities of social change in terms of the great perennial rhythms. He is not frightened of the new even when it appears, like the railway, in the form of power. The politics which sustains this sense of change is based upon the values of plenitude, variety; it is a popular Romanticism of bustle and hubbub. So it is not a case of an "organic society" destroyed by the Industrial Revolution, Chestertonian stagecoaches banished by steam engines: the circulation of life, effected by the railway, is as natural as the circulation of the blood. If we remark that Dombey and Jo Bagstock go to Leamington by train and that the railway is a congenial part of Dombey's world, we should also note that the railway has done the Toodles no harm; on the contrary, they enjoy a better life now that Toodle is an engine driver. The train destroys only those like Mr. Carker the Manager who are already damned.

The contrast between Dombey and the Toodles is sharp, then, but it is not blatant. Propaganda is not intended; Dickens's aim is to bring the two nations together at last. But the immediate obstacles must be acknowledged. Dombey and everything he represents must be seen as intractable, consumed with pride of station. In the encounters with Edith one form of pride meets another. Dombey's pride is categorical, Edith's is consistent with her sense of herself as fatally corrupted. Edith's pride is modern in the sense that it is self-aware, ironic; Dombey's is beyond self-criticism, coinciding too neatly with his character. But before these encounters Dombey is revealed in relation to his wife and children. The crucial passage comes in chapter 3 after Mrs. Dombey's death. Dombey recalls the last scene, Florence and her mother clasped together:

Let him be absorbed as he would in the Son on whom he built such high hopes, he could not forget that closing scene. He could not forget that he had had no part in it. That, at the bottom of its clear depths of tenderness and truth, lay those two figures clasped in each other's arms, while he stood on the bank above them, looking down a mere spectator—not a sharer with them—quite shut out.   (29)

The passage should be read with an earlier reference in mind—the last sentence of chapter 1:

Thus, clinging fast to that slight spar within her arms, the mother drifted out upon the dark and unknown sea that rolls round all the world.   (10)

Dombey is safe upon the bank, he runs no risk of drowning, but his safety is bought at the cost of always remaining on the surface of things. Here and throughout the main body of the novel he is held to the surface, cut off from the depths, the sources of life and feeling. Man of the City, he is alien to the Sea. What is appalling in him is the terrible penury of the symbolism by which he lives; he has so little in that way that he must hold to what he has with insistence of will. W. H. Auden has argued that most of the troubles of the world are caused by our "poverty of symbols"; we have to entrust our entire emotional lives to the few symbols we possess. The difference between Dombey and Florence is the difference between a wretchedly penurious symbolism and a symbolism at least adequately wide and deep—*adequately* meaning that Florence's symbols are enough to sustain the range and depth of her allegiance. Dombey has paid for what he has with what he is. Florence has committed herself to a life of feeling and to a correspondingly responsive symbolism. Note, for instance, of Dombey that Dickens never gives him a childhood, a father, a mother. Moving on a bleak surface, he is denied whatever makes for density of experience. He is thin and brittle. Florence and Paul, deprived in every domestic way, inhabit the depths. In book 2, chapter 7 of *Hard Times* Dickens says of James Harthouse and Louisa: "To be sure, the better and profounder part of her character was not within his scope of perception—for in natures, as in seas, depth answers unto depth." Dombey feels toward Florence, Dickens says,

an uneasiness of an extraordinary kind. He almost felt as if she

watched and distrusted him. As if she held the clue to something secret
in his breast, of the nature of which he was hardly informed himself.
As if she had an innate knowledge of one jarring and discordant string
within him, and her very breath could sound it.   (29)

The knowledge is innate because it lives and moves far below the
ostensible surface; when we think of Florence's patience and sensi-
tivity, we find her character in her symbols. Her kinship with Paul
is a shared symbolism, a secret lore.

Paul is constantly associated with depth, the sea, and death.
Miss Blimber reports that "he is singular (what is usually termed
old-fashioned) in his character and conduct" (184) and Paul
wonders what this "old fashion" can be which others find in him.
We have assumed, with Henry James, that Paul is merely precocious and therefore obnoxious. But if we repudiate Paul we
separate ourselves from the fundamental symbolism of the novel.
The O.E.D. cites Miss Blimber's report for one meaning of old-
fashioned, that is, "having the ways of a grown-up person; hence,
precocious, intelligent, knowing." But in the novel it rather means
having the ways of a person born for death. Chapter 17 ends:

The golden ripple on the wall came back again, and nothing else
stirred in the room. The old, old fashion! The fashion that came in
with our first garments, and will last unchanged until our race has run
its course, and the wide firmament is rolled up like a scroll. The old,
old fashion—Death!
Oh thank God, all who see it, for that older fashion yet, of Immortality! And look upon us, angels of young children, with regards not
quite estranged, when the swift river bears us to the ocean!   (226)

If we choose to be embarrassed by this aspect of the novel, we must
bear the consequences. In fact Paul cannot be received on any
terms but his own. His life is a free-flowing current rushing to the
sea. "Why, will it never stop, Floy," he asks; "it is bearing me away,
I think" (222). He sees a boat at sea and, in vision, his mother
shining upon the water.

The symbolism is perennial. Emily Dickinson has a poem which
begins: "My River runs to thee—/Blue Sea! Wilt welcome me?
(No. 162). Paul asks Florence: "The sea, Floy, what is it that it
keeps on saying?" (109) Florence does not gloss the waves; like old
Glubb she probably "knows a great deal about it" (152) but there
are no translations for these sounds. Waves say whatever the
listener is capable of hearing. Dr. Blimber hears them saying,

"Gentlemen, we will now resume our studies"; to Mr. Toots they speak of a time when he was brighter; to Florence they recite Paul's story and finally the grand story of love, "eternal and illimitable, not bounded by the confines of this world, or by the end of time, but ranging still, beyond the sea, beyond the sky, to the invisible country far away!" (811) To Paul the waves speak of death, "the old, old fashion," and then of immortality, but they also rehearse the movements of life, the succession of days and nights, the rhythm of the seasons, the mystery, the secret doctrine of things. His own feeling merges in the feeling of the sea. In "The Masthead" chapter of *Moby-Dick* Ishmael thinks of a young, absent-minded Platonist manning the masthead, lulled "by the blending cadence of waves with thoughts" until, losing his identity, he "takes the mystic ocean at his feet for the visible image of that deep, blue, bottomless soul, pervading mankind and nature." Paul Dombey, a child Platonist, is old fashioned in this sense too; the new fashion is temporal, empiricist, and willful. So while Paul is associated with currents, rivers, seas, and death, his father is associated with surface and ice: "he might have been hung up for sale at a Russian fair as a specimen of a frozen gentleman" (57). One glance from her father is enough to freeze Florence's tears (30). When Captain Cuttle shakes Dombey's hand, "at this touch of warm feeling and cold iron, Mr. Dombey shivered all over" (134).

Indeed the action of the book may be stated in these terms. The novel tells how Dombey's pride and his will are at last dissolved by the flow of Florence's feeling. At the end "the white-haired gentleman" playing with his two grandchildren loves to see them "free and stirring" (878). More generally I would argue that this pattern of action is central in Dickens's fiction. His concern is to bring the two nations together by making them share certain perennial feelings and sentiments. Feeling could be shared, he believed, so fully that the sharing would dissolve the artificial barriers of class, money, and prejudice.[2] He was not alone in this conviction.

---

[2] I use the word "feeling" in this essay to refer to "the primary feelings," in Alfred North Whitehead's phrase, except that I emphasize the sense in which the word is a verbal noun, a term of action, rather than a noun. In part 3 of his *Process and Reality: An Essay in Cosmology* (Cambridge, 1929), Whitehead deals with the Theory of Prehensions, comprising the Theory of Feelings, the Primary Feelings, the Transmission of Feelings, Propositions and Feelings, and the Higher Phases of Experience. "A feeling," he says, "is the appropriation of some elements in the universe to be components in the real internal constitution of its subject. The elements are the initial data; they are what the feeling feels.... The essential novelty of a feeling attaches to its subjective form. The initial data,

The fifth chapter of John Stuart Mill's *Autobiography* deals with a crisis in his "mental history." The crisis began in the autumn of 1826 when Mill felt that, as he wrote, "my love of mankind, and of excellence for its own sake, had worn itself out." This sense of attrition was related to his fear that "the habit of analysis has a tendency to wear away the feelings." The crisis, he says, left him in the condition which Coleridge describes in his "Dejection" ode. The first relief came when he was reading that passage in Marmontel's *Memoires* where, after his father's death, the young boy assures his family that he will be everything to them, that he will "supply the place of all that they had lost." Mill's response to this passage was so strong that it released the flow of feeling which in the crisis had been frozen. From that time, he says, "I gave its proper place, among the prime necessities of human well-being, to the internal culture of the individual." He ceased "to attach almost exclusive importance to the ordering of outward circumstances, and the training of the human being for speculation and for action." The cultivation of the feelings became, he reports, "one of the cardinal points in my ethical and philosophical creed." Mill then goes on to say that his reading of Wordsworth's miscellaneous poems, in the two-volume edition of 1815, proved a crucial event in the development of his creed:

---

and even the nexus which is the objective datum, may have served other feelings with other subjects. But the subjective form is the immediate novelty; it is how *that* subject is feeling that objective datum" (327).

Whitehead then distinguishes "three primary types of feeling which enter into the formation of all the more complex feelings.... (i) that of simple physical feelings (ii), that of conceptual feelings, and (iii) that of transmuted feelings." He continues: "In a simple physical feeling, the initial datum is a single actual entity; in a conceptual feeling, the objective datum is an eternal object; in a transmuted feeling, the objective datum is a nexus of actual entities. Simple physical feelings and transmuted feelings make up the class of physical feelings. In none of these feelings, taken in their original purity devoid of accretions from later integrations, does the subjective form involve consciousness. Although in a propositional feeling the subjective form may involve judgment, this element in the subjective form is not necessarily present" (328).

To come to Dickens: the "primary feelings" are especially relevant to community and communication because, in Whitehead's terms, the "elements" are universal and universally available, and the process of appropriation is the same in kind for everyone, though different in degree. When people are divided by the machinery of society, the differences may be reduced by emphasizing the "natural" affinities between one man and another. Thus Dickens treats divisions as artificial, affinities as fundamental. In a full account of the matter it would be instructive to refer to two major works which throw strong if indirect light upon the politics of Dickens's fiction: Susanne K. Langer's *Mind: An Essay on Human Feeling* (Baltimore, 1967) and Otto Gierke's *Natural Law and the Theory of Society 1500–1800* (Boston, 1957).

What made Wordsworth's poems a medicine for my state of mind, was that they expressed, not mere outward beauty, but states of feeling, and of thought coloured by feeling, under the excitement of beauty. They seemed to be the very culture of the feelings, which I was in quest of. In them I seemed to draw from a source of inward joy, of sympathetic and imaginative pleasure, which could be shared in by all human beings; which had no connexion with struggle or imperfection, but would be made richer by every improvement in the physical or social condition of mankind.

It is a celebrated moment in the history of nineteenth-century sensibility. I place it now beside another occasion, hardly less celebrated and equally pertinent to the present consideration of Dickens. Wordsworth is writing in the preface to the second edition of *Lyrical Ballads:*

If the labours of Men of science should ever create any material revolution, direct or indirect, in our condition, and in the impressions which we habitually receive, the Poet will sleep then no more than at present; he will be ready to follow the steps of the Man of science, not only in those general indirect effects, but he will be at his side, carrying sensation into the midst of the objects of the science itself.

The two passages are congenial. Together they propose a function for poetry which is peculiarly relevant to the nature of nineteenth-century society. Mill and Wordsworth, starting from different positions, reach the same conclusion: that the principal function of literature in an apparently intractable age is the cultivation of the feelings. The pleasure of this cultivation, the "inward joy" available from that source, could be "shared in by all human beings." The artist's role in a new Age of Science rests upon this fact. I would maintain that this is essentially the role which Dickens proposes to himself, especially in his later novels. The more recalcitrant the conditions, the more urgent the medicine. Two nations, separated more rigidly than ever before, might still be brought together by sharing feelings common to all.

The continuity between *Lyrical Ballads* and Dickens's novels is based upon this conviction that the flow of feeling may still dissolve the frozen places of life. Feeling is a form of energy at once natural and occult; issuing from "the buried life," it transforms the daily rote of surface, like water in Auden's poem "In Praise of Limestone." Feeling, indeed, is a kind of religion, with one advantage in that comparison: that it is shared, in some measure, by everyone. There is never enough feeling to satisfy Dickens or to melt, with ease, a hard world; like Christianity feeling often lies inert and terrified before its enemies. But it may be encouraged and provoked. Dickens and Wordsworth knew in their different ways and degrees that nineteenth-century society insists upon its industrial triumph and that it must be made to respect the old fashions, it must become sensitive to the human cost of its success; otherwise it would lose its soul. With whatever differences, Dickens and Wordsworth put their trust in feeling, as Henry Adams staked all, with less confidence, upon intelligence. Dickens and Wordsworth were luckier than Adams, because they had merely to provoke their society to increase and release and share the feelings it already had—free, unearned, and as yet unfulfilled. Adams had to demand that his society live by novelty, producing an active, governing intelligence where it had only promised to produce force and power. Dickens and Wordsworth asked society to remember its buried life and live for continuity and plenitude. Adams asked society to admit for its own salvation a force of sentiment which he called, in chapter 25 of the *Education*, the Virgin. "Symbol or energy," he writes, "the Virgin had acted as the greatest force the Western world ever felt, and had drawn man's activities to herself more strongly than any other power, natural or supernatural, had ever done. . . ."

In such a program the first requirement was to curb the will. The will must be relaxed, assuaged. There is a relevant passage in Huysmans's *À Rebours* where Des Esseintes, at the Bodega, orders a glass of amontillado. A mental traveler, he has been thinking of London as represented in Dickens's novels, imagining various characters from *David Copperfield, Martin Chuzzlewit, Bleak House,* and *Little Dorrit.* But after living for a while in his London of the imagination, he looks at the glass of sherry, and he recalls Poe's story of the cask of amontillado. Dickens's novels now seem to him merely lenient and consoling by comparison with Poe's stories, abrasive and desperate. En route to Decadence, Des Esseintes abandons Dickens at this point, because Dickens proposes, at least as a final possibility, a continuous movement of feeling among his characters. The characters are isolated at the start because that is their hard condition, but some of them, at least, are reconciled at the end. Poe's characters are walled in dungeons, utterly dependent upon the violence of their wills;

there is no question of mutual feeling or community. Des Esseintes, heading toward Baudelaire, Mallarmé, and Verlaine, finds Dickens first a consolation, then an amusement, but finally a scandal. To Dickens feeling can be questioned but cannot be doubted; its eloquence takes the form of action rather than knowledge, and like the sound of the waves it cannot be construed. Life is not naturally or necessarily, he asserts, a function of the predatory will. In chapter 47 of *Dombey and Son* he writes:

Not the less bright and blest would that day be for rousing some who never have looked out upon the world of human life around them, to a knowledge of their own relation to it, and for making them acquainted with a perversion of nature in their own contracted sympathies and estimates. (648)

This is his characteristic note; the later novels strive to reach conclusions in which it is heard.

But the "true voice of feeling" must be defined by distinguishing it from its false appearances. This is the purpose served by Mrs. Skewton in *Dombey and Son:* to represent in one character everything spurious which parades itself as "the language of the Heart." "I want Nature everywhere," she says (289). "With all those yearnings, and gushings, and impulsive throbbings that we have implanted in our souls, and which are so very charming, why are we not more natural?" she asks Dombey, as if he knew or she cared (293). Her praise of the past humiliates it; of Queen Bess she exclaims, "Dear creature! She was all Heart!" (387) In *Little Dorrit* Mrs. Merdle is put to the same use, and Mr. Pecksniff in *Martin Chuzzlewit*. "I am very impressible myself, by nature," Mrs. Merdle says in book 1, chapter 20, the great scene with the parrot. Dickens is anticipating criticism, making the obvious case first against himself. An exponent of true feeling must protect his truth by exposing falsity; otherwise his enemies are likely to undertake the task on their own terms. In Mrs. Skewton, Dickens takes the risk of showing his own values dangerously compromised, but temporarily and as a challenge, to deny his enemies the pleasure of casting the first stone. After Mrs. Skewton, no reader could accuse Dickens of being a slave to the language of delicacy. He is now free to represent the form of genuine feeling and its practical success in the world.

There is, as one example among many, Harriet Carker's success

with Alice Brown. At the end, after years of bitterness, Alice is
assuaged. In the last scene Harriet is associated with Christ as she
reads to the dying Alice from the New Testament, "the blessed
history, in which the blind lame palsied beggar, the criminal, the
woman stained with shame, the shunned of all our dainty clay, has
each a portion, that no human pride, indifference, or sophistry,
through all the ages that this world shall last, can take away"
(826). There is also Florence's influence upon Edith, short of
practical success. Chapter 30 describes again the nature of Edith's
pride, and then asks: "Was this the woman whom Florence— an
innocent girl, strong only in her earnestness and simple truth—
could so impress and quell, that by her side she was another creature, with her tempest of passion hushed, and her very pride itself
subdued?" (423) In contrast, Dombey fails to "correct and reduce"
Edith; she cannot be subdued by force of will (646).

It is a common pattern in Dickens's novels, the simple, innocent
girl who melts stern hearts; we cannot disown it. Florence's effect
upon Edith is a minor version of the major success which she at
last gains with Dombey. Constantly described as an angel, she becomes Dombey's Guardian Angel when she prevents him from
killing himself. She melts his frozen heart. Taine says that Dombey becomes the best of fathers and spoils a fine novel, but this is
unjust; Dombey cannot be separated from the angel who ministers
to him or from the pattern of reconciliation which he embodies. It
is hardly a question of character at all; it is the grand design of the
book, already anticipated, in miniature, by several episodes before
the end. The point to make is that Dickens is evoking certain
sensations, associations, and states of feeling which move at a level
far below the distinctions of society and class. The continuity of
these feelings marks for him the essentially human element. Together in feeling, people may freely differ in opinion; it matters
little. Everything beyond feeling is a later gloss upon the old text,
the old fashion.

That Dickens was deeply disturbed by the venom of class and
caste which embittered English society is clear in his later novels,
especially in *Our Mutual Friend*, his most elaborate engagement
with a question of class. But his rhetoric implies that England may
still make a genuinely popular success of itself by retaining direct
contact with its sources in feeling. Like Wordsworth's ballads,
Dickens's novels hope to save the harsh world by stirring the

fundamental rhythms of life; acting upon a realm of sentiment far below the divisions of telegrams and anger, Marshalsea Prisons, class, money, and Circumlocution Offices. Edmund Wilson has argued that in the later novels Dickens changes his political stance; the novelist now hopes that, as Wilson says, "the declassed representatives of the old professional upper classes may unite with the proletariat against the commercial middle class." But the essential movement of feeling on Dickens's part is beneath class altogether; he now wants to ground his appeal upon those sentiments and sensations which are common to all men regardless of class. The point about Dombey is that he takes so long to recognize his humanity. Like Wordsworth, Dickens asserts the essential basis of human life in terms of being and nature; in that context distinctions of class become secondary matters. Hopefully the two nations and all classes meet in the community of these feelings. In the last chapter of *Dombey and Son*, Dombey, old Sol, Captain Cuttle, and Toots join in drinking the last bottle of old Madeira, toasting Walter and Florence. In the City class distinctions persist, but in Sol's house the classes meet in good will. Classes persist, Dickens seems to say, but they do not matter, they do not touch the depths of humanity. He does not hope to rid England of class but to make the divisions of class as narrow as possible. People are not required to deny their "natural" class or to move above it, especially if the effort results, as it generally does, in the loss of natural feeling. Walter's role in *Dombey and Son* is important in this regard. "Awfully serene and still" (508) now that his quality has been proved by experience, he is deputed to redeem the City, setting it moving again in a new spirit. Another firm of Dombey and Son is promised, rising "triumphant," but it will enjoy the triumph while retaining a sense of the human values within its care. Dickens is not offering an Arcadian pastoral, a return to cows instead of capital, bowers instead of dustheaps. He has no quarrel with railways or the City so long as they keep in mind the community they serve.

This marks the continuity between Dickens's novels, early and late, despite their obvious differences. The two Scrooges are not totally apart. The aim of Dickens's fiction applies to the entire body of his work: to bring people together by making them share those feelings which, except by denying their humanity, they cannot fail to possess. The same motive relates many things in the fiction: the good cheer represented in *Pickwick Papers* by the

Christmas party at Manor Farm; Dickens's praise of wonder and
fancy, banished by Gradgrind in chapter 8 of *Hard Times;* the
selfless vitality of Mr. Sleary's circus-folk; the lenient image at
the end of *Dombey and Son.* For the later novels one moment is
especially significant. In *Our Mutual Friend* Eugene Wrayburn
has married Lizzie Hexam; the marriage is scandalous to Society.
The last chapter is called "The Voice of Society," the question
being: who really speaks on such a matter with the voice of
Society? The chapter recites several voices, each in a note of
predictable hauteur. But Twemlow defends the marriage: "If this
gentleman's feeling of gratitude, of respect, of admiration, and
affection," he says, "induced him to marry this lady, . . . I think he
is the greater gentleman for the action, and makes her the greater
lady." "I beg to say," he continues, "that when I use the word
gentleman, I use it in the sense in which the degree may be at-
tained by any man." This moment is important in Dickens because
it advances the concept of a gentleman as a moral term rather than
a term of class. The morality can only be a matter of feeling.
Toodle, for instance, is a gentleman by Twemlow's definition. So is
Dombey, after Florence's ministry.

My account may suggest, however, that Dickens's design upon us
is all too clear, too palpable, that his novels, if my view holds,
strive to complete themselves as fables and parables. The question
then arises: if so, what relation persists between the grand design
and the novelist's sense of circumstance, his recognition of the
unpredictable fact which threatens design and embarrasses parable? It has often been held that the books are full of irrelevant life,
incidents which have nothing to explain their presence but the
fact that Dickens's plenary imagination brought them forth. But
the chief characteristic of the later novels is the remarkable balance
which they maintain between these rival considerations. These
novels are still rich in circumstance, but the circumstance always
admits the pressure of a governing design. Admittedly if the design
is meant to define the social function of feeling, it is capacious
enough for almost any circumstance. But Dickens's artistic scruple
is evident. Our impression persists that in these novels there is a
splendid "wooing both ways" between incident and design. Incidents are rarely intimidated by the design; the relation is not

harsh. On the contrary incidents have an air of free development, short of total freedom.

To mention one example: Some readers have been scandalized by the fact that Florence continues to love her monstrous father. This can only be explained, they maintain, by the insistence of the fable. According to the Orphic design of the book, it is obviously necessary that Florence should love her father if she is to win him over at the end. Angels do not give up easily. Furthermore it may be urged that Florence loves her father, rigid and proud as he is, because it is natural for her to do so. In this she is indeed natural except that she is an extraordinary case of the natural. But in fact Florence's feeling is not so monolithic as those readers say. There are gradations. After Dombey strikes her, she continues to love him but not to expect anything from that love; it makes a difference. Even before that incident there are gradations, notably in a remarkable passage in chapter 47 where Dickens describes how the picture of Dombey, to Florence's still loving eyes, has become abstract, receding from the present tense: "Florence loved him still, but, by degrees, had come to love him rather as some dear one who had been, or who might have been, than as the hard reality before her eyes" (649). The paragraph which follows that sentence is one of the finest things in the book. Dickens's art, which has so often been supposed to deal in rough and ready effects, is here a matter of precise and delicate adjustment as Dombey's presence to Florence becomes dim and virtual. The adjustment is made by the grammatical forms which disengage the image of Dombey from the present tense until it recedes through the past to become, like the grammatical mood itself, subjunctive.

The point is that Dickens's sense of his large design is indeed imposing limits upon his freedom; his zest, his delight in gusto and proliferation, are curbed. But the restriction brings reward, for within these self-imposed limits he gains a new power of adjustment and nuance. As a novelist he assents to limitation; he does not chafe under restriction now. In *Little Dorrit,* for instance, the persuasions of design are strongly operative when the house falls upon Blandois, killing him; when Mrs. Clennam confesses her crime to Amy; when Amy marries Arthur. These events are rhetorically congenial, and the design requires them. But while a suggestion of parable hovers about Blandois's death, as about Carker's death in *Dombey and Son,* it does not inhibit Dickens's sense of circumstance too severely. One recalls the great moment when Mrs. Clennam says, "Flintwinch, it is closing in." Dickens is like a man who, believing in Destiny, chooses to call it Providence. The given world is still his oyster, but he lives in it now with a sense of providential will. He strives to accommodate himself to the will of Providence as to a structure of values independent of his consciousness. He assents to the structure because he has not made it; he has merely sensed its presence. Feeling is common to circumstance and to the grand design; palpable in the content of circumstance, it may be sensed in the design too. So Dickens reconciles man's individual feeling to a providential pattern in which the feeling suffers as little restriction as possible and gains in the end what it lacked of form and meaning. So too the narrator in *Dombey and Son* speaks as he does, not because he pretends to be God but because he assents to Providence and offers himself as its witness. Design or Form is the artistic correlative of Providence. Dickens trusts in the community of feeling because it is at once particular and general; there can be nothing more intimate than feeling and at the same time nothing more universal. The design is compounded of feeling; feeling aspires to the success of design. The art of Dickens's later novels is based upon his sense of the continuity of earth and sky, land and sea, fact and type. The "popular" nature of his art depends upon this sense.

If so much depends upon feeling, Florence's burden is enormous. She must feel nearly everything, and Dickens is bound to place her in a position to do so. She is present when her mother dies, when Paul dies, when her father comes home with a new wife, when contention arises between Dombey and Edith, when Walter comes back, when Dombey tries to kill himself, and so forth. She must feel everything whether she expresses what she feels or not. Like Fanny in *Mansfield Park* she must contain within herself what other characters release in action and words. In the preface to *What Maisie Knew* James speaks of Maisie as "really keeping the torch of virtue alive in an air tending infinitely to smother it; really in short making confusion worse confounded by drawing some stray fragrance of an ideal across the scent of selfishness, by sowing on barren strands, through the mere fact of presence, the seed of the moral life." James's novel proves, if proof is demanded, what can be done by the mere fact of presence. In *Dombey and Son*

Florence registers everything by holding it within herself. Nothing is ever lost or forgotten. Florence is given to us not as a remarkable "vessel of consciousness" but as someone who lives in the depths. She feels and fears and contains what Dombey merely confronts as obstacles on the surface.

In chapter 35, for instance, Dombey and his wife have returned from their honeymoon. Edith has told Florence that she cannot teach her how to "become dearer to Papa." That night Florence dreams of Paul, her father, Walter, and Edith: "In every vision, Edith came and went, sometimes to her joy, sometimes to her sorrow, until they were alone on the brink of a dark grave, and Edith pointing down, she looked and saw—what!— another Edith lying at the bottom" (508). Edith has admonished Florence "never seek to find in me what is not there," meaning presumably her better self, already corrupted and destroyed. Like Dombey in an earlier instance of the same figure, Edith is standing upon the brink looking at the self she has killed. The woman on the brink is the Edith who defeats Dombey by running off with Carker, whom she detests. The same figure is invoked on several occasions in the novel and especially when Edith sees in the depths of her hatred for Carker "the dark retaliation" she is about to practice upon Dombey. Florence feels this too and is confirmed in fear when she sees Carker coming from Edith's room.

It may be argued that poor Florence is simply incapable of sustaining these burdens. But we should not forget the narrator, who feels so strongly in her behalf that the effect is almost as if she were more than herself. The narrator goes before her, preparing her way, removing obstacles; what Florence feels is echoed and amplified in his feelings. He "sets the scene" for her. In chapter 47, for instance, he arranges the action as a miniature drama in five acts, but he also introduces the play, prepares our minds to receive it. In the first paragraphs he comes before us as an orator, a preacher, but especially as an impresario. "Oh for a good spirit who would take the house-tops off, with a more potent and benignant hand than the lame demon in the tale,[3] and show a

---

[3] The lame demon is Asmodeus in Le Sage's *Le Diable Boiteux*, translated as *Asmodeus, or The Devil upon Two Sticks*. In chapter 3 and thereafter Asmodeus, for Signor Leandro's edification and enlightenment, lifts the housetops and reveals the inhabitants, the springs of their actions, and their secret thoughts (I am indebted to Harry Stone for this ascription; see his *Charles Dickens' Uncollected Writings from "Household Words": 1850–1859*, 2 vols. [Bloomington, 1968], 2: 488, n. 11).

Christian people what dark shapes issue from amidst their homes, to swell the retinue of the Destroying Angel as he moves forth among them!" (648) And lo the narrator proceeds to take the Dombey house-top off, revealing the dark shapes.... And since the story has a moral, the impresario gives it at once: if Christians knew the truth, they would "then apply themselves, like creatures of one common origin, owing one duty to the Father of one family, and tending to one common end, to make the world a better place!" (648) Now the house-top is lifted. Act 1: Edith and Florence. "Forgive me," Edith says, "for having ever darkened your dark home—I am a shadow on it, I know well—and let us never speak of this again" (651). Act 2: at the dinner table, Dombey, Edith, Florence, and Carker. This act works up to a climax when Edith, throwing her jewels to the ground, leaves the room, but the climax is prefigured by the detail of the quarrel between Edith and Dombey. The quarrel is strong stuff, enlivened by the shift from direct speech to oblique speech when the participants address each other through the sinister agent, Carker; enlivened too by our sense of Florence's presence, silent and distraught, until Dombey orders her to leave the room. Act 3: Florence sees Carker on the staircase. Act 4: Florence, meeting Edith on the stairs, is "transfixed before the haggard face and staring eyes," as Edith shrieks, "Keep away! Let me go by!" (662) Act 5: Edith has run off with Carker. Dombey strikes Florence, who rushes out of the house.

I have described this chapter as if it were a Victorian melodrama mainly to concede that the basis of Dickens's art is, as many readers have said, theatrical. Concession may go further. George Eliot complained that Dickens always stopped at the surface of things, never revealed the hidden self in his characters. Henry James agreed with her, compounding the charge by equating the hidden self with intelligence and intelligence with "nature." "Where in these pages," James asked in his review of *Our Mutual Friend*, "are the depositaries of that intelligence without which the movement of life would cease? Who represents nature?" [4] Now it is obvious that Dickens did not think of intelligence as having the place in life which James ascribed to it. He does not show his characters putting much trust in ratiocination. His art is most congenially employed when a character is revealed by action, gesture, idiosyncrasy. He seldom presents a character by showing him

---

[4] *The Nation* I (21 Dec. 1865):787 (unsigned review).

in relation to himself. His characters are not introspective by nature, though they may occasionally be forced to look within by
circumstance. Normally a character in Dickens is disclosed in relation to other characters, or in relation to his setting, or in relation
to certain figures and images which surround him. Normally too
the characters depend for their lucidity upon the way in which
the narrator presents them, the degree of light and shade which
he allows them. They need not do everything for themselves. We
are dealing, it is apparent, with a kind of fiction which delights in
conditions and conventions; the impresario loves to be seen at
work. Robert Garis has described this aspect of Dickens in *The
Dickens Theatre*. The only point I would make is that Dickens's
theater, like most theaters, is animated by feeling rather than by
intelligence. The most "intelligent" character in *Dombey and
Son* is the narrator in the sense that he knows precisely what he is
doing: deploying and controlling the figures, relationships, motifs.
But Dickens does not believe that intelligence is the principle
"without which the movement of life would cease." It would not
cease, unless it were also deprived of feeling. In chapter 47 none
of the characters says anything remarkable; there is very little
evidence of intelligence as the moving principle of life. Except
for Florence these dark shapes are contorted in one degree or
another; those are doomed who are congealed in their characters. But Florence escapes from the ruined house and "in the wild-
ness of her sorrow" seeks old Sol's Midshipman, the only place
which, she knows by instinct, will welcome her. So the principle
of feeling is preserved—by Florence, Captain Cuttle, Mr. Toots,
not least by Diogenes. All that Dickens asks of Florence is that in
behalf of England she keep the lines of feeling open—silently,
if silence is congenial to her circumstance.

Hard Times and the Factory Controversy

Dickens vs. Harriet Martineau

K. J. FIELDING and ANNE SMITH

HARD TIMES is possibly now accepted as the most central of Dickens's works to an understanding of his attitude to society. It has been studied, for example, in relation to his beliefs about education, the Preston strike, disputes between capital and labor, and his general views on the quality of nineteenth-century urban industrial civilization. Yet one obvious gap remains in investigations about the beliefs and experience that lay behind the creation of the novel: his attitude to the workers themselves, the lives they led, and the conditions they worked in. In general, critics are so dismayed by the saintly character of the power loom weaver, Stephen Blackpool, that they do their best to ignore this part of the novel. Whether in Dickens's day or ours, they (like John Ruskin) think of Stephen as "a dramatic perfection" rather than "an honest workman," or (like George Orwell) dismiss him as "merely pathetic," or (like Harold Perkin) assume that in *Household Words* (in which *Hard Times* appeared) Dickens simply purveys "edifying tales, and cautionary advice against strikes." [1]

This is quite true about Stephen Blackpool though much too simple a generalization about *Household Words*. But if we are to consider the novel at all seriously as a study of the "times," it needs some explanation, if not defense, for the way in which parts of it are so vehemently simplified. This is too large a prob-

[1] Ruskin, *"Unto This Last": Four Essays on the First Principles of Political Economy* (London, 1862), p. 14; Orwell, "Charles Dickens," in *The Collected Essays, Journalism, and Letters of George Orwell*, 4 vols. (London, 1968), 1:426; Perkin, *The Origins of Modern English Society: 1780–1880* (Toronto, 1969), p. 307.

lem for the present essay. It includes the question of Dickens's changing attitude to changing industrialism, a question which needs a fuller examination if it is to be understood. But within this last question lies another which brings us down to the simpler detail of the rights and wrongs of a dispute in which he was involved when he was writing *Hard Times*. The dispute had a direct effect on the novel, and it may even have helped to form and alter Dickens's opinion about the subject he had taken up. It also leads one to a better understanding of Dickens's attitudes to the new world of large-scale industry. This is, perhaps, a subject within our scope.

As far as Dickens's own response to the wonders of the industrial revolution goes, there is no doubt that he welcomed them at the beginning of the 1850s. Dickens had a pride in progress even though he opposed any mechanization of the spirit. It is no doubt true, as Herbert L. Sussman says, that "although he saw the factories of England and America at first hand, his imagination never thrilled to mechanized manufacturing as it did to the railway." [2] All the same, when he began *Household Words* he made some striking affirmations in "A Preliminary Word" in the first number (30 March 1850). He welcomes the "stirring world around us"; he expresses faith in the "progress of mankind" and gratitude for "the privilege of living in this summer-dawn of time"; he reminds his readers that the "mightier inventions of this age are not all material"; and he feels that "all the voices *we* hear, cry Go on!" Later, in the third volume in an article written jointly with R. H. Horne, "The Great Exhibition and the Little One," the two countries which showed respectively "the greatest degree of progress and the least," England and China, are compared, and Dickens's optimism is even more explicit:

That we are moving in a right direction towards some superior condition of society—politically, morally, intellectually, and religiously— that newly turned-up furrows of the earth are being sown with larger, nobler, and more healthy seed than the earth has ever yet received, we humbly yet proudly, and with heartfelt joy that partakes of solemnity, do fully recognise as a great fact.[3]

[2] *Victorians and the Machine* (Cambridge, Mass., 1968), p. 61

[3] *Household Words* (hereafter *HW*) 3 (12 July 1851):356, comparing the Great Exhibition with one in the Chinese Gallery, Hyde Park Place; cf. Dickens's "The Chinese Junk," *Examiner*, 24 June 1848, which takes the same view.

With *Bleak House* (1852–53) it is reasonable to read the novel as showing that, as between the old order and the new, Dickens's sympathies are with the Ironmaster. Yet in *Hard Times,* barely a year later, we can see him revealing a much greater awareness of what this new order was to cost. It is true that the novels are set in different times, with the industrialist in each of them shown in a different social and fictional context. Yet the change may well be thought to suggest that Dickens's position had shifted: that the author of *Hard Times* apparently holds different beliefs and that as far as these went he is hardly the same man as the author of "A Preliminary Word" in 1850.

Another way in which we can see this change illustrated is in Dickens's relations with Harriet Martineau as a contributor to *Household Words.* Miss Martineau, then in her late forties, was a forceful journalist whom Dickens had been glad to enlist when the periodical was founded. She had a ready pen, wrote clearly, and even more evidently than Dickens she was a firm believer in progress. In 1855 she wrote in her *Autobiography:*

It appears to me now that, while I see much more of human difficulty from ignorance, and from the slow working (as we weak and transitory beings consider it) of the law of Progress, I discern the working of that great law with far more clearness, and therefore with a far stronger confidence, than I ever did before.[4]

In her obituary in the *Daily News* (29 June 1879), which she wrote herself, she echoes this earlier statement of faith: "She saw the human race, as she believed, advancing under the law of progress" (*Autobiography,* 3:470). But in spite of this shared belief, the temporary and uneasy alliance (for five years) between Dickens and Harriet Martineau came to be sharply broken, and the main reason for the disruption appears to have been their disagreements arising from the publication of *Hard Times* and certain articles associated with it. For the novel, as Harriet Martineau writes, "startled" her (2:419).

Her own account of the break is given in her *Autobiography,* where she explains that it was finally caused by what she saw as Dickens's prejudice against Roman Catholics. Yet, as she says, for a long while before this she had been "uneasy about the way

---

[4] *Harriet Martineau's Autobiography with Memorials by Maria Weston Chapman,* 3 vols. (London, 1877), 2:447; further references are in our text by volume and page numbers.

'Household Words' was going on" (2:418). She ascribes her growing concern to three causes: Dickens's attitude to the social role
of women, allegedly expressed in a number of articles; his account of the Preston Strike;[5] and his treatment of the "Factory
and Wages controversy" in *Hard Times*. Writing in the *Autobiography,* she declares that she thought the proprietors of *Household Words* "grievously inadequate to their function, philosophi-
cally and morally" (2:418). She is more specific in an earlier
comment in the same work in which she says that *Hard Times*
shows Dickens's "vigorous erroneousness about matters of science"
in connection with "the controversies of employers" (2:378). She
also attacks him for showing "irresponsible sentimentality": "Nobody wants to make Mr. Dickens a Political Economist; but there
are many who wish that he would abstain from a set of difficult
subjects, on which all true sentiment must be underlain by a sort
of knowledge which he has not" (2:378).

What is rather strange is that in her account of their differences,
Harriet Martineau, the exact and high-principled economist, is
almost inconceivably irresponsible or forgetful about matters of
fact. For example, she says in the *Autobiography:*

In the autumn of 1849, my misgivings first became serious. Mr. Wills
[subeditor of *Household Words*] proposed my doing some articles on
the Employments of Women, (especially in connexion with the Schools
of Design and branches of Fine-Art manufacture;) and was quite unable to see that every contribution of the kind was necessarily excluded
by Mr. Dickens's prior articles on behalf of his view of Woman's position; articles in which he ignored the fact that nineteen-twentieths of
the women of England earn their bread, and in which he prescribes
the function of Women; viz., to dress well and look pretty, as an
adornment to the homes of men. I was startled by this; and at the
same time, and for many weeks after, by Mr. Dickens's treatment in
his Magazine of the Preston Strike, then existing, and of the Factory
and Wages controversy, in his tale of "Hard Times." (2:419)

She goes on to say that a "more serious incident still occurred in
the same autumn" and then tells how a story she had written for
a Christmas number was rejected because it gave a favorable view

---

[5] "On Strike," *HW* 8 (11 Feb. 1854):553–59; see also James Lowe's "Locked Out,"
HW 8 (10 Dec. 1853):345–48. All articles were published anonymously; identification is from a typed copy of the *HW* Contributors' Book, the original of which
is now in the Princeton Univ. Library. Harriet Martineau did not know which articles
were by Dickens and which by other contributors. For "the social role of women"
see n. 6.

of the Roman Catholic faith. Later in this passage she writes that
the time of this occurrence was "at the end of 1853" (2:421), as it
was.

Now all this is rather astonishing. It is hard to accept that a
regular journalist and the author of *The Thirty Years Peace* could
not remember the year when *Household Words* began (March
1850). It is odd that she should say that William Henry Wills ap-
proached her in 1849 when he had not even been engaged as sub-
editor by then. Her apparent belief that Dickens wrote certain
articles on "his view of Woman's position" is part of the same
muddle, since he had written none at all, nor had he published
any, and it is hard to imagine what articles she may have meant
of a subsequent date. She even seems to have thought that the
Preston Strike happened in 1850 instead of 1853–54. It leaves one
nonplussed. "Vigorous erroneousness" was almost her own special-
ity, and it must briefly be said that her paragraph is extremely
confused. The tone of respect in which she was treated throughout the subsequent controversy and with which she has sometimes
been treated since (merely with regard to that controversy) is un-
deserved, and, as this passage suggests, her grasp of the situation
was incompetent.[6]

There are several excuses to be made for her. Although she had
many years in which to revise the *Autobiography*, she did not
bring it out herself. She had been very ill, she composed it hastily,
and the period at which she wrote it (according to Mrs. Fenwick
Miller) "was the most aggressive and unpleasant of her whole
life."[7] W. R. Greg, who reviewed the *Autobiography* for *Nine-*

[6] For the date of Wills's engagement see Dickens to Wills, 22 Jan. 1850, *The Letters of Charles Dickens*, ed. Walter Dexter, 3 vols. (Bloomsbury [London], 1938), 2:200. The remarks about Dickens's "articles" on women can refer to at most only one by him, which was partly about an American emancipationist, Mrs. Amelia Jenks Bloomer ("Sucking Pigs," *HW* 4 [8 Nov. 1851]:145–47), and there do not appear to be any of the kind by other contributors. It is true that Harriet Martineau may have been rather vexed by Mrs. Jellyby's specifically feminist activities referred to in the last chapter of *Bleak House*, as she shows by her remarks in *The Factory Controversy: A Warning Against Meddling Legislation* (Manchester, 1855), pp. 35–36 and 45, though she cannot spell her name. For the factory articles see n. 11 below. Her last contribution to *HW* was "The Rampshire Militia," 10 (13 Jan. 1855): 505–11. Harriet Martineau's own "erroneousness" has corrupted her biographers such as R. K. Webb, who writes in his *Harriet Martineau: A Radical Victorian* (London, 1960): "The connection ceased in 1857 when, alarmed by the anti-Catholic bias of the paper, she turned her artillery of principle on W. H. Wills, the editor, while Dickens ran increasingly afoul of her for his crudity, his attitude towards women, and his sentimentalizing about factories in *Household Words*" (312); the date and the plain statements here are wrong.

[7] *Harriet Martineau*, 4th ed. (London, 1896), p. 176.

teenth Century in 1877, commented that in speaking of herself
she gave a false impression of ill nature, bitterness and deprecia-
tion, but added that "in conveying this impression she does herself grievous injustice. There has seldom been a more kindly-
hearted or affectionate person" (2:100). She is possibly, as Walter
Houghton suggests, a typical example of the Victorian who was
dogmatic or rigid because he felt that he must hold fast to his
own convictions in the midst of confusion.[8] In addition she may
well have regarded herself as an acknowledged authority whose
position was being undermined, and the controversy which arose
out of the *Household Words* articles and *Hard Times* possibly
affected her even more acutely because she herself had written
a somewhat similar story with a very different outcome over twenty
years before.[9] All of which both helps to excuse and explain her;
yet it does not prevent her account of her relations with Dickens
from being misleading.

What had really happened was that they *had* differed very
sharply indeed over Dickens's views on political economy, factory
employment, workmen's compensation, and certain manufacturers' defiance of the law. And in spite of what she says about re-
jecting Wills's proposal, she *did* write a series of articles on factory
employment with some special reference to women between 1851
and 1852. All these incidents, taken together, are possibly as helpful to us now as they were to Dickens at that time in defining his
opinions. As Humphry House remarks of a similar situation, "if
we now wonder how Fezziwig's 'oily rich, fat, jovial voice' could
have seemed tolerable, even to Dickens, in the 'forties, we must
look for the answer in Harriet Martineau and the *Westminster
Review*." [10] Equally if we want to understand how Dickens could
so simplify Coketown and sanctify Stephen Blackpool we must
read Miss Martineau's *The Factory Controversy* and her articles
in *Household Words*.[11]

---

[8] *The Victorian Frame of Mind* (New Haven, 1966), pp. 137–80 (chaps. 6–7).

[9] *The Hill and the Valley*, vol. 1 of *Illustrations of Political Economy*, 9 vols.
(London, 1833). It is a story about a strike in a South Wales ironworks which
follows the death of a boy who, "most unfortunately ... was careless, and put himself in the way of a blow on the head, which killed him on the spot" (92). It is
written clearly and intelligently but entirely from the point of view of the fair-
minded, hard-working owner-employers who close down their factory when the
strike makes it impossible for them to go on. We owe this reference to Ada Nisbet;
no doubt detailed comparisons of interest might be made between *Hard Times* and
several of Martineau's stories.

[10] *The Dickens World* (London, 1941), p. 69, cf. pp. 74–75.

[11] These articles, published from 18 Oct. 1851 to 17 April 1852, are: "Flower

The dispute came into the open after she had finished her *Autobiography* (late 1855) and had published a pamphlet entitled *The Factory Controversy: A Warning Against Meddling Legislation* (issued by the National Association of Factory Occupiers, Manchester, 1855).[12] The pamphlet is largely made up of a scathing criticism of the so-called "editors" of *Household Words* for their publication of a series of articles on factory accidents advocating enforcement of the law requiring proper fencing-in of factory machinery.[13] In these articles Henry Morley, one of Dickens's regular assistants, argues on behalf of the enforcement of the Factory Act of 1844, which ruled that "all parts of the mill-gearing in a factory should be securely fenced." The factory inspectors had issued a circular on 31 January 1854 saying that they would have to "compel every shaft of machinery, at whatever cost and of whatever kind, to be fenced off," because of the annual toll of fatal accidents and mutilations (about forty) from unfenced machinery.[14] The reaction of the manufacturers to this belated decision to enforce the law had been to form an association. Morley makes no objection to the formation of a manufacturers' association for mutual insurance against claims, but he does object to the outright illegality of their express intention to resist the law by paying the fines imposed on any manufacturer for refusing to fence his machinery. He represents it as a threat to society and

Shows in a Birmingham Hot-House," 4:82–85; "The Magic Troughs at Birmingham," 4:113–17; "Wonders of Nails and Screws," 4:138–42; "The Miller and His Men," 4:415–20; "Gold and Gems," 4:449–55; "Rainbow Making," 4:485–90; "Needles," 4:540–46; "Time and the Hour," 4:555–59; "Guns and Pistols," 4:580–85; "Birmingham Glass Works," 5:32–38; "What There is in a Button," 5:106–12; and "Tubal Cain," 5:192–97. Similar "process-articles" (about factories and their manufactures) by Dickens and others had already been published.

[12] It was first sent to the *Westminster Review* and rejected. She then offered it on her own initiative to the National Association of Factory Occupiers which delightedly gave her a hundred guineas for it. It was set out in the form of a review of a variety of parliamentary, legal, and manufacturers' reports, newspaper reports, and four articles in *HW* 11 (1855): "Fencing with Humanity," 241–44; "Death's Cyphering Book," 337–41; "Deadly Shafts," 494–95; and "More Grist to the Mill," 605–6. Further references to the pamphlet are included in our text.

[13] Those listed in n. 12 above but with the addition of "Two Shillings per Horse-power," *HW* 12 (8 Sept. 1855):130–31. Dickens was the sole editor.

[14] *Reports of the Inspectors of Factories to Her Majesty's Principal Secretary of State for the Home Department for the Half-Year Ending 30th April 1854* quotes from a factory inspectors' circular (15 March 1854) "that above forty persons employed in factories annually lose their lives or suffer mutilations from unfenced shafts which the law requires to be securely fenced" (59); it adds that in the previous half year there had been six deaths and thirteen mutilations. Hereafter these semiannual inspectors' studies are referred to as *Reports*.

objects to the monstrosity of their risking even one death for the
sake of saving the expense of adequate fences.[15]

Harriet Martineau retaliated by defending the manufacturers,
arguing that they were not (as Morley said) "striking" against the
law but against an interpretation of it by men less qualified than
themselves. Speaking for the factory owners, she agrees with their
interpretation of the law to mean that it was enough for the machinery to be encased to the height of seven feet. She then argues
the question of moral responsibility on the grounds that if any
workman (or child) climbed above the height of seven feet, even
if in the course of his work, he was responsible for his own safety.
Writing specifically against Dickens (although *Household Words*
was not alone in its protest but had fairly widespread support including that of Leonard Horner, the most active of the factory
inspectors), Miss Martineau says that she holds Dickens "alone"
to be "answerable" for the "disgrace" of the series of articles in
Household Words:

He uses the opportunities of the subject in the palpable way which
a just-minded writer would scrupulously avoid,—vividly describing the
crushing of bones and the rending of flesh, and the tearing of joints
out of their sockets, carrying this method so far as to speak of the
members of the Association as "men not squeamish about a few spots
of spilt brain, or a leg or an arm more or less upon a poor man's body."
(37)

Here Harriet Martineau represents the inhuman school of political economy which Dickens often satirizes so bitterly. The contrast between the two points of view is plain, and surely there is
nothing out of place in Morley's plea for a greater assumption of
responsibility on the manufacturer's part to avoid scenes like the
one she objects to:

Perhaps it is not good [writes Morley] when a factory girl, who has
not the whole spirit of play spun out of her for want of meadows,
gambols upon bags of wool, a little too near the exposed machinery
that is to work it up, and is immediately seized, and punished by the
merciless machine that digs its shaft into her pinafore and hoists her

---

[15] Cf. Maurice W. Thomas, *Early Factory Legislation* (Leigh-on-Sea, 1948), and
John Trevor Ward, *The Factory Movement: 1830–1855* (London/New York, 1962);
but although these partly help to confirm what was said in the dispute, they add
little in detail and nothing in sophistication. More important are the Factories
Acts and the *Reports* reviewed by Martineau (n. 12, p. 410) as well as those for the

up, tears her left arm at the shoulder joint, breaks her right arm, and beats her on the head.[16]

This was in fact an incident (typical of several in the factory reports) which Dickens originally meant to carry right into *Hard Times*, for the manuscript and extant corrected proofs of book 1, chapter 13, show him as not only identifying this girl as Rachael's younger sister but intending to footnote the text with a reference to Morley's article.[17] Why he finally cut it out is now impossible to say. Partly it may have been because he disliked footnotes in fiction and partly also because it would have been too specific, whereas in *Hard Times* he wanted to avoid (as he says) incidents being "localised." [18]

Whatever the reason, Harriet Martineau accuses the author of the *Household Words* articles (Dickens, "or," as she says, "his contributor") of "unscrupulous statement, insolence, arrogance, and cant" (35). She turns on him directly with the old charge that his inaccuracies in past novels were always excused because "he was a novelist; and no one was eager to call to account on any matter of doctrine a very imaginative writer of fiction.... But Mr. Dickens himself changed the conditions of his responsibilities and other people's judgements when he set up 'Household Words' as an avowed agency of popular instruction and social reform" (36). In her outrage she deplores the lack of room (in fifty pages) "to convict the humanity-monger ... of all his acts of unfairness and untruth" (44). It is only the "benevolence of their employers" which "has generated a mutual understanding" that saves "Mr. Dickens's representations" from causing "deadly mischief" among the workers (45).

Dickens was in Paris at the time the pamphlet was published,

---

rest of 1855 and 1856. Although the *Reports* are cited by Martineau, they offer evidence to show that the fencing asked for and refused did reduce accidents, and they clarify both the legal and moral positions, even though written by men who believed (as did Leonard Horner, the chief factory inspector) that the "law is an interference with private enterprise only justified by a strong moral necessity" (*Reports ... Ending 30th April 1855*, p. 5).

[16] "Ground in the Mill," *HW* 9 (22 April 1854):224; almost certainly taken from "Extracts from Reports of Certifying Surgeons," in *Reports ... Ending 31st October 1853*, about a young girl who had been "playing ... above some bags of wool" and whose injuries were "left arm torn out at shoulder joint, right arm fractured, and contusion of head" (113). The *Reports* are outspoken in detailing injuries, and apart from their "personifying" the machine, there is nothing "sentimental" about Morley's or Dickens's remarks.

[17] George Ford and Sylvère Monod, eds., *Hard Times* (New York, 1966), p. 252 (textual notes). This edition also includes part of Martineau's pamphlet, pp. 302–5.

[18] To Peter Cunningham, 11 March 1854, *Letters*, 2:546.

and it was left to Wills to ask Morley to write a reply and have it set up in proof. He then sent it to Dickens, who was in the middle of writing *Little Dorrit* and who replied expressing the wish "to avoid reading Miss Martineau's outpouring of conceit" and saying that he was putting it by for a while "without opening it." [19] But three days later he went carefully over Morley's draft reply, evidently making revisions and additions, returning it to Wills with the remark, "I do suppose that there never was such a wrong-headed woman born—such a vain one—or such a Humbug." [20]

The reply written by Morley and Dickens appears in *Household Words* as "Our Wicked Mis-Statements," [21] and the position taken is that "it is strictly within the province of the law to protect life." It is a humble position, arguing against her insistence that Factory-owners should refuse to obey "meddling legislation":

Might we not say ... that a writer who believes in his heart that resistance to a given law dooms large numbers of men to mutilation, and not few to horrible deaths, may honestly speak with some indignation of the resistance by which those deaths are produced; and that the same right to be angry is not equally possessed by an advocate who argues that the deaths cannot be helped, and that nobody has a right to meddle specially in any way with a mill-owner's trade?   (14)

Now, after over a hundred years, it is possible to make a careful, point by point reading of the original articles by Morley, the pamphlet by Harriet Martineau, and the Morley-Dickens reply, and to try to come to an impartial conclusion. It is only too clear that neither his privately expressed opinion that she was a conceited "Humbug" nor her public charges that he was unscrupulous, untruthful, and unfair, are dispassionate, but it is our judgment, without going into every detail here, that the arguments used by Miss Martineau and her accusations against Dickens are wrong.

For his part Dickens (with Morley) notes how quick Miss

---

[19] 3 Jan. 1856, *Letters*, 2:720.

[20] 6 Jan. 1856, *Letters*, 2:721.

[21] 13 (19 Jan. 1856):13–19; see also *Charles Dickens' Uncollected Writings from "Household Words": 1850–1859*, ed. Harry Stone, 2 vols. (Bloomington, 1968), 2: 550–62. The article is listed in the Contributors' Book as solely by Henry Morley, probably because the first draft to be set up in type was written entirely by him on Wills's initiative. But from Dickens's letters and from internal evidence it seems clear that Dickens took an effective part in modifying it. See Stone, with whom we agree.

Martineau is to take up the Bounderby view that the factories
might as well be thrown into the Atlantic if their owners have to
bear the expense of protecting their own workers.[22] For she clearly
says, on behalf of the factory-owners, that "if the charge is thrown
upon the employers of industry, they will retire from occupations
so intolerably burdensome" and that everyone with "any common
sense" could see that "our manufactures must cease, or the Factory
Laws, as expounded by Mr. Horner, must give way" (46). Yet the
expense of complying with the ten-year-old law was certainly
small,[23] and the positions she takes on the practical difficulties of
applying the law and on the liability of employers to pay compensation were both shown (in the course of a few years) to be
unfair in the light of "common sense" and untenable in principle.
In their use of facts, dates, figures, statistics, and references to the
law, Dickens and Morley are well informed, restrained, and accurate.[24]

On her part there is a personal element in Harriet Martineau's
attack in the way in which she lays down that Dickens must "con-
fine himself to fiction" (38), declaring that "as a matter of taste" it
was "a pity ... that a writer of fiction should choose topics in which
political philosophy and morality were involved" (36). Dickens
replies by pointing out that she herself was extremely well known
as the author of *Forest and Game-Law Tales* and "many volumes
of Stories on Political Economy"; but Miss Martineau evidently
regarded her own fiction as somehow "true," since the doctrines or
principles it teaches were, as she thought, scientifically established.
This dogma is given *ex cathedra* and is closed to any rational examination; and in some ways her arguments can best be understood as the embodiment of all that the fable of *Hard Times* rejects. It is remarkable that Dickens did not foresee from the first
that there was this risk in inviting her to be a contributor, and

---

[22] P. 16: "We believe it was Mr. Bounderby who was always going to throw his
property into the Atlantic."

[23] See *Reports ... Ending 31st October 1855*, pp. 56 and 110.

[24] See Ward, pp. 401–3. In the short run the Association was actually successful
in some of its aims, but by 1860 Rev. George Stringer Bull could fairly claim that
"there is now scarcely a manufacturer who does not thank God for the factory
regulations which were forced from an unwilling government" (*Richard Oastler:
A Sermon* [Bradford, 1861], p. 12). That Dickens was well informed is shown not
only by his part in the articles written by Morley and himself which can be checked
against the *Reports*, but also from his letters (e.g., to Wills, 10 Jan. 1856, *Letters*,
2:724–26); he was clearly quick to see points involved and understood, e.g., the
implications of Lord Campbell's Act, 9 and 10 Vict. 93, which for the first time
allowed the relatives of someone killed at work to sue for compensation.

it is not less surprising that she should have agreed to become
one in spite of knowing very well from his earlier works that as
soon as either of them touched on political economy they were
bound to be in fundamental disagreement. It was inevitable therefore that their relationship should end sooner or later with exasperation on Dickens's side and disdainful withdrawal on hers.

As we have already noted, difficulties first came into the open
when her story for the Christmas number of 1853 was rejected,
when she says that she decided that she could "never again write
fiction" for *Household Words* "nor anything in which principle
or feeling were concerned"; although it is characteristic that, as
she correctly explains elsewhere in the *Autobiography*, she had in
fact already given up submitting fiction. Their final rupture came
only in 1854, apparently over another difference about Roman
Catholicism, following which, since she received no expression of
"repentance or amendment" (*Autobiography*, 2:422), she at last
withdrew.

Now, leaving on one side the question of Dickens's prejudice
against Roman Catholicism (about which she may have been in the
right), her treatment of contemporary industrial life in her contributions remains most interesting. Even as subedited by Wills
and Dickens they are a remarkable illustration of some of the assumptions of the class and world of Bounderby and Gradgrind.
In fact, so marked are these assumptions and so strikingly do they
conflict with Dickens's editorial views that they suggest that dif-
erences about political economy must have underlain and caused
the whole disagreement.

At first, as we have seen, Dickens and Harriet Martineau had
been united by a faith in progress. Yet by 1854 Dickens was increasingly concerned with reports of industrial strife, and, with a
visit to Preston and publication of his article "On Strike" (11
February 1854), he began to put forward his opinions about political economy again more clearly. They may seem moderate now,
but there are three references in the article which must have been
extremely disturbing to Miss Martineau. The first of these is similar to Sissy Jupe's attempted definition of statistics in *Hard Times*
(book 1, chap. 9) and is a protest against the undue veneration
claimed for the subject. Dickens remarks that: "Political Economy
was a great and useful science in its own way and in its own place;
but ... I did not transplant my definition of it from the Common

Prayer Book, and make it a great king above all gods." Then, although admitting that political economy was useful, Dickens maintains that its validity is severely limited by its usual exclusion of the human factor, stating his belief that

into the relations between employers and employed, as into all the relations of this life, there must enter something of feeling and sentiment; something of mutual explanation, forbearance and consideration; something which is not to be found in Mr. M'Culloch's dictionary, and is not exactly stateable in figures; otherwise those relations are wrong and rotten at the core and will never bear sound fruit.

Dickens also stresses that unless political economy "has a little human covering and filling out," it is a "mere skeleton." This was a fundamental belief. He writes to Wilkie Collins about this time of his sympathy for "the working people" with "their wretched arena chalked out for them . . . by small political economists." [25] There is also a letter to Charles Knight about his scorn for mere "figures and averages," respected by "addled heads who would take the average of cold in the Crimea during twelve months as a reason for clothing a soldier in nankeens on a night when he would be frozen to death in fur." [26] Such a point of view is completely antipathetic to Harriet Martineau's, as can be seen in her pamphlet in which she complains that "Mr. Dickens cannot endure a comparative number which may diminish the show he makes with a positive one" (38). For, rather like Mr. M'Choakumchild (*Hard Times*, book 1, chap. 9), she demonstrates that although there might be over four thousand workers a year injured by machinery in textile factories, "only" twelve of that number were killed because machinery was still unfenced and that in "no other" occupation was "the proportion of deaths so small" (*Factory Controversy*, 9).

Harriet Martineau's pamphlet did not, of course, appear until well after *Hard Times;* it was partly a consequence of the novel, not a provocation. But although she was a self-appointed spokeswoman, she graphically represents views already held by the factory-occupiers who welcomed her support. It is not surprising, therefore, if Dickens's exasperation with such views led him into the trap of idealizing Stephen Blackpool, nor that his severe judg-

---

[25] 17 Dec. 1854, *Letters*, 2:609.
[26] 30 Jan. 1855, *Letters*, 2:620.

ment of utilitarianism in *Hard Times* should aggravate the an-
noyance given Miss Martineau by the earlier *Household Words*
articles on workers' injuries in factories.

At the same time, although the break between them was not final
until early 1855, Dickens had been growing increasingly disillusioned with her contributions. The opening paragraphs of "Our
Wicked Mis-Statements" are determinedly fair:

> We have a respect for Miss Martineau, won by many good works she
> has written and many good deeds she has done, which nothing that
> she can now say or do will destroy; and we most heartily claim for her
> the respect of our readers as a thing not to be forfeited for a few hasty
> words.

Yet his letters to Wills show his private complaints about her being
"grimly bent upon the enlightenment of mankind." [27] There are
possibly two reasons for this alteration in his attitude. One is the
change in Dickens himself, which we have already glanced at, and
the other is an increased awareness that they were both looking
very differently at the industrial scene. It is true that for a time
Dickens almost became what Ruskin was to call him, "the leader
of the steam-whistle party *par excellence*." [28] But at no time in his
career did he forget the nature of human participation in industry.
As early as the absurd Miss Monflathers, for example, in *The Old
Curiosity Shop* (chap. 31) he had satirized those who *did* forget:

> "Don't you feel how naughty it is of you," resumed Miss Monflathers,
> "to be a wax-work child, when you might have the proud conscious-
> ness of assisting, to the extent of your infant powers, the manufactures
> of your country; of improving your mind by the constant contempla-
> tion of the steam-engine; and of earning a comfortable and independ-
> ent subsistence of from two-and-ninepence to three shillings a week?"

There is much more to Dickens's view than this, but for the
moment it may be illuminating to turn aside and see what Harriet
Martineau wrote for him in her series of factory articles in *Household Words*. It reveals how narrow but how vitally important the
divisions could be among those who sincerely believed in progress, especially when some of them remained so severely aloof

---

[27] 14 Oct. 1854, *Letters*, 2:597.
[28] Letter to Charles Eliot Norton, 19 June 1870, *The Works of John Ruskin*, ed.
E. T. Cook and Alexander Wedderburn, 39 vols. (London/New York, 1903–12), 37:7.

from the workers who helped to make it possible. It reminds us that although Dickens kept a close control over *Household Words*, it cannot be argued that every word in it gives opinions he approved; it may help to suggest how his views were often shaped by a response to others; and it makes clear how Miss Martineau was welcomed as a contributor at first, even though disagreement seems to have been inevitable as they went on.

Harriet Martineau's first contributions to *Household Words* (begun as early as 25 May 1850) are in the form of fiction: four of her stories appear in the first three volumes, seven in the first six up to December 1852. Her series of factory articles began on 18 October 1851. She later explains that after giving up fiction she decided that "a full, but picturesque account of manufactures and other productive processes might be valuable, both for instruction and entertainment" (*Autobiography*, 2:385). So she visited her brother in Birmingham and with the advantage of his introductions and technical knowledge went to work on the series there. Her titles give some idea of her approach to the subject. A description of the manufacture of papier-mâché tea trays, for example, is "Flower Shows in a Birmingham Hot-House," electroplating is dealt with as "The Magic Troughs of Birmingham," and a visit to a nail factory is entitled "Wonders of Nails and Screws." It was an interesting approach, and was no doubt (as she says) "eagerly accepted." The articles were good publicity for the firms concerned, and she received pressing invitations from other districts. But she and Dickens prudently agreed that "our chief textile manufactures were already familiar to every body's knowledge" (2:388).

Yet in this series of articles she is doing more than writing clear descriptions of little-known processes. She writes persuasively, using what are now some of the familiar techniques of advertising or public relations. Some of the unpleasant aspects of the factories are noted, but quickly erased from a reader's impression by pleasing contrasts with other parts of the work or by thoughts of their ultimate contribution to progress. Miss Martineau herself was not only deaf but had no sense of smell (she was assisted on her visits by her sister-in-law and nieces); thus much unpleasantness may have escaped her notice.

The articles are remarkably detailed and vivid. In "Rainbow Making" we see how she offsets a recognition of the physical discomfort by an excited appreciation of the brilliance of dyed silks:

"From trough to trough we go, breathing steam, and stepping into puddles, or reeking rivulets rippling over the stones of the pavements; but we are tempted on, like children, by the charm of the brilliant colours that flash upon the sight whichever way we turn." An assumed childlike awe at the accomplishments of British manufacture pervades every article. "There is a mystery in most houses of business," she writes in "Time and the Hour." And in "The Magic Troughs": "As for the gilding and silvering chambers, they are like seats of magic. One might look on for a year, and have no idea of the process, but that it must be done by magic." Of the machine process of worming screws, she declares "it is wonderful to see." Every process has her unbounded admiration: "But, oh! the beauty of those candlesticks, and of the ornamented parts of the gas-fittings, and of the most massive of the chains. And the ingenuity too!—the cleverness with which the tubing is concealed in gas-furniture" ("Tubal Cain"). Even the outside of the factories could be attractive—seen in a certain light. After a walk through the ancient streets of Coventry, she remarks: "It is strange, after this, to see the factory chimney, straight, tall and handsome, in its way, with its inlaying of coloured bricks, towering before us, to about the height of a hundred and thirty feet" ("Rainbow Making").

Outside the factories with their "Magic Troughs," workmen are "improvident"; inside they have something of a Carlylean dignity, and craftsmen become artists: "The chasing of the cast articles is one of the most astonishing processes . . . it seems as if every man . . . must be an artist." She has great patriotic pride. The contribution of each factory to the Great Exhibition has a proud notice.

All this, it hardly needs saying, is in strong contrast with *Hard Times,* in which Coketown is "a town of machinery and tall chimneys," savage, monotonous, and dirty (book 1, chap. 5), where the chimneys are "built in an immense variety of stunted and crooked shapes," like "the kind of people who might be expected" to live there; where it is only to "travellers by express-train" that the great factories look "illuminated, like Fairy Palaces"; and where those who work in them leave their shifts, like Stephen, with "the odd sensation . . . which the stoppage of the machinery always produced . . . of its having worked and stopped in his own head" (book 1, chap. 10).

To Harriet Martineau the workpeople are most admired when

they do go like machinery. There is little difference in the kind of admiration she has for the human and for the mechanical as long as each is performing its function. In the button factory she is delighted with the row of "harping lathes" which in "their clean and rapid work are perhaps the prettiest part of the whole show." Her approval of the human machines in the screw factory is expressed in much the same tones:

The job looks anything but a tidy one, while we regard the process alone. But it is different when we stand aside, and survey the room. Then we see that these six score women are neatly dressed; hair smooth, or cap clean—handkerchief or little shawl nicely crossed over, and fastened behind; faces healthy, and countenances cheerful.

In the same piece she may reveal her identification of women and machines by the use of metaphor:

As we turned away from the hundreds of women thus respectably earning their bread, we could but hope that they would look to it that there was no screw loose in their household ways, that the machinery of their daily life might work as truly and effectually as that dead mechanism which is revolving under their care, for so many hours of every day.

A passage in "Gold and Gems" shows the total identification of worker and product in the author's mind, as she describes women who give a special polish to metalware by burnishing it with their bare hands:

What curious finger-ends they have—those women who chafe the precious metals into their last degree of polish! They are broad—the joint so flexible that it is bent considerably backwards when in use; and the skin has a peculiar smoothness: more mechanical, we fancy, than vital. However that may be, the burnish they produce is strikingly superior to any hitherto achieved by friction with any other substance.

Elsewhere a machine is seen as almost human: "Probably the first thing every stranger does on entering the grinding-room is to burst out a-laughing,—the machinery is so grotesque;—so like being alive and full of affectations" ("Birmingham Glass Works"). The description has a Dickensian touch that is not unlike the pistons of the Coketown factories, working "monotonously up and down like the head of an elephant in a state of melancholy madness" (book 1, chap. 5), except that in Coketown it does not seem so amusing.

Yet people are not nearly so reliable as machinery; as they age they are less productive:

We saw a woman in her own home ... tacking the buttons on their stiff paper, for sale ... This woman sews forty gross in a day. She could formerly, by excessive diligence, sew fifty or sixty gross; but forty is her number now—and a large number it is, considering that each button has to be picked up from the heap before her, ranged in its row, and tacked with two stitches. ("What there is in a Button")

It does not occur to the author to wonder whether this employment has anything to do with the woman's deterioration as well as age. Ruskin, faced with his Birmingham nail makers, is saddened by their "manufacturing toil" which left them with "no form of comeliness." [29] Dickens sees Blackpool imaginatively as "Old Stephen" (at forty) since "he had had a hard life" (book 1, chap. 10). But Harriet Martineau appears as cooly detached as Gradgrind in his Stone Lodge and as warmly disapproving of any self-indulgence of the workers as Mr. Bounderby with his comments on "turtle-soup and venison" (book 2, chap. 2).

Harriet Martineau never stresses the dangers of industrial work, merely notes them occasionally in passing, and rejoices to report when the manufacturer has made conditions better. She describes such conditions as those she finds at the glassworks:

We find ourselves on a sort of platform, in front of six furnace mouths, which disclose such a fire within as throws us into a secret despair; despair for ourselves, lest we should lose our senses, and for the men, because it seems impossible to live through the day in such a heat. ("Birmingham Glass Works")

Similarly with the women who work in the heavy air of the lacquering-room at a brass foundry: "There sit companies of women.... One wonders that they can be healthy, sitting in such a heat, and in such a smell. They earn good wages" ("Tubal Cain"; the wages were 11 shillings per week). It is always implied that the workpeople are capable of adapting themselves to any conditions. In the description of varnishing and "stoving" tea trays she remarks: "This

---

[29] Letter 80 (16 July 1877), *Fors Clavigera: Letters to the Workmen and Labourers of England* (8 vols. [London, 1871–84]), in *Works*, 29:172 and 175.

must be unwholesome work to the superintendents of the process. The heat of the stove rooms is very great, and the smell of baked varnish is almost intolerable to novices." To Harriet Martineau accidents are all preventable by the workpeople themselves. As she describes the glass-blowing, she makes no mention of the dangers to the workmen, but she is well aware of them for herself:

All swing their glowing cylinders as if they were desperate or demented; a condition which we suspect we are approaching under the pressure of the heat, and the strangeness and the hurry of incessantly getting out of the way of red-hot globes, long pipes, and whirling cylinders.

Writing about wire drawing, she notes:

Women are preferred to boys for this work. Their attention is more steady, and they are more careful of their own flesh and blood. Boys are apt to make mischief; and, if they look off their work, it is too likely that they may lose their finger-ends. It is in this department of the business that most of the accidents happen. ("Nails and Screws")

Yet she does gives a lengthy description of the attempts made by needle manufacturers to get their employees to wear masks which would prevent their fatally inhaling tiny pieces of ground steel. In this case it is the employees who refuse the protection offered them —a fact which she makes much of. It is the employers who have "saved" the needle-grinders from "their own folly." [30]

Inevitably Harriet Martineau's justifications for the working conditions she found are that mass production made necessities cheaper and that all present-day working conditions are an improvement on the past: "Cyclopaedias of the present century—

---

[30] To be fair to Harriet Martineau, this was no doubt a genuine problem, and Dickens himself was to write about "knowing from the instance of the Sheffield Sword Grinders and their magnetic mask, and from other analogous cases, how difficult it is to induce ignorant people to take precautions provided for them when doing dangerous work" (29 Dec. 1868, *Letters*, 3:692). This letter was in reply to a reasoned protest from the proprietors of Limehouse lead mills who were disturbed by what Dickens had written about some cases of lead poisoning in "A Small Star in the East" (*All the Year Round*, n.s.1 [19 Dec. 1868], 61–66). It is worth remarking that Dickens taking a doctor with him had visited some of the victims and talked to them in their own homes. He came back to the subject in "On an Amateur Beat" (*All the Year Round*, n.s.1 [27 Feb. 1869], 300–303) after a further visit to the mills when he noted the precautions taken and praised the employers' care but still concluded that the work was highly dangerous. His remarks ended by looking to "American inventiveness" for an advance which would make the production of white lead possible "entirely by machinery."

within the last thirty years, even—give such an account of the formation of a needle, as appears quite piteous to one who was at
Redditch yesterday." Manufacturers are never blamed for bad
working conditions; they are invariably praised for their care.
Good working conditions are noted with complacency. Winding
silk is "easy work," many of the women are allowed to sit at their
reels, and the air is "pure and cool." She congratulates the employees in the needle factory: "Those who work on Mr. James's
premises are well off for air, light, and cheerfulness." Similarly
where labor relations are good, the credit goes to the employer.
It is true that the employer, himself, may say that their improved
"health, understanding, and morals" is simply the result of "Sunday schools . . . and the good free-school"—and he may be right.
But she thinks that: "There is something in the tone of the intercourse between himself and everybody on his premises, which con-
vinces a stranger that there is also somebody else to thank for the
improvement, which drives out all the stranger's preconceptions
of the wretchedness of needle-makers" ("Needles"). All the best
points of the employers are dwelt on, their ingenuity, enterprise,
and economy being judged the most praiseworthy. Her series is
thus an enormously forceful exaltation of "the entrepreneurial
ideal," [31] appearing in the same journal that was to call the Preston
Strike an employers' "Lock-Out," to deride a sympathizer of the
factory-occupiers (in "On Strike") as "Mr. Snapper," to suggest
that strikes might even be justified, and to ridicule the "masters"
in Josiah Bounderby. Yet to Harriet Martineau the only fault of
the masters is that they are too complacent about their workers'
improvidence: "It is too common to hear employers speak coolly,
if not with satisfaction, of this state of things, because it keeps the
workmen dependent and humble, and lessens the dangers of those
strikes about wages, which are the plague of the manufacturer's
life" ("The Magic Troughs at Birmingham").

The same series of articles shows her severity when she has to
remark on any legislative interference in trade. She objects particularly to taxation and import dues. The paper duty forces the
manufacturer to use cheap materials. Coventry ribbon-workers are
blamed for their "tenacity about protective duties." A whole page
in "Time and the Hour" is devoted to commenting on "legislative
impediments which annoy the manufacturer. . . . What confusion,

---

[31] Perkin, *Origins*, chap. 8.

and trouble, and waste, are caused by all these legislative med-
dlings!" The only answer is Free Trade. In her last process article
("How to Get Paper"), which Dickens found so "grimly determined," she writes against the paper tax once more. This was a
tax which, in spite of the unpopularity it brought him, Dickens de-
fended in preference to other forms of taxation which he judged
bore more heavily on the poor.[32] It is one instance of the way in
which he did *not* insist that no contributor should express views
contrary to his own.

In all these articles there is not even the Smilesian encourage-
ment to the worker to "come and join the masters," although
they are written in the belief that society's problems can be solved
only by self-help. Their author may have been cut off by her deaf-
ness, yet, even though writing for such a popular periodical as
Household Words, she shows no personal interest in the people she
meets, notes no conversations with the workers, and merely expresses the hope that they can be improved by education. In her
eyes the workers appear difficult children, and she is the teacher,
as when she cheerfully lectures them on how they must adapt
themselves to the machine: "Here must be no Monday laziness
after Sunday's rest; no caprice as to going to work or staying away.
Like time and tide—like brewing and dyeing—the work at Messrs.
Elkington's cannot wait for men's humours" ("Magic Troughs").

Nothing could be more dissimilar to Dickens's approach, whether
in his own journalism in which the personal interest is emphasized
or in his admission in *Hard Times* that he entertains "a weak idea
that the English people are as hard-worked as any people on whom
the sun shines" (book 1, chap. 10). Being the daughter of a ruined
manufacturer may have helped to shape Harriet Martineau's ideas
of the relations between "masters and men"—as much as Dickens's
childhood experiences affected his. What is curious, though not
altogether surprising, is that Harriet Martineau's nonfiction, which
is supposedly the work of a dispassionate observer, may be thought
to be as strongly marked by its author's characteristic preferences
as Dickens's fiction.

Part of the interest of all this lies, moreover, in the change (as
we have explained) that had been taking place in Dickens. And it
could hardly be more strikingly shown than in his having allowed
Harriet Martineau her head in her factory articles for *Household*

[32] To Charles Knight, 8 Feb. 1850, *Letters*, 2:205.

important

Words and then having felt driven to repudiate everything she stood for in *Hard Times*. For as he shows in "A Preliminary Word," he had also been fascinated by "the mightier inventions of the age"; he had been ready himself to pay tribute to the manufacturers; and early in 1853 he could speak of seeing "in the factories and workshops of Birmingham such beautiful order and regularity, and such great consideration for the workpeople provided, that they must be justly entitled to be considered educational too." [33] And of course he never questioned that, with good will, the interests of all classes "are identical."

The difference that existed from the first between him and those who thought like Miss Martineau lay chiefly in his deep concern both for the individual and for the quality of working-class life. It shows chiefly in his novels, but it is also reflected in such *Household Words* articles as "The Amusements of the People—I" (30 March 1850) in which he says that the people have "a right to be amused," or in "To Working Men" (7 October 1854) in which he declares that they have "a right to every means of life and health that Providence has afforded." He can write of such a city as Manchester in 1852 as an "awful machine," kept "in harmony" only with the help of such institutions as its new Public Library;[34] and fascinated as he may be by the new inventions he refuses to admit that "the hardest workers at this whirring wheel of toil" are to be "excluded from the sympathies and graces of imagination" ("A Preliminary Word," 30 March 1850).

But with *Hard Times* a change arose. He decided to write it for *Household Words* because the journal was thought to be declining; and he may have thought that with contributors such as Miss Martineau it had become rather too complacent about workingmen and the conditions in which they lived and worked. He certainly found himself, as he wrote to Mrs. Gaskell (21 April 1854), rebelling against "the monstrous claims at domination made by a certain class of manufacturer," [35] and he declared that the "idea" of the novel had "laid hold" of him "by the throat in a very violent manner." [36]

Nor was this quite all. For one of the consequences of the

[33] 3 Jan., *Speeches of Charles Dickens*, ed. K. J. Fielding (Oxford, 1960), p. 160.

[34] *Speeches*, pp. 153–54, Pierpont Morgan Library, ms quoting letter to Miss Coutts, 3 Sept. 1852.

[35] *Letters*, 2:554.

[36] To Hon. Mrs. Richard Watson, 1 Nov. 1854, *Letters*, 2:602.

Martineau dispute was that he certainly recognized where his
sympathies lay when the spinners and piecers struck in Manchester
(November 1855 to January 1856) following a reduction in wages
at a time of higher prices. So when Morley sent him the draft of an
article about the strike, at about the same time as his draft of "Our
Wicked Mis-Statements," Dickens was uncompromising in his
demand that Morley's article be rewritten. The creator of Slack-
bridge, the union agitator, and of the antiunionist Stephen Blackpool gives very clear instructions in a letter to Wills that this strike-
article cannot possibly put forward the opinion that "all strikes
among this unhappy class . . . are always necessarily wrong." [37] He
is clearer than ever before that to open such a piece "by saying
that the men are *of course* entirely and painfully in the wrong'
. . . would be monstrous." Nor would he concede that they were
wrong because such a strike would throw other men out of work
without their consent, exclaiming "O Good God when Morley
treats of the suffering of wife and children, can he suppose that
these mistaken men don't feel it in the depths of their hearts, and
don't honestly and honorably—most devoutly and faithfully—believe—that for those very children when they shall have children,
they are bearing all these miseries now!" Morley's draft was immediately revised and published as "The Manchester Strike" (2
February 1856); from it we can see the curious result that the editor
(and in some instances author) of articles on the wonders of new
manufacturing processes is now represented as holding that "un-
wholesomely cheap production" is "a perversion of the common
law of trade, which will in the course of time be blotted out by the
advance of education." He is shown as arguing that though free
competition is healthy, the unskilled worker is at such a disadvantage that he has no freedom to compete, and that ("O, political
economist!") such a class must be protected.

To account in this way for what happened in the Dickens-
Martineau dispute is not merely to offer a small gathering of facts
as part of a centenary tribute. In the course of their differences
we can see a development in Dickens which also partly underlies
his fiction. It is evident that this was a period of crisis for him. Of
course it is obvious how painfully inadequate Stephen Blackpool
is, but we have also to consider how extraordinarily confined up to
this time had been the imaginative understanding even of Dickens

[37] 6 Jan. 1856, *Letters*, 2:721–22.

and certainly of most of his readers when faced with the results of the industrial revolution. Industrial life was a new experience for the imaginative writer; its achievements were at first a matter of simple wonder to everyone; and the break with the dominant "entrepreneurial deal" was something which not only had to occur within Dickens's own general editorial policy but within himself, and this was in defiance of the very strongest tendencies of the age as well as his own. The effects of the break can be seen in *Hard Times;* also in *Little Dorrit* in the partnership of the inventor Daniel Doyce and the factory manager Arthur Clennam; they can even be seen in *Great Expectations* and certainly in the spirit of the *Uncommercial Traveller*. George Orwell may be right in saying that Dickens was "not mechanically minded," [38] but he had to adapt to the machine age. That he did so deserves to be recognized more clearly by those who now read Dickens's novels at all closely.

[38] *Collected Journalism,* 1:444.

Dickens and
the Voices of Time

GEORGE H. FORD

IN THE LAST FEW YEARS the topic of time has become almost alarmingly fashionable. We are discovering that our views of time can provide insights into our casts of mind as individuals or as members of societies in different ages and places, and also provide a key to literary works. Our preoccupation with problems of time may derive from an obsessive sense that modern life is being transformed, as Philip Rahv says, at such vertiginous speed we feel as if the past "were being ground to pieces in the powerhouse of change" [1]—a sense that the Victorians, I think, also experienced. And another critic has commented that "the displacement of the sense of recurrence as the dominant human awareness is . . . probably the major crisis in the arts today." [2]

In any event the proliferation of studies of time in literature has been marked in recent years. Such studies include those of the literary critic Georges Poulet of Zurich (that this eminent expert on time should be stationed in Switzerland seems almost bizarre). Poulet's works have been followed by studies on time and literature by J. Hillis Miller, Jerome Buckley, Frank Kermode, John Raleigh, K. J. Fielding, and many others.[3] Seminars on time and literature have been held at M.I.T. under the direction of an

---

[1] *The Myth and the Powerhouse* (New York, 1965), p. 14.

[2] Walter J. Ong, "Evolution, Myth, and Poetic Vision," *CLS* 3 (1966):6.

[3] See Poulet, *Studies in Human Time*, trans. Elliott Coleman (Baltimore, 1956) and *The Interior Distance*, trans. Coleman (Baltimore, 1959); Buckley, *The Triumph of Time: A Study of the Victorian Concepts of Time, History, Progress, and Decadence* (Cambridge, Mass., 1966); Raleigh, *Time, Place, and Idea: Essays on the Novel* (Carbondale, Ill., 1968); Kermode, *The Sense of an Ending: Studies in the Theory of Fiction* (New York, 1967); Fielding, "Dickens and the Past: The Novelist of Memory" in *Experience in the Novel: Selected Papers from the English Institute*, ed. Roy Harvey Pearce (New York, 1968), pp. 107–31. In its original form my essay was read as a paper at the University of Edinburgh several years ago. In subsequently revising it I have profited in particular from Fielding's suggestive discussion, although my approach to our common topic is generally from an angle different from his.

engineer, J. T. Fraser, whose book *The Voices of Time* (New York, 1966), from which my title derives, compiles discussions of time by scientists, philosophers, psychiatrists, musicologists, and theologians.

For a convenient mode of classifying our senses of time, Raleigh's book is useful. According to Raleigh the three different ways in which man has viewed time are the linear, the cyclic, and the durational. Or we can take a leaf from the anthropologists and also use their terms for classifying different societies: the future-oriented society (whose view of time corresponds to the linear); the past-oriented (corresponding to the cyclic concept of time); and the present-oriented (corresponding, but not so neatly, to the durational concept of time).

Literary historians, like the anthropologists, may rest content with classifying authors under these three categories. Literary critics, however, may wish to go beyond classification and resort to evaluation. Thus the eminent literary critic, Father Ong, argues in a lively article on time in literature that a writer's responsibility to society requires his adopting a future-oriented linear view of time. A writer such as Yeats, with his cyclic view of time, is to Father Ong deplorable ("spectacularly and desperately anti-evolutionary" he says).[4] It is interesting to hear Father Ong urging writers of the 1960s not to follow the bad examples of Yeats, Joyce, and Lawrence, and instead to move forward into the future under the banner of the linear time-sense.

For our purpose what is most interesting in Father Ong's article is his discovering in Tennyson and other Victorians a future-oriented time-sense which he extols at the expense of the brooding, cyclic sense of twentieth-century writers. I think Ong is wrong, although that's much too emphatic (if irresistibly alliterative). I should say rather that he is half right, for in the major Victorian writers we encounter two, perhaps three, of these attitudes toward time, attitudes that may account for the different voices we listen to in their literature. To make my point I propose to restrict most of my discussion to Dickens, and I hope the reader will bear with me as I come to it via what may seem an oblique line by considering the tone of his prose style. For a writer's style or styles can provide insight, I think, into his sense of time or senses of time

---

[4] P. 9.

and finally to his stance or stances toward the role of the artist in society.

❧

In an excellent essay in his book *The Lost Childhood* Graham Greene praises Dickens for what he calls his "secret prose" and speaks of its "delicate and exact poetic cadences, the music of memory, that so influenced Proust." [5] *His secret prose*—it is a fine and striking phrase. But its calls for illustration and also for some inquiry into the circumstances which produced it.

Here is a brief and familiar example of the music of memory from *David Copperfield*. In this novel, as Randolph Quirk notes, there are no less than four chapters entitled "Retrospect," chapters in which by switching from past to present tense or to a series of present participles, the novelist contrives to halt the movement of time in his narrative.[6] In the midst of describing to us his impressions of his first visit to the fishing town of Yarmouth, David remarks:

I don't know why one slight set of impressions should be more particularly associated with a place than another, though I believe this obtains with most people, in reference especially to the associations of their childhood. I never hear the name, or read the name, of Yarmouth, but I am reminded of a certain Sunday morning on the beach, the bells ringing for church, little Em'ly leaning on my shoulder, Ham lazily dropping stones into the water, and the sun, away at sea, just breaking through the heavy mist, and showing up the ships, like their own shadows.

Such a passage has its own glow, and if we are rereading the novel as we reread a poem, there is an additional association when we remember that this idyllically quiet beach is the same one on which the battered body of Steerforth will be washed ashore, years and chapters later: "And on that part of it where she and I had looked for shells, two children. . . . I saw him lying with his head upon his arms, as I had often seen him lie at school." The timeless quality of the original scene at Yarmouth is specified by the novelist himself when he comments: "The days sported by us, as if Time had not grown up himself yet, but were a child too, and

[5] "The Young Dickens," rpt. in *The Dickens Critics,* George H. Ford and Lauriat Lane, Jr. (Ithaca, N.Y., 1961), pp. 246–47.
[6] *Charles Dickens and Appropriate Language* (Durham, Eng., 1959), p. 10.

always at play.... We had no future.... We made no more provision for growing older, than we did for growing younger." In
addition it may be noted that this timeless moment at Yarmouth
is created for us in purely visionary terms. Elsewhere Dickens often
relies upon senses other than the visionary. In *Little Dorrit* when
Arthur Clennam revisits the home of the girl he loved twenty years
before, he imagines that he can smell "its jars of old rose-leaves and
lavender" even before the door opens, and when he does cross
the threshold "those faded scents in truth saluted him like wintry
breath that had a faint remembrance in it of the bygone spring."
And in *Great Expectations* when Pip's argument with Biddy
prompts her to crush a black-currant leaf in her hands, he remarks
in passing: "the smell of a black-currant bush has ever since recalled to me that evening in the little garden." Similarly Proustian
is Pip's account of his sister's funeral: the smell of sherry on Uncle
Pumblechook's breath and the parlor in which the air was "faint
with the smell of sweet cake."

And again, one other example from *Great Expectations*, this
time less sensuously evocative yet with the kind of haunting effect
that is especially noticeable in that novel. One of the many ironies
of *Great Expectations* is embodied in its very title. "Great Expectations" seems to promise a Horatio Alger story of an energetic
young Victorian pushing his way up into heady heights of success.
Pip's story does move forward in time, of course, but instead of
the fast-paced progress that the title might lead us to expect, the
narrative keeps hovering back over the past, a past of unidentified
guilt and of shame and fear. When Pip is apprenticed to Joe the
blacksmith, he is filled with discontents:

What I wanted, who can say? How can *I* say, when I never knew? What
I dreaded was, that in some unlucky hour I, being at my grimiest and
commonest, should lift up my eyes and see Estella looking in at one
of the wooden windows of the forge. I was haunted by the fear that
she would, sooner or later, find me out, with a black face and hands,
doing the coarsest part of my work, and would exult over me and
despise me. Often after dark, when I was pulling the bellows for Joe,
and we were singing Old Clem, and when the thought how we used
to sing it at Miss Havisham's would seem to show me Estella's face in
the fire, with her pretty hair fluttering in the wind and her eyes scorn-
ing me,—often at such a time I would look towards those panels of
black night in the wall which the wooden windows then were, and

would fancy that I saw her just drawing her face away, and would
believe that she had come at last.

A characteristic touch in this passage is the accusing face at the
window (everyone will recall the hair-raising scene in *Oliver Twist*
where Fagin and Monks stare in through a window at the boy
Oliver, asleep in his seemingly secure haven). In *Great Expectations* it is a detail which can make us aware too of the auto-
biographical significance of the scene. The principal trauma of
Dickens's own childhood had been his menial employment in a
blacking warehouse in a workroom through the windows of which
he could be watched by passers-by. In such scenes of *Great Expectations* Dickens is tapping the springs of what Proust calls the
"involuntary memory" or what Matthew Arnold calls (in one of
his poems) "the buried life." What Pip finally uncovers from his
buried life when he encounters his secret sharer, Magwitch, leads
him to realize that the black coaldust of the blacksmith's forge is
clean by comparison with the stain and the smell of Newgate prison
which, later in the book, he tries to brush from his clothes and
exhale from his lungs. And on this occasion he is once more concerned about a meeting with Estella whose face he will see watching him through the window of a coach.

The aspect of Dickens's writing which we are seeking to identify
may be regarded by some readers as an inconsequential one. Certainly his secret prose is not the typical attribute of his novels that
would come first to mind; we should think rather of the great
humorist or of the social critic and satirist. As I have noted elsewhere, fervent expression of moral indignation is said to be a
popular indulgence of the middle classes (as letters to the editor
in any newspaper will illustrate), and for many readers perhaps
the chief satisfaction in reading Dickens's novels are the "adrenal
excitements" stimulated by them. When the boy Jo dies in *Bleak
House*, Dickens's rhetoric whips us up into a fury against irresponsible authorities: "Dead, your Majesty. Dead, my lords and
gentlemen. Dead, Right Reverends and Wrong Reverends of every
order. Dead, men and women, born with Heavenly compassion
in your hearts. And dying thus around us every day." Our juices
flow in response to this voice. It is the fearless voice of the great
Victorian reformer who is fighting to correct the ills of social, eco-
nomic, and political life so that mankind can continue its progress.

It is also the voice to which Robert Garis devotes almost exclusive attention in his book, *The Dickens Theatre: A Reassessment of the Novels* (Cambridge, Mass., 1965), for it involves the novelist's being fully aware that he is facing an audience. It is a public voice; it is future-oriented, a voice that would satisfy the requirements of Father Ong—and also the requirements of Jeremy Bentham, one might add. It is a voice not unique in Dickens's writing, for one encounters it in other Victorian novels. Hillis Miller in his latest book on Victorian fiction notes that in Thackeray and Trollope and Eliot and Meredith the narrator is often a spokesman embodying the "collective consciousness" and "general judgment of the community." [7] By contrast, the other voice in Dickens, the one we are trying to identify, is a private voice reporting a private vision which through fiction is shared with us: the secret prose. [8]

The range of Dickens's prose style is of course vast and diversified, but if we accept the simplification, we can say that his prose moves between these two poles of public and private, each with its own wavelength.

The more typical and well-known prose style developed early, as the example I shall cite will illustrate. In 1834 as a young newspaper reporter twenty-two years of age, Dickens was sent to Edinburgh to report upon a banquet given in honor of Earl Grey. The guest of honor was late, and the hungry banqueters finally lost patience. Here is the report of the scene by the irreverent young writer:

[One guest] . . . overcome by the cold fowls, roast beef, lobster, and other tempting delicacies . . . appeared to think the best thing he could possibly do, would be to eat his dinner, while there was anything to eat. He accordingly laid about him with right good-will, the example was contagious, and the clatter of knives and forks became general. Hereupon, several gentlemen, who were not hungry, cried out "Shame!" and looked very indignant; and several gentlemen who were hungry cried "Shame!" too, eating, nevertheless, all the while, as fast as they possibly could. In this dilemma, one of the stewards mounted a bench and feelingly represented to the delinquents the enormity of their conduct, imploring them, for decency's sake, to defer the process of mas-

---

[7] *The Form of Victorian Fiction: Thackeray, Dickens, Trollope, George Eliot, Meredith, and Hardy* (Notre Dame, Ind., 1968), pp. 53–88.

[8] See John Stuart Mill's essay "What Is Poetry," *Monthly Repository* (Jan. 1833), for his discussion of the difference between eloquence and poetry: "Eloquence supposes an audience; the peculiarity of poetry appears to us to lie in the poet's utter unconsciousness of a listener."

tication until the arrival of Earl Grey. This address was loudly cheered, but totally unheeded; and this is, perhaps, one of the few instances on record of a dinner having been virtually concluded before it began.[9]

In this early reporting we can notice already developed the characteristically jaunty Dickensian tone of good-humored amusement in the presence of some absurdity, especially the absurdity of inflated language, the language of after-dinner speakers, of addresses to clubs, or of lawyers and Parliamentarians such as Sergeant Buzfuz or the Eatanswill candidates in *Pickwick*. As Alice Meynell notes, Dickens invented his own style by making fun of Gibbon's style, or more specifically, of Gibbon's nineteenth-century imitators.[10]

In the more serious social criticism, especially in the somber later novels,[11] the air of detached amusement often gives way and passes over into a harsh, sardonic manner in which a coating of irony is too transparent to conceal the indignation against abuses that seethes underneath it, as for example in the great opening chapter of *Bleak House* with its jabbing staccato sentences or in *Hard Times* in this characteristic description of the clock in Mr. Gradgrind's study: "a deadly statistical clock . . . which measured every second with a beat like a rap upon a coffin-lid."

This is a style which even carries over into snatches of stylized dialogue such as those we listen to at Mr. Merdle's receptions and dinners in *Little Dorrit*. Here is a passage in which three or four nameless guests discuss Mr. Merdle's financial triumphs:

There was a dinner given in the Harley Street establishment . . . and there were magnates from the Court and magnates from the City, magnates from the Commons and magnates from the Lords, magnates from the bench and magnates from the bar, Bishop magnates, Treasury magnates, Horse Guards magnates, Admiralty magnates,—all the magnates that keep us going, and sometimes trip us up.

"I am told," said Bishop magnate to Horse Guards, "that Mr. Merdle has made another enormous hit. They say a hundred thousand pounds."

[9] In Edgar Johnson, *Charles Dickens: His Tragedy and Triumph*, 2 vols. (New York, 1952), 1:96.

[10] "Charles Dickens as a Man of Letters," *The Dickens Critics*, pp. 107–8.

[11] Cf., however, K. J. Fielding's interesting suggestion in "Dickens and the Past" that in his last novels Dickens's concern for social issues is considerably diminished, a development which Fielding traces to the self-examination Dickens had undergone in writing *David Copperfield* and *Little Dorrit*: "For, as he understood himself, and withdrew into himself, more, he became less interested in the world about him" (108).

Horse Guards had heard two.

Treasury had heard three.

Bar, handling his persuasive double eye-glass, was by no means clear but that it might be four.... But here was Brother Bellows, who had been in the great Bank Case, and who could probably tell us more. What did Brother Bellows put this new success at?

Brother Bellows was on his way to make his bow to the bosom, and could only tell them in passing that he had heard it stated, with great appearance of truth, as being worth, from first to last, half-a-million of money.

Admiralty said Mr. Merdle was a wonderful man. Treasury said he was a new power in the country, and would be able to buy up the whole House of Commons. Bishop said he was glad to think that this wealth flowed into the coffers of a gentleman who was always disposed to maintain the best interests of Society.

This brilliantly diversified public voice is the principal voice in these novels, and behind it is a set of attitudes appropriate to it including attitudes toward the past and future. Dickens's attitude toward the past is actually complex and contradictory. Much of the time he seems to embody the attitude of Carl Sandburg that the past is a bucket of ashes and to agree with Henry Ford that history is bunk. His potboiler effort in writing pure history, *A Child's History of England,* would certainly reinforce this generalization. The book is a curiously naive production often displaying "an amused contempt" for earlier ages, and, like Mark Twain in *The Connecticut Yankee,* the author appears, as Humphry House says, "as a proud Victorian, conscious of living in a progressive age." [12] In the same vein one can mention Dickens's library at Gadshill. A boyish joke in a grown man's library was his set of imitation books with imaginary titles making fun of the past iniquities of man's history (*The Wisdom of Our Ancestors: Ignorance, Superstition, et al.*) On the evidence of this boyish joke John Raleigh concludes that Dickens's sense of time is purely linear and that he has no interest in the past. [13] And Edgar Johnson

---

[12] *The Dickens World,* 2d ed. (London, 1960), p. 34. The attitude toward the past of his *Child's History* also colors Dickens's two historical novels. In *A Tale of Two Cities* and *Barnaby Rudge,* where we might expect to find his awareness of time most fully developed, we find more often instead the other voice of Dickens, the stridently expressed contempt for the blunders made by earlier generations of men. But see also Robert Alter's impressive analysis of Dickens's treatment of history: "The Demons of History in Dickens' *Tale,*" *Novel,* 2 (1969): 135–42.

[13] Pp. 46–48. In his journalism, as might be expected, Dickens frequently sounds his steam whistle. An article written for *Household Words* (with Charles Knight), in which he contrasts the stagnation of past-oriented China with the progress of future-oriented England, is representative of this vein and aligns him with such

argues that the principal difference between Scott and Dickens is their contrasting views of the past. "For Dickens" says Johnson, "the good old times were the bad old times." [14] Also relevant is the observation made by Alexander Welsh that Dickens's view of time is that of a city man, someone constantly exposed to change and uprooted from traditional recurring patterns of experience.[15]

On these grounds, Ruskin, the Tory Socialist, was right to complain that Dickens was, as he says, "a pure modernist—a leader of the steam-whistle party *par excellence*—and he had no understanding of any power of antiquity except a sort of jackdaw sentiment for cathedral towers. . . . His hero is essentially the ironmaster." [16] And yet the recurring expressions of contempt for the past, of which Ruskin is complaining, do not provide the whole story. In this respect Dickens is very much like one of his twentieth-century admirers, George Orwell. The principal conflict in Orwell's thinking was his divided allegiance toward past and future. As a socialist he had to assert a faith in progress and linear time, and also a repudiation of outmoded ways of life. But by instinct Orwell was a man whose nostalgic preferences were for older and established ways of life, especially the Victorian modes which he loved. One of the most effective symbols in *1984* is the Victorian glass paperweight which the hero discovers in a junk shop, a foolish and nonfunctional ornament, but for Orwell's hero it is almost a secular equivalent of a fragment of the true Cross to a Christian pilgrim.

Dickens, as I said, anticipates Orwell's sense of divided allegiance. In chapter 28 of *Bleak House* he offers a striking scene of the self-made Ironmaster, Mr. Rouncewell, confronting Sir Leicester and Lady Dedlock in the reception room of their ancient country estate. What is noteworthy in this confrontation is its bringing into conflict not only two contrasting ways of life but two contrasting views of time, a contrast that occurs often in Victorian

contemporaries as Herbert Spencer and John Bright (reported in *Charles Dickens' Uncollected Writings from "Household Words": 1850–1859*, ed. Harry Stone, 2 vols. [Bloomington, 1968], 1: 329). See, e.g., Bright's speech on progress as reported in the *Times* (London), 3 Jan. 1865.

[14] "Dickens and the Spirit of the Age," in *Victorian Essays: A Symposium*, ed. Warren D. Anderson and Thomas D. Clareson (Kent, Ohio, 1967), p. 29.

[15] "Satire and History: The City of Dickens," *VS* 11 (1968): 382. See also John Gross and Gabriel Pearson, eds., *Dickens and the Twentieth Century* (London, 1962), p. xii.

[16] *The Works of John Ruskin,* ed. E. T. Cook and Alexander Wedderburn, 39 vols. (London/New York, 1903–12), 37:7.

life and literature (and, as Orwell's case suggests, in our own as well).

The future-oriented factory owner, Mr. Rouncewell, is invited by the Dedlocks to relax and spend the night at Chesney Wold, but he declines. "In these busy times," he says, ". . . I have to travel all night, in order to reach a distant part of the country, punctually at an appointed time in the morning." These were the men, celebrated by Carlyle as the Plugsons of Undershot, who were making England into a great power, and it is evident in this scene that the novelist expects us to applaud their superabundant energies. Throughout the scene Mr. Rouncewell seems to breathe like a railway engine impatiently waiting to take off from a station, ready to roar away into the future down the ringing grooves of change. The older traditional sense of time, embodied in the aristocracy, seems feeble and outmoded: "there is no hurry there [at Chesney Wold]; there, . . . in that quiet park, where the ivy and the moss have had time to mature." In this scene we are guided by the novelist to side against the old leisurely time, embodying rhythm, order, and possibly boredom, and to side with the new time sense embodying change, exhilaration, and possibly ulcers. But there are other later scenes which cancel out this facile solution. When Mr. Rouncewell's brother, Trooper George, visits his factory, there is a counterpointed confrontation of time values, and the past-oriented is given its due. For the future-oriented Ironmaster one senses the novelist's admiration, but for the past-oriented soldier, Mr. Rouncewell's brother George, one senses instead the novelist's affection.

In both Dickens and Orwell the conflict between past and future was never resolved, and I am not concerned here with trying to suggest a resolution. For our purposes the important point is that Dickens was by no means a loyal member of the steam-whistle party, and his mixed feelings, his divided allegiance, enabled him to add a dimension to his writing of extraordinary consequence.

What I am suggesting is simply that the development of the secret prose, the music of memory, as a counterbalance to the vigorous Whig tone with its castigations of the outmoded, which seems more typical of Dickens, was dependent upon a different attitude toward the past, especially his own past, on Dickens's part.

T. S. Eliot's *East Coker* opens with the motto of Mary Queen of Scots: "In my beginning is my end." And Dickens had to learn this wisdom, as Keats would say, on his pulses.

When did he learn it? In *Pickwick Papers* there is very little sense of it, I think. Although set in the recent past, *Pickwick Papers* is really the story of a perpetual present. When it first appeared as a serial, as John Butt has shown, the very seasons in which the Pickwickians were pursuing their adventures were made to correspond to the seasons in which the monthly numbers would be published.[17] And recollections of past time are rare and inconsequently conventional, as for example when Mr. Wardle reminds his elderly mother of her childhood: "The tear which starts unbidden to the eye when the recollection of old times and the happiness of many years ago is suddenly recalled, stole down the old lady's face as she shook her head with a melancholy smile." *Pickwick Papers* thus demonstrates Dickens's affinity to his favorite novelist of his early years, Smollett, and the line of his later development is his growth away from this early model not so much by a repudiation of Smollett's space world as by an assimilation of it into a world where we become aware of time, and of movement in time, as well as of movement in space.

What produced the change? Biography, although not conclusive, suggests one clue and allows us to guess. When the seventeen-year-old Mary Hogarth died in his arms, Dickens was himself twenty-five years of age. He had encountered death before, of course, but this event exposed him not only to what Edgar Johnson calls intimations of mortality but, because of his unusual relationship with this girl, to an awareness of a road not taken that cannot be taken, an awareness which as we shall see becomes one of the principal springs of his secret prose. The more immediate repercussion of Mary's death in his novels was his account of the death of Little Nell in *The Old Curiosity Shop*. For this scene we are less grateful to Mary Hogarth; it is one of the least-admired of his productions today. Yet one feature of the scene does deserve pausing over: the handling of time. Nell dies in a Gothic cottage in the country, a setting which Dickens says arouses "that solemn feeling with which we contemplate the work of ages that have become but drops of water in the great ocean of eternity." More specifically, as Nell's would-be rescuers approach the cottage and

---

[17] John Butt and Kathleen Tillotson, *Dickens at Work* (London, 1957), p. 73.

churchyard on the night of her death, time seems to be blotted
out by snow and night:

The old church tower clad in a ghostly garb of pure cold white, again
rose up before them, and a few moments brought them close beside
it. . . . An ancient sun-dial on the belfry wall was nearly hidden by the
snow-drift, and scarcely to be known for what it was. Time itself
seemed to have grown dull and old, as if no day were ever to displace
the melancholy night.

The suspension of clock-time in conjunction with death is an effective touch. It is one later to be exploited much more fully in
connection with Miss Havisham in *Great Expectations*. In fact
most of the setting for Nell's death is effectively represented; the
trouble is with the foreground figures. The staginess of these
makes the promising background, with its emphasis on past time,
seem stagy too.

In 1843, however, with the fable of *The Christmas Carol*, we
find evidence of Dickens moving more specifically in the direction
we are trying to track down. His aims in this story, as he explains
in a letter, were as follows: "I converted Mr. Scrooge by teaching
him that a Christian heart can not be shut up in itself, but must
live in the Past, the Present, and the Future, and must be a link
of this great human chain, and must have sympathy with everything." The fable remains a simple fable, yet of Scrooge, no matter
how flat the character, we are made aware (as we are not made
aware in Quilp's case, for example) that the miser is a product of
past experiences. The story centers upon Scrooge's having to confront that past, and when he sees the image of his own childhood,
he mutters, "I wish . . . but it's too late now." In *The Christmas
Carol*, as it happens, it isn't too late. In the novels it usually is too
late, as when Gradgrind misses the chance of a "wavering moment" to get to know the heart of his daughter when he is outlining to her Mr. Bounderby's proposal of marriage: "and the
moment shot away into the plumbless depths of the past, to mingle
with all the lost opportunities that are drowned there."

Sometimes a moment of realization may provide a brief release
through a character's freshly acquired awareness, but the release
is an impermanent one. Near the end of *Great Expectations* Miss
Havisham suffers from remorse and makes desperate efforts to re-
pair some of the harm she has caused Pip, but it *is* too late. She

has spent her life, as Hillis Miller says nicely, with her grief crystallized "into an eternal moment of shock and sorrow, like those of Faulkner's characters who remain immobilized with their backs to the future, facing some terrible event in the past which has determined the meaning of their lives." [18]

⌘

The difference between these later time-conscious novels and the early *Pickwick Papers* might be concisely described as the difference between a tour and a pilgrimage.[19]

How does a pilgrimage differ from a Smollett-like tour? Both involve a series of seemingly disconnected incidents, but the pilgrimage adds a new comprehensiveness beyond the scope of the tour because of the pilgrim's immersion in time as well as in space. The true tourist does not pause to reflect; he simply rushes forward collecting labels upon his baggage to reassure himself, as Conrad noted in *Lord Jim*, that he has his tokens for having paid the expected visits. The pilgrim, on the contrary, if he is to reach his Heavenly or earthly city, pauses on occasions and becomes aware of the burden of the past he carries on his back, occasions when he broods upon that burden and its contents of pains and pleasures. Action is halted, and into the hero's consciousness there floods an awareness of a past to which he must try to adapt before he can confront future experience. Time seemingly stands still or, more exactly, expands into a new dimension. Pip in *Great Expectations* becomes aware of this new dimension after he has spent what he calls a "memorable day" in the dazzlingly sadistic company of Estella and Miss Havisham. When he has returned home to his bed, the minutes expand into vastness, and normal clock-time is suspended—an experience which in Dickens is not a mystical one but rather, if the contrast may be allowed, a human one:

I fell asleep recalling what I "used to do" when I was at Miss Havisham's; as though I had been there weeks or months, instead of hours: and as though it was quite an old subject of remembrance, instead of one that had risen only that day. That was a memorable day to me,

---

[18] *Charles Dickens: The World of His Novels* (Cambridge, Mass., 1958), p. 256.

[19] Dickens of course continued himself to write of his own tours as in his *American Notes, Pictures from Italy*, and *The Lazy Tour of Two Idle Apprentices.* In *Little Dorrit* he develops the familiar comparison of life with a pilgrimage in order to account for the strange meetings that occur during this journey of all of us who are "restless travellers through the pilgrimage of life."

for it made great changes in me. But it is the same with any life. Imagine one selected day struck out of it, and think how different its course would have been. Pause, you who read this, and think for a moment of the long chain of iron or gold, of thorns or flowers, that would never have bound you, but for the formation of the first link on one memorable day.[20]

Georges Poulet speaks of duration as a "chaplet of instants." [21] Dickens's figure of the chain of memorable moments is comparable, and we find the thing, if not the terms, in Wordsworth's poetry and also in Browning's. In twentieth-century literature, James Joyce has made us acutely aware of these memorable moments and categorized them for us as epiphanies. And T. S. Eliot, in his *Four Quartets* speculates on the moment in the rose garden in a passage I sometimes think I understand, although I'm not sure:

> To be conscious is not to be in time
> But only in time can the moment in the rose-garden
> The moment in the arbour where the rain beat,
> The moment in the draughty church at smokefall
>   Be remembered; involved with past and future.
> Only through time, time is conquered.[22]

A striking feature of Dickens's presentation of memorable moments is that in his writings the moment in the rose garden—the ecstasy of love or of religious experience—is rarely described. His subject, instead, is the moment missed. To cite another twentieth-century poet:

---

[20] Cf. Thackeray's version of the "memorable day" in *Henry Esmond:* "There is scarce any thoughtful man or woman, I suppose, but can look back upon his course of past life, and remember some point, trifling as it may have seemed at the time of occurrence, which has nevertheless turned and altered his whole career. 'Tis with almost all of us . . . a *grain de sable* that perverts or perhaps overthrows us" (bk. 1, chap. 12).

[21] *Studies,* p. 14; see also Gaston Bachelard, *The Poetics of Space,* trans. Maria Jolas (New York, 1964), pp. 15–17.

[22] An awesome passage in *Hard Times* can be cited as almost a gloss on Eliot's lines. It describes how time passed during the eight weeks of Louisa Gradgrind's engagement to Mr. Bounderby, an engagement distinctly lacking in any moment in a rose garden: "Mr. Bounderby went every evening to Stone Lodge, as an accepted wooer. Love was made on these occasions in the form of bracelets. . . . The Hours did not go through any of those rosy performances, which foolish poets have ascribed to them at such times; neither did the clocks go any faster, or any slower, than at other seasons. The deadly statistical recorder in the Gradgrind observatory knocked every second on the head as it was born, and buried it with his accustomed regularity."

> Two roads diverged in a wood, and I—
> I took the one less traveled by,
> And that has made all the difference.

The heroes of Dickens's mature novels seem to grope their way painfully back to that diverging path Robert Frost described and to wonder sadly about the gates of a rose garden that closed against them or never opened, the experience missed. As Dickens himself wrote sadly to his friend Forster: "Why is it, that as with poor David [Copperfield], a sense comes always crushing on me now, when I fall into low spirits, as of one happiness that I have missed in life, and one friend and companion I have never made?" It is not often that we encounter complaints such as this in Dickens's letters. Self-discipline and a conviction that a cheerful front is essential for daily living kept in check this side of the man's utterances. But in his fiction it was not to be suppressed. Here for example is Arthur Clennam after he has spent an evening with the young girl, Pet Meagles. When he recognizes that it would be pointless to pursue her, his thoughts become suicidal:

He softly opened his window, and looked out upon the serene river. Year after year so much allowance for the drifting of the ferry-boat, so many miles an hour the flowing of the stream, here the rushes, there the lilies, nothing uncertain or unquiet. Why should he be vexed or sore at heart? It was not his weakness that he had imagined. It was nobody's, nobody's within his knowledge, why should it trouble him? And yet it did trouble him. And he thought—who has not thought for a moment, sometimes? —that it might be better to flow away monotonously, like the river, and to compound for its insensibility to happiness with its insensibility to pain.

The lonely isolation of the hero of *Little Dorrit*, rendered by his perspective of the London scene, would indicate that he is altogether different from Dickens himself, and yet, as Lionel Trilling has noted, the two have much in common.[23] Clennam, in his early forties, has returned to London to confront his past, that of his mother's jail-like home and that of his early love. The figure used to describe his searching review of his life is strikingly chill: "To

---

[23] *The Opposing Self: Nine Essays in Criticism* (New York, 1955), pp. 60–62. Trilling cites a letter from Dickens to Macready: "However strange it is never to be at rest, and never satisfied, and ever trying after something that is never reached, and to be always laden with plot and plan and care and worry, how clear it is that it must be, and that one is driven by an irresistible might until the journey is worked out."

review his life was like descending a green tree in fruit and flower, and seeing all the branches wither and drop off one by one, as he came down towards them." And the interior landscape in which his withering recollections unfold is, as usual in Dickens, functional to the same end:

When he got to his lodging, he sat down before the dying fire, as he had stood at the window of his old room looking out upon the blackened forest of chimneys, and turned his gaze back upon the gloomy vista by which he had come to that stage in his existence. So long, so bare, so blank. No childhood; no youth, except for one remembrance; that one remembrance proved, only that day, to be a piece of folly.... That he should have missed so much, and at his time of life should look so far about him for any staff to bear him company upon his downward journey and cheer it, was a just regret. He looked at the fire from which the blaze departed, from which the afterglow subsided, in which the ashes turned grey, from which they dropped to dust, and thought, "How soon I too shall pass through such changes and be gone!"

In such reflective passages as these we should note the characteristically nostalgic tone. There is no Hardy-like shaking of the fist at God or Fate; there is, rather, a sad awareness of deprivation and loss which stamps the secret prose with its distinctive mark.

The sources of this kind of writing in Dickens's own life seem then traceable to his response to Mary Hogarth's death and also to the two well-known traumatic experiences of his childhood and youth to which he returns: the blacking warehouse incident reflecting the hero's sense of shame or fear (the accusing face at the window) and the incident of his frustrating boyish love for Maria Beadnell to which he returns in various guises. The Dora of *David Copperfield* is one version; the Flora of *Little Dorrit* is another, and here the cauterizing agent of comedy seems to conceal the wounding ("Flora, whom he had left a lily, had become a peony"). But the comedy in *Little Dorrit* is reserved for the present 1855 version of the fat and florid Maria Beadnell, encountered again after twenty-four years. The 1832 version, preserved intact in memory, evoked a different response and a different style, "this first face" as Arthur Clennam's recollection has it, "that had soared out of his gloomy life into the bright glories of fancy." Or as Dickens himself admitted in a letter of the 1850s: "I cannot see the face ... without going wandering away over the ashes of all that youth and hope." This same figure of the ashes reappears in

a late story and is there combined with an expression made current
in contemporary criticism by Northrop Frye—the *Green World*.
At the end of this story, *Mrs. Lirriper's Legacy,* a man on his
deathbed is thinking back over his wasted life: "But now that he
... looked back upon the green Past beyond the time when he
had covered it with ashes, he thought ... of his young wife in the
early days of their marriage."

As a final example from Dickens, let us look at a paragraph in
Bleak House. The method of narration in *Bleak House* provides
what seems to be a precise demonstration of the division of voices
in Dickens's work of which I have been speaking. Half of the
book is told by Esther Summerson in her quiet-toned recollections,
and the other half by a loud-spoken public-voiced narrator whose
indignant observations are accentuated by his use of the present
tense.[24] But the division does not remain so clear cut, for Esther's
cheerfulness (a somewhat irritating cheerfulness) forbids her "wandering back," as she says, to the icy experiences of her unhappy
childhood. "It was not for me," she observes rather coyly, "to muse
over byegones." And on the other hand the speaker in the public-
voiced half of the book sometimes modifies his staccato mode into
slower-paced rhythms as he pauses with backward glances into the
past. Sometimes, as in Hardy's poems, there is a linking of the
dead and the living which is almost tender. In chapter 40, one
of the finest chapters in this novel, Dickens sets his stage at Chesney
Wold for the exposure of Lady Dedlock by Mr. Tulkinghorn. The
evening sun lights up the portraits of the dead Dedlocks on the
walls and later the moonlight and candlelight illuminate the faces
of the living Dedlocks ("winking cousins, batlike in the candle
glare, crowd round" Lady Dedlock to give her a glass of water)—
and it is hard to tell which are more unreal or more "stony," the
living or the dead. But satire of a decadent aristocracy is not the
whole story, for the scene opens with this paragraph:

This present summer evening, as the sun goes down, the preparations
are complete. Dreary and solemn the old house looks, with so many

---

[24] William F. Axton nicely makes the distinction between the two "rhythms";
the pace of Esther's narrative, he notes, suggests an "order and direction inhering in
events" which contrasts with the sense of disorder in the narrator's portion where
we get an effect of "the forward tumble of time without that sense of proportion
and order imparted to events by hindsight" (*Circle of Fire: Dickens' Vision and
Style and the Popular Victorian Theater* [Lexington, Ky., 1966], p. 223). See also
Taylor Stoehr, *Dickens: The Dreamer's Stance* (Ithaca, N.Y., 1965), pp. 48–50.

appliances of habitation, and with no inhabitants except the pictured forms upon the walls. So did these come and go, a Dedlock in possession might have ruminated passing along; so did they see this gallery hushed and quiet, as I see it now; so think, as I think, of the gap that they would make in this domain when they were gone; so find it, as I find it, difficult to believe that it could be, without them; so pass from my world, as I pass from theirs, now closing the reverberating door; so leave no blank to miss them, and so die.[25]

The unusual shift into the first person in this paragraph (although the reflections are assigned to a living Dedlock) links the public-voiced commentator with man's ordinary lot instead of leaving him, as he often seems to be, outside of it or above it. Awareness of time passing and of death coming makes the public voice momentarily a private voice.

This, let me admit, verges on a highly indelicate subject. One can give a public lecture on the sex life of Lady Chatterley without a ripple of alarm from one's audience. But to discuss publicly the nostalgic emotions aroused by the life of Lady Dedlock is dangerous, almost indecent. Since the 1920s we have not been afraid of the ancient mariner with his glittering eye, but we are curiously afraid of the man with the misty eye, and we exclude him from wedding feasts and polite conversation. The 1920s are some distance behind us now, however, and perhaps we can subdue our embarrassment and allow the nostalgic novelist back with us for short intervals.

An alternative solution or mode of defense would be to stress parallels between this phase of Dickens and the same quality in some eminent twentieth-century writers or writers favored by twentieth-century tastes. The recognition by Edmund Wilson and other critics that Dickens is like Kafka or Dostoevsky or Faulkner or Proust or Angus Wilson has been of immense service to his high status today among critical readers. It assures us that to read Dickens is not only respectable but fashionable. Having served its function of propping him up, however, perhaps the time has come when the twentieth-century buttressing can be removed and we can allow Dickens to stand alone or at least allow him to stand among

---

[25] Cf. Trevor Blount, "Sir Leicester Dedlock and 'Deportment' Turveydrop: Some Aspects of Dickens's Use of Parallelism in *Bleak House*," *NCF* 21 (1966): 153–54.

his Victorian contemporaries (which should no longer be an un-
kind comment to pass upon any writer).

For the two voices of Dickens that I have been trying to illustrate in this discussion are a clue not only to a reading of Dickens
but to much Victorian literature. This point could be expanded
into a book, but let me merely touch on it quickly, offering three
brief examples from Victorian works, all written in the same de-
cade as Dickens's *Great Expectations*.

The usual schoolboy summary of the Victorian age is more than
half right. It was a thrusting, energetic, forward-looking age, confident in its power and capacity to subdue the world of nature and
of lesser breeds in every continent of the globe. Our great-grandfathers spoke to headwaiters in a way that makes our more mousey
generations wince, and they spoke confidently too about all manner of subjects. They knew, or they acted as if they did, and Macaulay was their spokesman. And this future-oriented confidence
infected the artists of the age with a marked sense of their responsibilities to the public. Even Thackeray, whose cast of mind
seems vastly different from that of Macaulay (or of Dickens for
that matter), could affirm in a letter of 1847 that the novelist's role
was "as serious as the Parson's own," and "having such a vast
multitude of readers" he must "not only amuse but teach." [26]

Almost equally important in their literature, however, if less evident in their political and religious speeches, was another kind of
voice: tentative, uncertain, nostalgically evocative of something lost
and of paths not followed. We encounter it unexpectedly in Carlyle,
perhaps the loudest-voiced of Victorian writers, and one of Dickens's
few masters, the one whose public prose most deeply affected
Dickens's public prose. Looking through the letters and papers of
his dead wife, the old warrior is moved to write in a different vein of
gnawing remorse:

It was strange how she contrived to sift out of such a troublous forlorn
day as hers ... little items ... and to have them ready for me in the
evening, when my work was done, in the prettiest little narrative anybody could have given of such things. Never again shall I have such
melodious, humanly beautiful half-hours; they were the rainbow of
my poor dripping day, and reminded me that there otherwise was a
sun. ... I doubt, candidly, if I ever saw a nobler human soul than this

[26] *The Letters and Private Papers of William Makepeace Thackeray*, ed. Gordon
N. Ray, 4 vols. (Cambridge, Mass., 1945–46), 2:282.

which (alas, alas, never rightly valued till now!) accompanied all my steps for forty years. Blind and deaf that we are ... [we see] when it is too late! [27]

Or consider Tennyson, who used to be conveniently condemned as a blatantly cheerful exponent of progress, the steam-whistle poet (as he sometimes is), but whose major bias was of course toward the past—his own, his country's, and the whole of mankind's. One can select almost at random (there are closed rose gardens in *Maud* for example), but here is a stanza from a late lyric "In the Valley of Cauteretz." This anthology piece was written when he was revisiting a valley in Spain where he and an undergraduate friend had shared a day together years before. Addressing the stream, he writes:

> All along the valley, stream that flashest white
> Deepening thy voice with the deepening of the night,
> All along the valley, where thy waters flow
> I walked with one I loved two and thirty years ago.
> All along the valley, while I walked today
> The two and thirty years were a mist that rolls away.

The past here is relived because refelt. A similar situation is also evident in John Henry Newman's recollection of his first meeting with John Keble, a recollection stretching back even further than Tennyson's: "How is that hour fixed in my memory after the changes of forty-two years, forty-two this day on which I write!"

Newman is a most suitable figure to provide for us a final brief example, again another anthology piece. Moving out from the dust of the arena in which he carried on his ever-skillful debates on nice points of theology, Newman confronts in his *Apologia* the story of a memorable day. It is the day in 1846 (twenty years earlier) of his final departure from the Oxford college he had dearly loved. Confronting the major turning point in his life and the implications of a garden shut forever, he writes a brief prose elegy (and here, note, it is literally a closed garden):

In him [an Oxford friend] I took leave of my first college, Trinity, which was so dear to me.... There used to be much snap-dragon growing on the walls opposite my freshman's rooms there, and I had taken

---

[27] *Reminiscences*, ed. James Anthony Froude, 2 vols. (New York, 1881), 2:227, 260.

it as the emblem of my perpetual residence even unto death in my University. On the morning of the 23rd I left the Observatory. I have never seen Oxford since, excepting its spires, as they are seen from the railway.

Poulet says of the Renaissance that man learned during that age a double concept of time.[28] He learned first the joyous sense of becoming, of thrusting forward into a challenging future. And he also learned the anguish of living in time. The Victorian age, our second Renaissance, shared to the full this double awareness. And Dickens was a good Victorian.

---

[28] *Studies,* p. 10.

Dickens and
the Passions

BARBARA HARDY

> There was a fiction that Mr. Wopsle "examined" the
> scholars, once a quarter. What he did on those occasions was
> to turn up his cuffs, stick up his hair, and give us Mark
> Antony's oration over the body of Caesar. This was always
> followed by Collins's Ode on the Passions, wherein I par-
> ticularly venerated Mr. Wopsle as Revenge, throwing his
> blood-stained sword in thunder down, and taking the War-
> denouncing trumpet with a withering look. It was not with
> me then, as it was in later life, when I fell into the society
> of the Passions, and compared them with Collins and
> Wopsle, rather to the disadvantage of both gentlemen.
>
> *Great Expectations* (Chap. 7)

MY SUBJECT IS Dickens's treatment of passion, or strong
feeling, but since the question of feeling in fiction has been
neglected, I have to begin with a few rough assertions, hoping that
they will create, however crudely, some kind of context for the
present analysis.[1] I assume that the importance of the passions in
fiction has been passed over for two reasons: one, the thematic and
structural concerns of novel criticism; two, the subordinate and
sporadic place of feeling in the narrative medium.

We can—and indeed must—look at a lyric poem or an Elizabethan tragedy as a trajectory of passion, but the novel has such
narrative commitments to history, moral judgment, and psychological analysis that the track of feeling may be discontinuous and even
subdued. However, the nature of that track of feeling varies from
novel to novel and from novelist to novelist. There are novels
where we are hardly in touch with feeling at all, and others where
feeling flows in a continuum very like that of lyric or drama. In
Wuthering Heights, Sons and Lovers, North and South, and *How
It Is* the narrative constructs and generates feeling in a constant and

---

[1] This essay will form part of my forthcoming book, *Feeling in Fiction*.

continuous flow. In *Tom Jones, The Antiquary,* and *Daniel Deronda* there is a combination of passionate and dispassionate presentation. To make a further distinction: in *Wuthering Heights* and *How It Is* the passions are wholly dramatized through character; in *Tom Jones* and *Daniel Deronda* there is a recession from the dramatized passions of the characters to the dramatized passions of the narrator, who stands in varying relation to the inferred or un-inferred author, whose feeling may be supposed to make up the drift, motive, or main direction of the novel. Heathcliff's fury of passion, at one time, comes to us through the medium of Isabella's gloating triumph, which in its turn comes through the cool, tired, tough, partly guilty, confident, and doubtful sympathy of Nelly Dean, which in its turn comes to us through Lockwood's patronizing but not blunt interest and disinterest. Behind and in all is Emily Brontë's reckless vitality and so on. We receive Tom Jones's sorrow at leaving Sophia in a more distanced and more cheerful medium, that of Fielding's experienced assurance and amusement. (I am happy to note that Collins includes Cheerfulness and Mirth among his Passions.) We see Gwendolen's recklessness or self-regard in the medium of her author's wise compassion. And in the cases of Fielding and of George Eliot we can say, I think, that the prevailing feeling explored and generated in the novel often breaks through into explicit dramatization. In the case of Hardy, however, I take it we have an author whose feeling about the universe doesn't quite get expressed by Jude and Sue, who prove something to him, and for him, but whose spectrum of passion may seem larger or smaller than his; that is to say, the novel expresses a sense of barely tolerable but necessary and, alas, common waste and frustration, while Sue and Jude mostly express disappointed purpose and love, willful self-destruction or passive drifting with the destructive current.

The meaning of a novel is expressed in terms of feeling as well as idea, and we can thus distinguish the hideous laughter of a Beckett from the compassionate calm of a Hardy, though their ideas about the Universe are far less dissimilar. Each novel has its characteristic passions, and Hardy's range will of course be more expansively and variously set out if we distinguish among the novels. Each novelist has his characteristic passions. There is a good deal of point in looking at the author's persona in terms of prevailing feeling: there is the sanguine, cheerful author, unshocked and on good terms with his characters, the reader, and God; there is the intense, earnest, soliciting one; the rough and rude, the violent; the teasing and leering, tickling rather than stirring passions; the hard-cool, and the soft-cool, and so on. We now begin to veer toward another tremendous aspect of the subject, that of the readers' feelings, and at this point I veer back to Dickens.

It seems useful to start with the simple and obvious question of the characters' passions. The larger issues are all of great interest for the critic of Dickens: the question of Dickens's indulgence, control, and exhibition of feeling and that of his dramatic exploration of passion as against his direct melodramatic manipulation of the readers' feelings are plainly central to his art. But in this essay I want only to look at the passions of the characters. Back to Wopsle, Collins, and *Great Expectations*.

"It was not with me then, as it was in later life, when I fell into the society of the Passions, and compared them with Collins and Wopsle, rather to the disadvantage of both gentlemen." It is one of those comments often thrown up by Dickens, accepted and scarcely noticed after its moment. I do not propose to take it as a neglected text in whose light the novel should now illuminatingly be read. On the contrary, I want it for my text, but it would scarcely seem to be Dickens's. In a novel by George Eliot or Meredith—it could very easily come into *Harry Richmond*, say—it would indeed be resonant and thematic. The characters in George Eliot and Meredith do simplify the passions in their extreme youth and come at least to recognize the subtlety and stubbornness of feelings once stereotyped and departmentalized. Moreover, George Eliot and Meredith are carefully engaged with the task of rendering this complexity as a part of characterization and argument. How Maggie simplified the process of Renunciation, how she selected from her readings and inexperience a dangerously romantic and sexless Love. How Dorothea was wrong about Love and Humility, how Lydgate was wrong about Ambition, Love, and their relation to each other. Like any Elizabethan dramatist George Eliot draws the mixture, tensions, arguments, fights, and harmony of the passions; they compose her psychological medium and her subject. And the process of showing the simplification of the Passions involves a complex passionate rendering; think of Lydgate's enslavement to his passion for Laure and his marginal sense that his habitual self waited him in the flatland below. But there is at first sight something ingenuous and casual in Dickens's criticism of Collins. Dickens himself never entirely throws off those simplicities, extremities, and physical demonstrations which are presumably what he is laughing at in Wopsle's performance of Collins's all-too-performable Passions.

But—as so often with Dickens—to say this is misleading. He never throws off the simplicities, extremities, and physical demonstrations, but along with them go subtle insights and subtle renderings. From *Pickwick* to *Edwin Drood* the Collins method is conspicuous. It is the theatrical and behavioristic rendering, and it has certain disadvantages. The characters rant, rave, groan, sigh, weep, laugh fiendishly, heave the bosom, flourish sticks and umbrellas, toss their heads, strike themselves, hit stones, cast themselves on the ground, writhe, and so on. The disadvantages of the rendering of passion by passionate conduct, for which Dickens's sources are probably theatrical, are plain. The conduct, as in acting, tends to be exaggerated and extreme, and the passions tend to appear simplified and separated. Moreover certain falsities arise: it gets to look as if passions are always acted out and formulated, never inner and introverted, private and secret. Almost any very passionate character in early or middle Dickens will illustrate all these disadvantages. Edith Dombey, for instance, is a most subtle case of moral pride, torment, and self-destruction, but the innerness of her complexity and conflict bears very little relation to her head-tossing, bosom-heaving, and bosom-striking. More oddly, there is no particular reason for all the passionate externals. These are not actors, this is not a stage. Dickens has access to all the novelist's means of rendering strong feeling.

Moreover, he uses them. Speech implies more than it says; take Louisa Gradgrind's famous failure to communicate her dangers to her father as she speaks of the smothered fires of Coketown, and he demonstrates his inability to use symbol and transcend fact. The author takes us into the character's mind and heart: Oliver's susceptibility to Fagin's treatment of neglect followed by friendliness, Dombey's repression, jealousy, shift from almost turning to Florence toward hating her, Clennam's depression—all are in part at least rendered by the narration, by telling as well as showing. So there is at times a gap between the external display and the inner description.

However, there are as many methods of rendering passion in

Dickens as there are methods of presenting character, and in this
essay I can only examine a few. I should like to take my examples
from a fair chronological range, if only in order to insist on the
difficulty of discussing Dickens's development in rendering passion.
I think we might safely say that *Pickwick Papers* separates and
departmentalizes the passions more than any other novel, partly
because of its formal division into melodrama and comedy, partly
because of the extreme simplifications of the characters and action
—often, apparently, a visual simplification. But from *Oliver Twist*
onward I would say that Dickens employs a mixture of methods,
external and internal. Sometimes the melodramatic acting of the
passion seems to go with a crudity of concept so that the staginess
or externality seems to express what limited insight about the feelings Dickens possesses. Sometimes we can say that a less behavioristic and more subtle rendering is uttering a complex insight,
refusing to simplify or even to name a passion, since it may be too
complex and related to other passions to come out in mere tossing
and turning. But there are many very interesting cases where the
chosen method and the insight are at variance, where there is the
display that meets the eye, but where there is also more than meets
the eye, or where we shift from what conduct and gesture can show
to some attempt at a notation of the inner feelings that do not get
shown at all.

To begin with the simple case, let us look at the jealous passion
of Sikes. It is expressed in speech: "I'd grind his skull under the
iron heel of my boot into as many grains as there are hairs upon his
head." It is expressed in movement and gesture:

> Without one pause, or moment's consideration; without once turn-
> ing his head to the right, or left, or raising his eyes to the ground, but
> looking straight before him with savage resolution: his teeth so tightly
> compressed that the strained jaw seemed starting through his skin;
> the robber held on his headlong course, nor muttered a word, nor re-
> laxed a muscle, until he reached his own door.

And in this same chapter 47 it is expressed in action, in the murder
of Nancy.

This is a typical and constant instance, to be found over a wide
range of characters throughout the novels, such as Oliver, Fagin,
Ralph Nickleby, Quilp, Nell, Jonas Chuzzlewit, Edith Dombey,
Carker, Rosa Dartle, Bradley Headstone, Rogue Riderhood. Ac-

tion is a mode of passionate expression used even for the more
naturalistic characters like Bella, Wrayburn, Clennam. It is occasionally used very subtly, as when the outward display cannot be
read by the other characters: Steerforth stirs the fire, but David
cannot read the sign. It is sometimes rather partial and discrepant,
as in Edith, but sometimes perfectly matched to the character and
moral, as in Sikes. Dickens describes Sikes as an utterly hardened
character—"Whether every gentler human feeling is dead within
such bosoms, or the proper chord to strike has rusted and is hard
to find, I do not know. . . ." ("The Author's Preface to Third Edition," 1841)—and the extreme violence and resolution in outward
action is fully expressive of the extremity of character.

But if Dickens sees Sikes as dead or rusted in gentler human feelings, he most certainly does not show him only as the violently
outraged and jealous murderer played on by events and by Fagin.
In his brilliant account of the flight of Sikes Dickens manages something very fine, very striking, and very characteristic. It is a largely
but not entirely histrionic and behavioristic display of strong but
mixed and indeed *unclassified* passions. The author contrives expressive actions that symbolize, precipitate, and blend the passions.
The result is twofold: not only is tension sustained and renewed
after the murder, but the interest is given a human focus, and the
character of Sikes expands in a form of psychological melodrama
where the stage is both interior and exterior. The events themselves
are highly vivid and exciting: the pursuit, the flight, the fire, the
trap, the death. But the inner register is also exciting and especially
so for not being simple or predictable. Dickens is not showing us a
brute nor indeed is he evoking easy compassion for a hunted man,
but he is keeping Sikes (and us) in touch with certain common features of human feeling: loneliness, alienation, need for human contact and activity, repression, energy, and always fear. Being
Dickens, he uses a whole range of effects from the ironic grim
comedy of the cheapjack who finds the bloodstain on Sikes' hat to
the fire-fighting at the end. In the fire we have perhaps the most
successful external showing of something too subtle and complex to
be analyzed or given a single name. Sikes seizes on the fire as an
opportunity to use his energy and join it with that of other people.
His is a kind of rudimentary innocent pleasure, familiar in guilty
or alienated states, in which participation in something detached
from personal problems gives enormous relief. But there is also

here the relief in sheer physical energy, which keeps us also in
touch with the man's brutality, his loss of gentle human feeling.
The effect of such unnamed and natural passions is surely itself
hard to name: in Coleridgean terms we are kept in the "highroad"
of human passions. We are induced to feel a kind of sympathy—
perhaps *Mitleid* rather than pity—and the violent action is given
inner life, the life of nerves and feelings.

For now, a vision came before him, as constant and more terrible
than that from which he had escaped. Those widely staring eyes, so
lustreless and so glassy, that he had better borne to see them than think
upon them, appeared in the midst of the darkness: light in themselves,
but giving light to nothing. There were but two, but they were everywhere. If he shut out the sight, there came the room with every well-
known object—some, indeed, that he would have forgotten, if he had
gone over its contents from memory—each in its accustomed place.
The body was in *its* place, and its eyes were as he saw them when he
stole away. He got up, and rushed into the field without. The figure
was behind him. He re-entered the shed, and shrunk down once more.
The eyes were there, before he had laid himself along.

So far this is brilliant criminal psychology: the involuntary
imagery of strong passion (here, of course, guilt) realizes and sub-
stantiates the hideously macabre presentation of the body with the
carefully placed "its" and the telling selection of the eyes. This
kind of inner drama is found over and over again in Dickens: it
is there at the end of this novel in Fagin's analyzed perceptions in
the court (also playing a variant on the image of eyes), in the analysis of Jonas Chuzzlewit's guilty terrors, in Scrooge's nightmare of
death, and in many other instances. Robert Garis, one of the few
critics to pay any attention to the feelings in fiction, suggests that
Dickens is especially good at showing the passion of anger. To this
we must add guilt and fear—or better, guilty fear. But in order to
clinch the point we should observe Dickens's marvelous blending
of the extraordinary and the ordinary in his rendering of such
extreme states of sensation and passion. After the paragraph I have
quoted comes this:

And here he remained, in such terror as none but he can know,
trembling in every limb, and the cold sweat starting from every pore,
when suddenly there arose upon the night-wind the noise of distant
shouting, and the roar of voices mingled in alarm and wonder. Any
sound of men in that lonely place, even though it conveyed a real

cause of alarm, was something to him. He regained his strength and
energy at the prospect of personal danger; and, springing to his feet,
rushed into the open air.

The broad sky seemed on fire. Rising into the air with showers of
sparks, and rolling one above the other, were sheets of flame, lighting
the atmosphere for miles round, and driving clouds of smoke in the
direction where he stood. The shouts grew louder as new voices swelled
the roar, and he could hear the cry of Fire! mingled with the ringing
of an alarm-bell, the fall of heavy bodies, and the crackling of flames
as they twined round some new obstacle, and shot aloft as though refreshed by food. The noise increased as he looked. There were people
there—men and women—light, bustle. It was like new life to him. He
darted onward—straight, headlong—dashing through brier and brake,
and leaping gate and fence as madly as the dog, who careered with
loud and sounding bark before him.

He came upon the spot. There were half-dressed figures tearing to
and fro, some endeavouring to drag the frightened horses from the
stables, others driving the cattle from the yard and outhouses, and
others coming laden from the burning pile, amidst a shower of falling
sparks, and the tumbling down of red-hot beams. The apertures, where
doors and windows stood an hour ago, disclosed a mass of raging fire;
walls rocked and crumbled into the burning well; the molten lead
and iron poured down, white-hot, upon the ground. Women and children shrieked, and men encouraged each other with noisy shouts and
cheers. The clanking of the engine-pumps, and the spirting and hiss-
ing of the water as it fell upon the blazing wood, added to the tremendous roar. He shouted, too, till he was hoarse; and, flying from
memory and himself, plunged into the thickest of the throng.

Hither and thither he dived that night: now working at the pumps,
and now hurrying through the smoke and flame, but never ceasing
to engage himself wherever noise and men were thickest. Up and down
the ladders, upon the roofs of buildings, over floors that quaked and
trembled with his weight, under the lee of falling bricks and stones,
in every part of that great fire was he; but he bore a charmed life, and
had neither scratch nor bruise, nor weariness nor thought, till morning
dawned again, and only smoke and blackened ruins remained. (*Oliver
Twist*, chap. 48)

Among the many features of this scene is the combination of implicit and explicit comment. Dickens tells us quite a lot: that Sikes
is energized at the thought of personal danger, that it is like new
life, that he is escaping from memory and himself. But he also
leaves a lot to the action's eloquence, and it tells us that Sikes could
only escape from one torment into another, that he needed men
and women, that a delirium of action worked, but did not last. It
is a perfect instance of Dickens contriving an event which despite

melodramatic violence and improbability makes itself accepted because it is such a good carrier of passion. That makes it sound too static: it is, rather, a generator of new passion. We see an aspect of guilt and fear; we also see the needs, sensations, and perceptions that join Sikes with common humanity. I need not labor the additional work Dickens gets out of his action: the fire-fighting gives symbolic expression to violence, destructiveness, desperation, and ruin; Sikes needs the fire, he is also like the fire—burning, raging, and rocking.

This kind of multiple expressiveness of passion recurs in other novels. Perhaps the two most striking examples come in *Dombey and Son* where they not only act locally but also link with one of the main themes and in addition link terrible hands from Dombey to Carker, opposed as apparent lover and cuckold, in rivalry and jealousy, joined as victims of Edith's self-punishing and other-punishing sexual pride and honor. The examples I have in mind are the two railway scenes, the first expressing Dombey's reaction to Paul's death, the second accompanying Carker's death.

The fire expressly exists in order to render Sikes; it is attached to no before-and-after realities in the scene, people, or action of the novel, and this is chiefly why I have called it melodramatic and even improbable. It has the status of sensitive scenery. Not so with Dombey's train journey. The railway is connected with the whole industrial scene of the novel, and we see it grow, make changes, and employ real people. More important though, Dickens makes quite plain the gap between the railway's symbolic rendering of Dombey and its larger life. The railway stands for Death, but like the fire it provides smaller symbolic nuances. Dickens picks up, for instance, the violence of its noise, the iron way, and the speed which "mocked the swift course of the young life that had been borne away so steadily and so inexorably to its fore-doomed end." He also makes it quite plain that Dombey's sensations and feelings are selecting the symbolic points, that the train's journey, landscape, and effects are not wholly or simply as Dombey interprets them:

He found no pleasure or relief in the journey. Tortured by these thoughts he carried monotony with him, through the rushing land-scape, and hurried headlong, not through a rich and varied country, but a wilderness of blighted plans and gnawing jealousies. . . .
Away, with a shriek, and a roar, and a rattle, from the town, bur-rowing among the dwellings of men and making the streets hum,

flashing out into the meadows for a moment, mining in through the damp earth, booming on in darkness and heavy air, bursting out again into the sunny day so bright and wide. . . .

Throughout the long descriptions of Dombey's journey in chapter 20 there are these and other broad and objective descriptions that make the selection plain: Dombey chooses the dark but there exists the light, there is a wilderness without like the wilderness within, but there is also richness and variety. When Dombey moves into the industrial horrors, Dickens make explicit what was formerly implicit.

There are dark pools of water, muddy lanes, and miserable habitations far below. There are jagged walls and falling houses close at hand, and through the battered roofs and broken windows, wretched rooms are seen, where want and fever hide themselves in many wretched shapes, while smoke and crowded gables, and distorted chimneys, and deformity of brick and water penning up deformity of mind and body, choke the murky distance. As Mr. Dombey looks out of his carriage window, it is never in his thoughts that the monster who has brought him there has let the light of day in on these things: not made or caused them. It was the journey's fitting end, and might have been the end of everything; it was so ruinous and dreary.
So, pursuing the one course of thought, he had the one relentless monster still before him. All things looked black, and cold, and deadly upon him, and he on them. He found a likeness to his misfortune everywhere.

This is more complex than the use of the fire, because Dickens is using the symbol and the appropriately violent thing and action not only in order to make the passions plain but also in order to say something about the symbol-making action of passion. It is a way of having your symbol and explaining it.
By the time the railway is used to render Carker's passions of fury and fear, it has picked up resonance from chapter 20. It has come to stand for a monstrous Death by both showing and telling.
The whole long episode following Edith's disclosure in the Dijon Hotel is both telling and yet obscure. Obscure because Carker's fear of Dombey seems excessive. From the moment when Edith warns him, "Look to yourself!" saying that she has seen her husband in the street, Carker is blanched and shaken by terror. A bell rings and goes on ringing, and with it starts a state of great physical terror which continues throughout the next chapter (55)

and which is marked by superstition and confusion. It still seems
out of proportion to any fear of Dombey, but Dickens tries to
account for this, rather cleverly, by relating it to the sexual humilia-
tion Carker has just suffered which seems to "have rent and
shivered all his hardihood and self-reliance":

Spurned like any reptile; entrapped and mocked; turned upon, and
trodden down by the proud woman whose mind he had slowly poi-
soned, as he thought, until she had sunk into the mere creature of his
pleasure; undeceived in his deceit, and with his fox's hide stripped off,
he sneaked away, abashed, degraded, and afraid.

The fear and panic are enlarged beyond the obvious cause and
like the sensations of Dombey in the earlier journey are enlarged
and generalized by the use of the railway. Only, on this occasion
the symbol's resonance appears before the train itself to increase
the irrational blurred force of Carker's feelings:

Some other terror came upon him quite removed from this of being
pursued, suddenly, like an electric shock, unintelligible and inexplicable, associated, with a trembling of the ground,—a rush and
sweep of something through the air, like Death upon the wing. He
shrunk, as if to let the thing go by. It was not gone, it never had been
there, yet what a startling horror it left behind.

Carker is afraid of death, and throughout the description of his
flight Dickens incorporates the unknown object of the fear into
the fear itself. He also makes excellent use of all the rational apparatus of fear. The man feels alienated chiefly because he has been
mortified and hit where he felt most confident, in his sexual vanity.
He also feels alienated because he is in a foreign country. And
Dickens also makes his very self-consciousness increase the feeling
of dissociation in a brilliant perceptive stroke: "The dread of being
hunted in a strange remote place, where the laws might not protect
him—the novelty of the feeling that it was strange and remote,
originating in his being left alone so suddenly amid the ruins of
his plans." Like Sikes the character opens out and largely by means
of acutely rendered new feeling. But the whole episode is also an
inner melodrama of violent fear and desperate turmoil of feeling
—the violence is right for Carker, as it was for Sikes, but it also
keeps us on the highroad of normal experience. Dickens exploits
the symbol's pre-echo; the rush, the bell, the sweep of "something

through the air" are only explained when Carker—like other strong characters in nineteenth-century fiction—is destroyed by the train. Before the train hits him and mutilates him Dickens describes his journey in terms rather like those of Dombey's, the inner feelings being expressed by the outer landscape, but the selectivity made quite clear. The journey is "like a vision, in which nothing was quite real but his own torment." Dickens rushes through pages of descriptive summary where the very rapid generalization serves excellently to convey featureless motion, monotony, haste, change, painfully incessant traveling.

When at the end the description stops and stills as Carker goes on an English train to a little inn where he hopes for rest, the descriptive detail has blurred and whirled into a correlative for his sensations. We are utterly convinced by the comment that "imbecile discomfiture and rage—so that, as he walked about his room, he ground his teeth—had complete possession of him," for what might seem melodramatic and external detail is by now the acceptable gesture of a familiar passion. Like Sikes and Dombey, Carker is possessed and obsessed: he cannot feel at a standstill but has to keep in motion, "riding on nevertheless, through town and country, light and darkness, wet weather and dry, over road and pavement, hill and valley, height and hollow, jaded and scared by the monotony of bells, and wheels, and horses' feet, and no rest." He forgets the day and the time, he increases his "disorder" with wine, he is lured down to the railway and seems to see the trains as Devils and to be fascinated and terrified, holding on to a gate "as if to save himself." Gradually a state of derangement is made clear, though it is finally neither the lure of the train nor the fuddled mind which brings him on the rail. He meets Dombey (and his eyes), staggers, slips, and then meets the red eyes of the train.

In these three very characteristic set pieces, where Dickens attenuates and heightens the action in order to dwell on a passion, there is outward and inward violence. But in two of the later novels, *Little Dorrit* and *Great Expectations,* Dickens becomes interested in strong feeling that cannot be expressed in external events of this kind, where the characters have to feel their passions without outlet. It is true that Dombey does a lot of secret thinking and feeling, and in him Dickens shows from time to time a silence or repose eloquent of repression and reserve. But when Dombey suffers on the railway journey, there is the correspondence of action with the inner passion. In Arthur Clennam's depression or Pip's misery there is no such outlet; the strong feeling cannot get expressed or acted out but leads its secret life, visible only to the reader to whom it is shown in appropriate quiet.

Little Dorrit allows Dickens to show Arthur's depression continuously but quietly because its total environment is a match for it: the miserable city buildings, the dark houses, the dank weather, the prison climate, all provide continuous expressive material. The prevailing passion of the main character is a version of the prevailing feeling and theme of the novel:

> It was a Sunday evening in London, gloomy, close and stale. Maddening church bells of all degrees of dissonance, sharp and flat, cracked and clear, fast and slow, made the brick-and-mortar echoes hideous. Melancholy streets in a penitential garb of soot, steeped the souls of the people who were condemned to look at them out of windows, in dire despondency. ... Nothing to see but streets, streets, streets. Nothing to breathe but streets, streets, streets. Nothing to change the brooding mind, or raise it up. Nothing for the spent toiler to do, but to compare the monotony of his seventh day with the monotony of his six days, think what a weary life he led, and make the best of it—or the worst, according to the probabilities.

This is the opening description in chapter 3 which is immediately followed by the arrival of Arthur Clennam. The anonymous example in the general picture conforms perfectly to the character who actually arrives. It is the kind of correspondence of small image and large character which animates George Eliot's commentary and links it to the scene and persons. Such links are not always present in Dickens. For instance, in the famous opening description of *Bleak House* there is no tiny image of Esther Summerson,[2] and I would suggest that one of the large weaknesses of that great novel lies in a certain discord of feeling, in which the cheerfulness of Esther constantly grates against the depression and anger that mark the narrator of the general narrative and are constantly invoked in the reader. It is of course not just a matter of the friction of passions but of the social attitudes they suggest. But in *Little Dorrit* there is a conformity of passion which makes the local happy-ever-after fit modestly and suitably into the darker and more melancholy larger scene. One is tempted to suggest that the passions of characters are

---

[2] I do not count "the death of the sun." My point is precisely that Esther triumphs and does not die.

vivid expressions of the central passion of the novelist. Even Flora
Finching's love-gush, for instance, is a sad business both in its fat
middle-aged self-knowledge, its goodbye to romance, and its acceptance of moderation as the best in this world. "It was not ecstasy
but it was comfort," she says so memorably of her marriage, while
her love for Arthur had been "the morning of life it was bliss it
was frenzy it was everything else of that sort in the highest degree."
(A beautiful comic example of the refusal to distinguish, separate,
and name the passions.)

Dickens's serious treatment of the tender passions is never his
strong point; he is much better on sexual jealousy, pride, revulsion,
fury, fear, gluttony, sloth—almost anything—than on Love. Just
as his cheerfulness, which is sometimes marvelous, sometimes (as
in Gilbert and Sullivan) maddening, begins to ebb out of the
novels, so a certain improvement can be seen in his treatment of
love. It is true, as Garis observes, that Arthur Clennam's subdued
love for Pet Meagles is very archly shown, but the feeling for Little
Dorrit perhaps needs some such preliminary. Dickens need not
have been so coy, certainly, but a feeling both tender and yet
untragic is just right for Arthur's middle-aged-but-not-all-that-
middle-aged controlled emotional activity. The feeling for Pet is
right because it allows him to suffer the right kind of blindness to
Little Dorrit (it is incomparably better done than David's blindness to his love for Agnes) and because it keeps him in the right
fairly depressed state. His visits to the Circumlocution Office and
his relations with Daniel Doyce also bring out his combination of
energy and depression. Arthur is not a cynic, because Dickens
thought cynicism too wicked to let his hero feel it (Gowan can, of
course), but he *verges* on cynicism. His energetic depression can
pick up images and occasions for its strength of feeling from the
environment and themes of the novel. Of course it also illustrates
the environment and themes. Arthur's disappointment and gloom
are fairly consistent but are gathered into the moral energy of his
desire to do things for people—not an optimistic but a muted
desire. Although he is a striking and central instance of reserve,
there is another. Dickens observes explicitly that his history must
sometimes see through Dorrit's eyes, and so it does. As Arthur sees
quite clearly, she is not used to dwelling on her emotions, and
there is one splendid instance of her reserve which can also illus-

trate the reserve[3] of her author. The instance is "The Story of the Princess."

In "The Story of the Princess" Dickens shows in the storytelling that he knows how fictions may be used to express wish-fulfillment or life-as-it-is, to relate passion obliquely or directly. Dorrit tells the story of a Princess because Maggie needs stories about Princesses, "beyond all belief, you know!" and with "lots of hospitals, because they're so comfortable." But for herself the story has to have "a poor little tiny woman," not at all beyond belief and not at all comfortable. The little woman's secret place—like the novel called *Little Dorrit*—has a shadow in it. The storytelling's impromptu making and the fits and starts and interruptions by Maggie (the Common Listener) is a reserved expression of Dorrit's own secret passion. Not a subtle expression but a quiet one and typical of the novel's prevailing feeling from beginning to end.

This kind of quietness and reserve also shows itself in *Great Expectations* in the form and the content of its passions. The form is chiefly an explicit one, since the novel is a first-person narrative. Pip keeps no secrets from the reader. We notice that he insists on certain complications in loving which the early Dickens would have passed over. Pip keeps on insisting, for instance, on the misery of loving Estella, and if we go right back to *Oliver Twist, Nicholas Nickleby, The Old Curiosity Shop,* and *Martin Chuzzlewit,* we will conclude that even this insight is an advance. But the novel is also full of insight into the general nature of passion. We are often shown the confusion and derangement that marked the extreme passions of Sikes and Carker and again shown Dickens's refusal to name, separate, and classify the passions. In chapter 49 Pip feels both amazement and—he adds—"even terror" when Miss Havisham begs his forgiveness on her knees. He leaves her and goes down "into the natural air" and walks round the wilderness of casks, wet and rotting, the cold, lonely, and dreary yard, and ruined garden. Then he sees the image of Miss Havisham hanging from the beam and comments that "the mournfulness of the place and time, and the great terror of this illusion, though it was but

---

[3] I must make it plain that the whole novel is not reserved in its expression of feeling. In chap. 31, where the Dorrit family rebuke Little Dorrit for walking arm-in-arm with Old Nandy, for instance, we find the characters starting, firing off words, head-shaking, trembling and turning pale, passing a handkerchief over the face, grasping convulsively, clenching, weeping, crying "half in a passion and half out of it" (Fanny), and gasping. Dickens uses the stage fire from beginning to end.

momentary, caused me to feel an indescribable awe as I came out between the open wooden gates where I had once wrung my hair after Estella had wrung my heart." Even the little joke is melancholy. The account of Pip's "fancy" is quieted as well as explained by the explanation.

This recognition of emotional complication comes into the grim account of Orlick's attack in chapter 53. Here Pip manages to describe a mixture of physical pain, religiously "softened" thoughts, detestation, despair, terror, and considerable mental activity. The varying passions are linked and rendered by this insistence on the way the mind worked "with inconceivable rapidity." He repeats the phrase, even outlining the range of subject-matter he covered in inner action during one of Orlick's short speeches. Pip is interested in the kind and quality of imagery, as well as the imagination's speed, and says:

My rapid mind pursued him to the town, made a picture of the street with him in it, and contrasted its lights and life with the lonely marsh and the white vapour creeping over it, into which I should have dissolved.

It was not only that I could have summoned up years and years and years while he said a dozen words, but that what he did say presented pictures to me, and not mere words. In the excited and exalted state of my brain, I could not think of a place without seeing it, or of persons without seeing them. It is impossible to over-state the vividness of these images, and yet I was so intent, all the time, upon him himself—who would not be intent on the tiger crouching to spring!—that I knew of the slightest action of his fingers.

It is always dangerous to speak of Dickens changing, and if we turn back to the end of *Oliver Twist* we find Fagin's terribly alerted perceptions described in the court scene. But there is a new control and restraint, I think, in Pip's self-analysis. More important, the interest in shifts and shades of feeling is not confined to this kind of crisis in action.

Take the very different scene in which Pip questions Jaggers about Estella's parentage. In chapter 48 there is the account of a dinner-party at Jaggers's house, and Pip's sudden suspicion that Molly is Estella's mother. The realization is shown to dawn in a slow but sure train of association: Jaggers mentions Estella's marriage and predicts that she has got in the Spider a husband who will either beat or cringe. With the subject of marital brutality silently in his mind, Pip notices Molly making a knitting movement with her hands and after a minute remembers that he has seen Estella's fingers moving like that as she really knitted when he last saw her at Miss Havisham's. The sense of discovery is accompanied by a fusing of all Pip's previous feelings of inexplicable connection. Once again we have not only the dramatized process but the explicit comment which controls and increases reserve: "I thought how one link of association had helped that identification in the theatre, and how such a link, wanting before, had been riveted for me now, when I had passed, by a chance, swift from Estella's name to the fingers with their knitting action, and the attentive eyes. And I felt absolutely certain that this woman was Estella's mother."

This sense of reserve and passion is continued through a conversation with Wemmick, through the next interview with Miss Havisham, where he touches on the subject, and then culminates in the interview with Jaggers in chapter 51. Dickens makes the point that Pip's appearance, arm bandaged and coat over shoulders, and the need to tell Jaggers about the fire at Satis House, made for a promising informality, "caused our talk to be less dry and hard." There is the small rich spurt of wit in the image of the two murderers' casts "congestively considering whether they didn't smell fire at the present moment." Pip then tells Jaggers that he has asked Miss Havisham about Estella and reveals his guess. When Jaggers still tries to turn back to business, Pip makes "a passionate, almost an indignant appeal to him to be more frank and manly with me." One of the vivid phrases in his paraphrased appeal to Jaggers is the phrase, "little as he cared for such poor dreams."

There follows a high point of narrative and emotional discovery. The scene is moving because Jaggers tells Estella's story, but also because in telling it he reveals that other side of himself, the side not shown, as it is in Wemmick, but from time to time implied. The language of the disclosure is legal—"Put the case"—and cautiously so. It is also impersonal—"he lived in an atmosphere of evil"—and cautiously so. The whole story expresses his sympathy and generosity and there are explicitly telling breaks, as when he picks up Pip's assumption that he would not care for the "poor dreams":

Mr. Jaggers nodded his head retrospectively two or three times, and actually drew a sigh. "Pip," said he, "we won't talk about 'poor dreams'; you know more about such things than I, having much fresher experience of that kind."

And again, in the middle of his story:

"But add the case that you had loved her, Pip, and had made her the subject of those 'poor dreams' which have, at one time or another, been in the heads of more men than you think likely, then I tell you that you had better—and would much sooner when you had thought of it—chop off that bandaged left hand of yours. . . ."

It is such implications of reserve, and of the capacity and history of the reserve, that show the other side of Jaggers. This show of restraint and passion makes not only that moving impression of the felt life and complexity of a minor character, but more importantly, for this novel, of the unprofessional and unconditioned "natural" life that the barrister shares with his clerk. Their affinity is made very plain when Pip tries to use Wemmick's Aged-Parent side to pry open Jaggers's heart, and Jaggers smiles in response. The point is reaffirmed at the end of the chapter when Wemmick challenges Mike's comment, "a man can't help his feelings," and says severely, "his what?" while Jaggers adds, "I'll have no feelings here."

It is tempting to exaggerate this restraint as a feature of the mature Dickens, but we must remember the feeling implicit in the brilliant comic reserve of Dick Swiveller and the Marchioness, one of Dickens's few moving love stories and one of his most eloquent appeals on behalf of the victimized child. What we can say with some certainty is that Dickens comes to provide a greater continuity of feeling in his later novels. A thematic analysis would point out the idea of nature and denaturing running not only through the stories of Pip, Estella, and Miss Havisham but also through the minor figures of Wemmick and Jaggers, but I prefer to stress the community of feeling created in this and other late novels. Perhaps after all Pip learnt something that Wopsle and Collins did not know about the adult passions—that they are *always* with us, whether spoken or acted out or not, that they are always with *all* of us, and that they do not come on one at a time.

The Fiction
of Realism:

Sketches by Boz, Oliver Twist,
and Cruikshank's Illustrations

J. HILLIS MILLER

...the illusion was reality itself.[1]

One important aspect of current literary criticism is the disintegration of the paradigms of realism under the impact of structural linguistics and the renewal of rhetoric.[2] If meaning in language rises not from the reference of signs to something outside words but from differential relations among the words themselves, if "referent" and "meaning" must always be distinguished, then the notion of a literary text which is validated by its one-to-one correspondence to some social, historical, or psychological reality can no longer be taken for granted. No language

---

[1] Charles Dickens, *Sketches by Boz*, The Oxford Illustrated Dickens (London: Oxford University Press, 1966), 493. Further quotations from this text will be identified as *SB*, followed by the page number. I wish to thank Mr. William E. Conway, Librarian of the Clark Library, and Mr. William D. Schaefer, Chairman of the Department of English, University of California, Los Angeles, for their many courtesies when I delivered the second part of this essay at a Clark Library Seminar. I owe thanks to Mr. Richard A. Vogler for valuable information and to Miss Ada Nisbet for her careful reading of my manuscript and for her expert advice on several important matters of detail. For all these helps and kindnesses I am extremely grateful, as well as for the pleasant opportunity provided by the Clark Seminars for the preparation of this paper.

[2] Among the scholars representing this development in criticism are Georges Blin, Roland Barthes, Jacques Derrida, Gilles Deleuze, Gérard Genette, and Paul de Man. Derrida's "La double séance," *Tel Quel*, 41-42 (Printemps; Eté 1970), 3-43, 4-45, and DeMan's "The Rhetoric of Blindness," forthcoming in *Poétique* and in his volume of essays, are particularly valuable for their formulations of the theoretical bases of such inquiries. My *The Form of Victorian Fiction* (Notre Dame, Ind.: University of Notre Dame Press, 1968) is an attempt to make suggestions along these lines for nineteenth-century English novels.

is purely mimetic or referential, not even the most utilitarian
speech. The specifically literary form of language, however, may
be defined as a structure of words which in one way or another
calls attention to this fact, while at the same time allowing for its
own inevitable misreading as a "mirroring of reality." "The set
(*Einstellung*) toward the MESSAGE as such," says Roman Jakobson, "focus on the message for its own sake, is the POETIC function of language."[3] Realistic fiction is a special case of the poetic
function of language. Its peculiarity may be defined as the reciprocal relation within it between the story narrated and the question
of what it means to narrate a story. One may say of realistic fiction
what Walter Benjamin says of Brecht's epic theater: its way of
establishing the set toward the message as such is "to underline
the relation of the represented action to the action signified by
the fact itself of representation."[4] This essay will attempt to test
these generalizations by a discussion of Dickens's *Sketches by Boz*
and, more briefly, *Oliver Twist*. I shall also investigate the relevance to the issue of realism in these texts of the admirable illustrations for them by George Cruikshank.

At first sight the *Sketches by Boz* seem an unpromising text
for such study. They seem still rooted in the journalistic mode
which was Dickens's first way of writing as a parliamentary reporter.[5] The *Sketches* are a representation in words of scenes,
people, and ways of living which really existed in London in the
eighteen-thirties. Here, even if nowhere else, Dickens seems to

---

3 "Closing Statement: Linguistics and Poetics," *Style in Language*, ed. Thomas A.
Sebeok (Cambridge, Mass.: The M.I.T. Press, 1966) , p. 356.
4 Cited by Jean-Michel Rey from the *Essays on B. Brecht*, in "La scène du texte,"
Critique, 271 (Décembre 1969), 1068.
5 See John Butt and Kathleen Tillotson, "*Sketches by Boz*: Collection and Re-
vision," *Dickens at Work* (London: Methuen, 1963) , pp. 35-61; Philip Collins, "A
Dickens Bibliography," *The New Cambridge Bibliography of English Literature*, ed.
George Watson, III (Cambridge: Cambridge University Press, 1969), cols. 786-787;
Appendix F, *The Pilgrim Edition of the Letters of Charles Dickens*, ed. M. House and
G. Storey, I (Oxford: Oxford University Press, 1965), for detailed information about the
writing of the *Sketches by Boz*, their publication in various periodicals, their revision
and collection in 1836 in the two-volume *Sketches by Boz*, First and Second Series, published by Macrone, their further revision for the edition of 1839 in monthly parts
published by Chapman and Hall and collected by them in the one-volume edition
of 1839, and the final revision of 1850. Mrs. Tillotson's essay (the preface of *Dickens
at Work* says it is mainly hers) is especially valuable for its discussion of the process
of revision which the *Sketches* underwent.

have been practicing a straightforward mimetic realism, especially
in the section of the collected sequence called "Scenes." Here the
reader may find vivid descriptions of many aspects of London life
at the period of Victoria's accession, descriptions which have great
value as "social history." There are sketches of old Scotland
Yard, of Seven Dials, of Astley's, of Greenwich Fair, of Vauxhall
Gardens, of omnibuses, cabs, coaches, and the people who run
them, of Newgate Prison, pawnbrokers' shops, old clothes shops
in Monmouth Street, of gin shops, private theaters, first of May
celebrations, and so on. No one can doubt the "photographic"
accuracy of these descriptions. Dickens has obviously seen what
he describes and reports it accurately with the good journalist's
sharp eye for detail. Moreover, originals for many of the public
figures alluded to in the *Sketches* or acquaintances used as models
have been identified.[6]

The habitual narrative structure of the *Sketches* objectifies
this journalistic model. The basic situation of the *Sketches* presents Boz as the "speculative pedestrian" (*SB*, 190) wandering the
streets of London. Boz is, like a good reporter, detached from
what he sees in the sense of not being caught up in the life he
witnesses, but this lack of involvement liberates him to see with
great clarity and to record exactly what he sees. There is a good
description of this way of being related to the world in a passage
in the periodical version of "The Prisoners' Van," a passage suppressed in the collected *Sketches*. "We have a most extraordinary
partiality for lounging about the streets," says Boz. "Whenever
we have an hour or two to spare, there is nothing we enjoy more
than a little amateur vagrancy—walking up one street and down
another, and staring into shop windows, and gazing about as if,
instead of being on intimate terms with every shop and house in
Holborn, the Strand, Fleet-street and Cheapside, the whole were
an unknown region to our wandering mind."[7] Boz looks at London as if he were a stranger in his own city. He has no business
to be where he is, and therefore he is a "wanderer," an "amateur
vagrant." He refers to himself here, as throughout, with the jour-

---

6 See *Dickens at Work*, pp. 46-48, 52-53, and the essays by W. J. Carlton in *The
Dickensian*, cited in Collins, *Bibliography*, col. 787.

7 Cited in *Dickens at Work*, p. 44.

nalistic "we," which depersonalizes him, reduces him from a private man to a function, and at the same time suggests that he is divided into two consciousnesses. One is the public role of journalistic recorder who speaks not for himself but for the collective experience of all the dwellers in the city, for the universal truth which all know but do not know they know until it has been articulated for them by Boz. Such a truth is shared by all but is visible only to those who are disengaged from immediate involvement in the life of the city. Behind this collective self is Boz's other self, the private man behind the public role, who watches the journalist at work, somewhat self-consciously. This deeper self, it may be, expresses his private experience or private peculiarities covertly by way of the conventional mask.

Another text from the "Scenes" will show the characteristically exact notation of dress, behavior, time, and locale which Dickens's amateur vagrant makes of what he sees. Roland Barthes has called attention to the role of the "irrelevant detail" in fiction or in history as a device for establishing the authenticity of what is reported and for conveying "l'effet du réel."[8] In such passages as the following the distinction between "relevant" and "irrelevant" detail seems in principle impossible to make. The entire purpose of the passage is to tell the reader that such scenes do in fact exist in the London streets on a Sunday afternoon and that Boz has watched them with an eye on which nothing is lost, no detail "irrelevant." Each item is able by the fact of its existence to contribute to Boz's amusement and to ours:

Can any one fail to have noticed them in the streets on Sunday? And were there ever such harmless efforts at the grand and magnificent as the young fellows display! We walked down the Strand, a Sunday or two ago, behind a little group; and they furnished food for our amusement the whole way. They had come out of some part of the city; it was between three and four o'clock in the afternoon; and they were on their way to the Park. There were four of them, all arm-in-arm, with white kid gloves like so many bridegrooms, light trousers of unprecedented patterns, and coats for which the English language has yet no name—a kind of cross between a great-coat and a surtout, with the collar of the one, the skirts of the other, and pockets peculiar to themselves.

8 In the essay of this title in *Communications*. XI (1968), 84-89.

Each of the gentlemen carried a thick stick, with a large tassel at the top, which he occasionally twirled gracefully round; and the whole four, by way of looking easy and unconcerned, were walking with a paralytic swagger irresistibly ludicrous. One of the party had a watch about the size and shape of a reasonable Ribstone pippin, jammed into his waistcoat-pocket, which he carefully compared with the clocks of St. Clement's and the New Church, the illuminated clock at Exeter 'Change, the clock of St. Martin's Church, and the clock of the Horse Guards. When they at last arrived in St. James's Park, the member of the party who had the best-made boots on, hired a second chair expressly for his feet, and flung himself on this two-pennyworth of sylvan luxury with an air which levelled all distinctions between Brookes's and Snooks's, Crockford's and Bagnigge Wells (*SB*, 218-219).

*

The *Sketches by Boz* seem firmly attached to the social facts of London in 1836. As such, they are apparently fully open to analysis according to a concept of interpretation which sets a solid reality on one hand and its mirroring in words on the other. The value of the *Sketches* is the exactness of the mirror's image. Such an analysis is confirmed by the rather slender tradition of critical comment on the *Sketches*. From the contemporary reviews down to the best recent essays they have been praised for their fidelity to the real. This critical line remains faithful to the linguistic doctrine of Plato's *Cratylus*, according to which "the correct name indicates the nature of the thing."[9] Things, in this case, as the critics note, are to be found especially in a region of lower middle class urban life which had not been much reflected before in fiction, in social history, or in journalism. This stratum of English life is that "Every-Day Life and Every-Day People" of which the *Sketches* are said in their subtitle to be "Illustrative." If there is a fallacy in the concept of realism, criticism of the *Sketches* from 1836 to the present provides an excellent example of the fallacy at its most straightforward. Here it affirms itself in the sunlight with a clear conscience. Nowhere is there evidence of an uneasy sense that something might be wrong with the formulas of realism.

Dickens himself may be said to have initiated this tradition of criticism, not only with the subtitle but also with his claim in the original preface of February, 1836, that "his object has been to

---

[9] *The Dialogues of Plato*, trans. B. Jowett, third ed., I (New York: Oxford University Press, [1892]), 374.

present little pictures of life and manners as they really are." As Kathleen Tillotson has observed, the early reviewers picked up this note and praised the *Sketches* for their "startling fidelity," for their power of "bringing out the meaning and interest of objects which would altogether escape the observation of ordinary minds," for their discovery of "the romance, as it were, of real life."[10] "The *Sketches*," says Mrs. Tillotson, "were acclaimed for their novelty and accuracy both in the kind of life observed, and the penetration of the observer accepting and transforming the commonplace. . . . Throughout the reviews there is gratitude for the discovery of 'every-day life' in neglected but immediately recognized pockets of urban and suburban society."[11] The fullest contemporary statement of this interpretation of the *Sketches* is that made by John Forster in his *Life*. "The observation shown throughout is nothing short of wonderful," says Forster.

Things are painted literally as they are. . . . It is a book that might have stood its ground, even if it had stood alone, as containing unusually truthful observation of a sort of life between the middle class and the low, which, having few attractions for bookish observers, was quite unhacknied ground. . . . It was a picture of every-day London at its best and worst, in its humours and enjoyments as well as its sufferings and sins, pervaded everywhere . . . with the absolute reality of the things depicted.[12]

One might expect Victorian accounts of the *Sketches* to be caught within the Cratylean myth of representationalism. All Victorian criticism of fiction, for the most part, remains enclosed within the formulations and judgments of that myth. The only frequently expressed alternative was the other form of representationalism which values a text for its accurate mirroring of the feelings or subjective perspectives of its author. Twentieth-century critics, however, might be expected to go beyond their predeces-

---

10 Quoted in *Dickens at Work*, p. 37, from *Metropolitan Magazine* (March 1836), p. 77; *Examiner* (28 February 1836), p. 133; *Spectator* (20 February 1836), p. 183. See Collins, *Bibliography*, cols. 786-787. for a fuller list of contemporary reviews, which were for the most part laudatory. Mrs. Tillotson is right to say that the *Sketches by Boz* rather than *Pickwick Papers* were Dickens's first popular success as a writer.

11 *Dickens at Work*, p. 37.

12 *The Life of Charles Dickens*, Library Edition, revised, I (London, 1876), Book I, Section V. According to Collins, *Bibliography*, Forster is also the author of the review in the *Examiner* cited above.

sors. Nevertheless, praise of the *Sketches* for their "fidelity to reality" persists with little change in the relatively sparse commentary the book has received in our own day. Thea Holme, for example, in the introduction to the Oxford Illustrated Edition of the *Sketches*, commends Dickens for

setting down . . . all the small events in the everyday life of common persons—bank clerks, shop assistants, omnibus drivers; laundresses, market women, and kidney-pie sellers: directing his powers of observation and description upon scenes and characters within the daily scope of any loiterer in London. . . . As an example of what is now called "documentary" the *Sketches* deserve a unique place in literature. It has been pointed out elsewhere that more than half this volume's contents are facts: facts observed with an astonishing precision and wealth of detail (*SB*, vii, viii).

Mrs. Tillotson uses the same kind of language as the nineteenth-century reviewers to identify the quality of the *Sketches*. "The tales and sketches themselves," she says, "without annotation, give us the world which the young Dickens saw."[13] Angus Wilson, in his recent lively study of Dickens, says of the *Sketches* that in them "we see how a brilliant young journalist's observation of London's movement is just on the point of taking wings into imaginative art."[14] An intelligent and sympathetic essay on the *Sketches* by Robert Browning, to give a final example, is constructed around the same assumptions. "The London of the *Sketches*," says Browning, "is not fictitious. . . .[Dickens] chronicles much that is small in scale and dull-toned with such fidelity, that it is the distinction of the *Sketches*, as it is that of Joyce's *Dubliners*, that the reader senses the life of a whole city. . . . It is the first recommendation for this volume, that in it [Dickens] gave such a lively account of what he saw and heard in London. . . . Dickens . . . felt the artist's primary need, to record."[15]

The *Sketches by Boz*, in their apparent nature, in what Dickens said he intended them to be, and in the traditional interpretation of them, seem to offer little opportunity for a putting in question of realism. Moreover, the theoretical schemas of a critic like

---

13 *Dickens at Work*, p. 37.
14 *The World of Charles Dickens* (New York: The Viking Press, 1970), p. 84.
15 "*Sketches by Boz*," *Dickens and the Twentieth Century*, ed. John Gross and Gabriel Pearson (Toronto: University of Toronto Press, 1962), pp. 20, 21, 34.

Jakobson allow for the existence of works of literature which refer outside themselves rather than remaining reflexive. In Jakobson's list of the six functions of language the "poetic" function, in which language is focused on itself, exists side by side with what Jakobson calls "a set (*Einstellung*) toward the referent, an orientation toward the CONTEXT—briefly the so-called REFERENTIAL, 'denotative,' 'cognitive' function."[16] Elsewhere in the same essay and at greater length in the influential discussion of two types of aphasia in *Fundamentals of Language,* Jakobson implies that there is a connection between this opposition of poetic and referential functions of language, on the one hand, and the distinction between two figures of speech, on the other. Metaphor is based on similarity and metonymy on contiguity. Poetry proper depends on metaphor, but realistic fiction defines people in terms of their contiguous environment. It favors metonymy over metaphor and the referential function of language over the set of language toward itself. Jakobson, it should be noted, allows for a complex relation between metonymy and metaphor, and for the use of both in poetry: "Similarity superimposed on contiguity imparts to poetry its throughgoing [sic] symbolic, multiplex, polysemantic essence."[17] In spite of this insight into the relation between the two tropes, however, he sees a tendency for language to split into two distinct regions, each governed by one of the "gravitational poles" of these fundamental figures of speech:

In manipulating these two kinds of connection (similarity and contiguity) in both their aspects (positional and semantic) —selecting, combining, and ranking them—an individual exhibits his personal style, his verbal predilections and preferences. . . . In poetry there are various motives which determine the choice between these alternants. The primacy of the metaphoric process in the literary schools of romanticism and symbolism has been repeatedly acknowledged, but it is still insufficiently realized that it is the predominance of metonymy which underlies and actually predetermines the so-called "realistic" trend, which belongs to an intermediary stage between the decline of romanticism and the rise of symbolism and is opposed to both. Following the path of contiguous relationships, the realistic author metonymically digresses from the plot to the atmosphere and from the characters to the setting in space and time. He is fond of synec-

---

16 *Style in Language*, p. 353.
17 *Ibid.*, p. 370.

dochic details.[18]

Here is a clue which, while granting the approximate correctness of the traditional interpretation of the *Sketches by Boz,* may allow criticism to proceed beyond general statements about their "faithful reproduction of the real." Following this clue, it may be possible to identify how this fidelity is expressed in certain habits of language. In any case, the *Sketches* offer an excellent opportunity to test the validity of Jakobson's historical and linguistic schematizations. They were written during the time which he says marks the ascendancy of "realism," and they seem on other grounds to belong unquestionably in that pigeon-hole.

*

In spite of some youthful crudities and some self-conscious awkwardness of style the *Sketches by Boz* are a characteristic expression of Dickens's genius. Moreover, they contain all of Dickens's later work in embryo—the comedy, the sentimentality, the respect for the vitality of his characters, however foolish or limited they are, the habit of hyperbole, the admirable gift for striking linguistic transformations, the notion of an irresistible social determinism in which the urban environment causes the sad fate of the unlucky people living within it. The *Sketches* provide an excellent opportunity to watch the development of a great writer and to see his characteristic ways with words at the level of emergence, where they may be more easily identified. The full implications of the *Sketches* are only visible in the light of their relations to the later work of Dickens. They inevitably derive some of their meaning for a twentieth-century reader from the fact that, for example, he may encounter in "The Hospital Patient" a preliminary sketch for the murder of Nancy in *Oliver Twist.* The *Sketches,* in spite of Dickens's well-known use of metaphor, are in fact based on a brilliant and consistent exploitation of what Jakobson calls "the metonymical texture of realistic prose."[19] Metonymy may be defined as a linguistic substitution in which a thing is named not directly but by way of something adjacent to it either temporally or spatially. Synecdoche, substituting part for

---

[18] Roman Jakobson and Morris Halle, *Fundamentals of Language* (The Hague: Mouton, 1956), pp. 77-78.

[19] *Style in Language,* p. 375.

whole, container for thing contained, attribute for substance, and so on, is an important subdivision of metonymy. In both cases the linguistic substitution is validated by an implied ontological link. Some relation of similarity or causality, it is suggested, actually exists in the real world between the thing and something adjacent to it.

If the *Sketches* are a work for the critic to explicate, searching for patterns dispersed in their multiplicity, London was for the young Dickens, in his disguise as Boz, also a set of signs, a text to interpret. The speculative pedestrian is faced at first not with a continuous narrative of the lives of London's people, not with the subjective state of these people at the present moment, and not even with people seen from the outside as appearance or spectacle. What he sees at first are things, human artifacts, streets, buildings, vehicles, objects in a pawnbroker's shop, old clothes in Monmouth Street. These objects are signs, present evidence of something absent. Boz sets himself the task of inferring from these things the life that is lived among them. Human beings are at first often seen as things among other things, more signs to decipher, present hints of that part of their lives which is past, future, or hidden.

The emblem for this confrontation of a collection of disconnected objects whose meaning is still to be discovered is the list. The many lists in the *Sketches* anticipate similar lists in Dickens's later novels, for example the description of the extraordinary things which tumble out of Mrs. Jellyby's closet in *Bleak House*. In *Bleak House*, however, the contents of Mrs. Jellyby's closet are immediately "readable" as evidence of her quality as a wife and mother. Her irresponsibility has already been encountered in other ways. In the *Sketches* the lists are often the starting point of an act of interpretation which moves beyond them to the hidden ways of life of which they are signs. The law of these lists is random juxtaposition. They are not so much metonymic in themselves as the raw material of metonymy, since there seems no meaningful connection between any one object and those next to it. Boz's task is to discover such connections, and at first the only metonymy involved seems to be the synecdoche whereby such lists stand for the apparent disorder of London as a whole. An admirable example of this motif is the description of a "broker's shop" in a slum neighborhood:

> Our readers must often have observed in some by-street, in a poor
> neighbourhood, a small dirty shop, exposing for sale the most extra-
> ordinary and confused jumble of old, worn-out, wretched articles,
> that can well be imagined. Our wonder at their ever having been
> bought, is only to be equalled by our astonishment at the idea of their
> ever being sold again. On a board, at the side of the door, are placed
> about twenty books—all odd volumes; and as many wine-glasses—all
> different patterns; several locks, an old earthen-ware pan, full of rusty
> keys; two or three gaudy chimney-ornaments—cracked, of course; the
> remains of a lustre, without any drops; a round frame like a capital O,
> which has once held a mirror; a flute, complete with the exception of
> the middle joint; a pair of curling-irons; and a tinder-box. In front
> of the shop window are ranged some half-dozen high-backed chairs,
> with spinal complaints and wasted legs; a corner cupboard; two or
> three very dark mahogany tables with flaps like mathematical prob-
> lems; some pickle-jars, some surgeons' ditto, with gilt labels and with-
> out stoppers; an unframed portrait of some lady who flourished about
> the beginning of the thirteenth century, by an artist who never flour-
> ished at all; an incalculable host of miscellanies of every description,
> including bottles and cabinets, rags and bones, fenders and street-door
> knockers, fire-irons, wearing apparel and bedding, a hall-lamp, and a
> room-door (SB, 178-179, and see also pp. 189, 382-383 for additional
> lists).

Though these things were made by man and once expressed
the quality of human life, they are now broken, incomplete, useless, detached from the environing context which gave them
meaning, and thrown together in pell-mell confusion. From such
unlikely material Boz must put together a coherent picture of
London life. The Sketch from which the list above is quoted
observes that the articles in such shops differ from place to place
in the city and may be taken as trustworthy signs of the quality
of life in that part of London. "Although the same heterogeneous
mixture of things," says Boz, "will be found at all these places, it
is curious to observe how truly and accurately some of the minor
articles which are exposed for sale—articles of wearing apparel,
for instance—mark the character of the neighborhood" (SB, 179).
He goes on to give as examples the theatrical character of the
things for sale in such shops in Drury Lane and Covent Garden,
the nautical character of the things for sale in the shops in Rat-
cliff Highway, and the way the shops near the King's Bench Prison

are full of things sold by the debtors imprisoned there:

Dressing-cases and writing-desks, too old to pawn but too good to
keep; guns, fishing-rods, musical instruments, all in the same condition; have first been sold, and the sacrifice has been but slightly felt.
But hunger must be allayed, and what has already become a habit is
easily resorted to, when an emergency arises. Light articles of clothing,
first of the ruined man, then of his wife, at last of their children, even
of the youngest, have been parted with, piecemeal. There they are,
thrown carelessly together until a purchaser presents himself, old, and
patched and repaired, it is true; but the make and materials tell of
better days; and the older they are, the greater the misery and destitution of those whom they once adorned (*SB*, 181).

Here the literary strategy of the *Sketches* may be observed in
little: first the scene, with its inanimate objects, then the people
of whose lives these objects are the signs, and finally the continuous narrative of their lives, which may be inferred from the
traces of themselves they have left behind. Boz's work is analogous
to that of a detective or archaeologist. From the bric-a-brac of a
dead civilization he resurrects a whole culture, an unrecorded
piece of history. This movement is recapitulated repeatedly. "The
Streets—Morning" (*SB*, 47-52), for example, begins with the
empty streets of London, an hour before sunrise, and as Boz
watches they gradually fill with the life that is lived there. "Shops
and Their Tenants" (*SB*, 59-63), to give another example, begins
with the description of a certain shop and then follows the history
of its successive tenants as they may be guessed from changes in
the outer appearance of the shop.

Perhaps the most striking example of this characteristic imaginative progression in the *Sketches* is the admirable "Meditations
in Monmouth Street" (*SB*, 74-80). This is one of the best of the
Sketches, a text already marked by the special qualities present
in Dickens's mature work. The organizing law of Boz's "meditations" is given early in the Sketch:

We love to walk among these extensive groves of the illustrious
dead, and to indulge in the speculations to which they give rise; now
fitting a deceased coat, then a dead pair of trousers, and anon the
mortal remains of a gaudy waistcoat, upon some being of our own
conjuring up, and endeavouring, from the shape and fashion of the
garment itself, to bring its former owner before our mind's eye. We
have gone on speculating in this way, until whole rows of coats have

started from their pegs, and buttoned up, of their own accord, round the waists of imaginary wearers; lines of trousers have jumped down to meet them; waistcoats have almost burst with anxiety to put themselves on; and half an acre of shoes have suddenly found feet to fit them, and gone stumping down the street with a noise which has fairly awakened us from our pleasant reverie, and driven us slowly away, with a bewildered stare, an object of astonishment to the good people of Monmouth Street, and of no slight suspicion to the policemen at the opposite street corner (*SB*, 75).

Confronted with the clothes of the dead, Boz's speculations bring to life in an instant the personages who once wore these clothes. The clothes are metonymically equivalent to their absent wearers and give Boz access to them. The life which properly belonged to the wearers is transferred to the clothes. These leap up with an unnatural vitality to put themselves on the ghostly owners conjured up by Boz's speculative imagination. The fitting of the old clothes to mental images of their former owners begins as a voluntary act. It is soon described as proceeding without intervention by Boz. It becomes a spectacle rather than an act. The text moves toward that personification of the inanimate which has often been seen as one of the major sources of metaphor in Dickens's work: "waistcoats have almost burst with anxiety to put themselves on."[20] The metonymic reciprocity between a person and his surroundings, his clothes, furniture, house, and so on, is the basis for the metaphorical substitutions so frequent in Dickens's fiction. For Dickens, metonymy is the foundation and support of metaphor.[21] The passage quoted above from the "Meditations in Monmouth Street" moves not only to free Boz's speculations from their voluntary basis and to make them into a self-generating reverie. As speculation becomes vision, quaint fancy becomes grotesque hyperbole, and Boz witnesses the macabre ballet of whole rows of coats, lines of trousers, and half an acre of shoes stomping noisily off on their own accord. Finally the

---

[20] For the seminal description of this aspect of Dickens's imagination, see Dorothy Van Ghent, "The Dickens World: A View from Todgers's," *Sewanee Review*, LVIII (1950), 419-438.

[21] Gérard Genette, in an excellent article, "Métonymie chez Proust, ou la naissance du Récit," *Poétique*, 2 (1970), 156-173, published since I completed this study, has called attention to a similar founding of metaphor on metonymic assumptions in *À la recherche du temps perdu*.

dream bursts of its own excess, and Boz finds himself back to himself, self-consciously aware that people are staring at his queer bewilderment. His return to himself gives him a guilty feeling that he must have committed some crime for which the policemen over the way may apprehend him as a danger to the community.

The initial description of the habitual progression of Boz's meditations in Monmouth Street is followed by a full-scale example of their operation on a particular occasion. From a row of old suits in a shop he identifies not only the person who must have worn them but his life story from his school-days to his death in banishment or on the gallows:

> We were occupied in this manner the other day, . . . when our eyes happened to alight on a few suits of clothes ranged outside a shop-window, which it immediately struck us, must at different periods have all belonged to, and been worn by, the same individual, and had now, by one of those strange conjunctions of circumstances which will occur sometimes, come to be exposed together for sale in the same shop. The idea seemed a fantastic one, and we looked at the clothes again with a firm determination not to be easily led away. No, we were right; the more we looked, the more we were convinced of the accuracy of our previous impression. There was the man's whole life written as legibly on those clothes, as if we had his autobiography engrossed on parchment before us (*SB*, 75).

The row of old suits is a legible text. Its reader is led first to the person who owned them, in a metonymic progression, and then on to the narrative of the man's life, given in this case, as in other similar cases in the *Sketches,* as a connected *récit.*

*

If a movement from things to people to stories is the habitual structural principle of the *Sketches,* the law which validates this movement is the assumption of a necessary similarity between a man, his environment, and the life he is forced to lead within that environment. As a man's surroundings are, so will his life be. This metonymic law functions implicitly everywhere, but it is presented explicitly in several striking formulations early in the *Sketches.* In one place Boz tells his readers that there is no reason to provide an analysis of a certain character's personality. An objective description of what he looked like and how he dressed will convey immediately his inner spiritual nature:

We needn't tell you all this, however, for if you have an atom of observation, one glance at his sleek, knowing-looking head and face— his prim white neckerchief, with the wooden tie into which it has been regularly folded for twenty years past, merging by imperceptible degrees into a small-plaited shirt-frill—and his comfortable-looking form encased in a well-brushed suit of black—would give you a better idea of his real character than a column of our poor description could convey (SB, 158-159).

In another Sketch the three-stage process is entered at the second stage, and Boz's clairvoyant eye sees through to the life story of a solitary clerk he glimpses in St. James's Park, "a tall, thin, pale person, in a black coat, scanty grey trousers, little pinched-up gaiters, and brown beaver gloves" (SB, 215). From the man's dress and behavior Boz can infer his whole way of existence. He states for the reader the close reciprocity which must exist between the two if his inferences are correct: "There was something in the man's manner and appearance which told us, we fancied, his whole life, or rather his whole day, for a man of this sort has no variety of days. We thought we almost saw the dingy little back office into which he walks every morning . . ." (SB, 216). A detailed narration of this man's day follows, including what he eats for dinner and the amount he tips the waiter. In "The New Year" Boz presents an elaborate description of a party in the house opposite his own on the basis of the fact that the house has green blinds. He knows the profession of the master of the house by a glimpse of his clothes, by his way of walking, and by means of those same green blinds: "We can fancy one of these parties, we think, as well as if we were duly dress-coated and pumped, and had just been announced at the drawing-room door. . . . The master of the house with the green blinds is in a public office; we know the fact by the cut of his coat, the tie of his neckcloth, and the self-satisfaction of his gait—the very green blinds themselves have a Somerset House air about them" (SB, 226). A final succinct statement of the law of metonymy on which the Sketches are built is given in the seventh Sketch:

The various expressions of the human countenance afford a beautiful and interesting study; but there is something in the physiognomy of street-door knockers, almost as characteristic, and nearly as infallible.

Whenever we visit a man for the first time, we contemplate the features of his knocker with the greatest curiosity, for we well know, that between the man and his knocker, there will inevitably be a greater or less degree of resemblance and sympathy (*SB*, 40).

Ex ungue lionem—as the whole beast may be conjured up from a single claw, or as an archaeologist reconstructs a vanished civilization from a few potsherds, so Boz can tell a man and all his life from even so small and peripheral a part of him as his door knocker. The *Sketches* are constructed around Boz's exercise of this power.

This law of metonymic correspondence underlies many other characteristic linguistic procedures in the *Sketches*. Many begin with a generalization about a certain class of Londoners and then narrow down to a characteristic case. Mr. John Dounce, for example, the hero of "The Misplaced Attachment of Mr. John Dounce" (*SB*, 244-249), is presented as one version of a whole class of Londoners, the "steady old boys." The part and the whole correspond, and John Dounce's nature and experiences seem determined by his membership in a class of which Boz could give many examples. Many of the characters in the *Sketches* are defined, in another form of metonymy, not as individual persons but as gestures, roles, or functions. One character says, "Yes, I am the upper-boots." He exists not as a man but as "a voice from inside a velveteen case, with mother-of-pearl buttons" (*SB*, 408). The guests at a benefit, in another Sketch, are described not as people but as the drinks they have ordered: "ninety-seven six-penn'orths of gin-and-water, thirty-two small glasses of brandy-and-water, five-and-twenty bottled ales, and forty-one neguses" (*SB*, 254). Here the part stands for the whole in a comic synecdoche which is a frequent stylistic resource in the later novels, as in the admirable metamorphosis of Sairey Gamp's husband, within her active imagination, into his wooden leg: "And as to husbands, there's a wooden leg gone likeways home to its account, which in its constancy of walkin' into wine vaults, and never comin' out again till fetched by force, was quite as weak as flesh, if not weaker."[22]

Metonymy provides a structuring principle for the *Sketches*

---

[22] *Martin Chuzzlewit*, chapter 40.

in still another way. If each Sketch often recapitulates the progression from scene to person to narrative, the *Sketches* as a whole
proceed through exactly this sequence. When Dickens collected
the various texts from their random appearance over a period of
three years in various periodicals, he rearranged the Sketches in
a way which does not correspond to the chronological order of
their original publication. The order finally adopted for the one-
volume edition of 1839 and maintained in subsequent editions
does match exactly, however, the sequence I have identified as
appearing within the individual Sketches. First come a group of
seven Sketches entitled "Our Parish," six of which had appeared
originally as a connected series in a single periodical, the *Evening
Chronicle*. The remaining Sketches are divided into three groups:
"Scenes," "Characters," and "Tales."[23] This grouping seems clear
evidence that Dickens had become to some degree aware of the
principle which had governed his imagination during the composition of the *Sketches*. From scene to character to tale—the
metonymic chain of substitutions could not be more clearly
named. The *Sketches* when they were first collected were set side
by side like the heterogeneous objects in a junk shop, but the
final ordering reveals a significant relationship among them which
was at first hidden but which can be revealed by their proper
juxtaposition.

   The clue taken from Roman Jakobson has seemingly sustained
a vindication of the traditional description of the *Sketches* as realistic copying and an identification of the basic trope whereby that
mimesis is performed. Moreover, it is easy to see how, in the case
of the *Sketches*, the predominance of metonymy reinforces that
deterministic vision of man's life which is often said to be an
essential aspect of realistic fiction. One narrative pattern recurring in the *Sketches* is an apparently inescapable progression of
the city dwellers step by step toward starvation, sickness, degradation, crime, depravity, suicide, or execution. A character caught
in this progression is "impelled by sheer necessity, down the
precipice that [has] led him to a lingering death" (*SB*, 78). Such a
sequence occurs in "Our Next-Door Neighbour," in "The Pawn-

   [23] See *Dickens at Work*, pp. 41-43, 56-57, for a discussion of the ordering and reordering of the *Sketches* in the collected editions of 1836 and 1839.

broker's Shop," in "The Hospital Patient," "The Prisoners' Van,"
and "The Black Veil," as the rather acerbic ending to a comic
tale in "A Passage in the Life of Mr. Watkins Tottle," and with
melodramatic emphasis in the last Sketch, "The Drunkard's
Death." There is a close relation between metonymy and this
form of narrative. The story of a man's degeneration "impelled
by sheer necessity" constitutes a spreading out on the diachronic
scale of the determinism implied synchronically in saying that
each man is defined by what is around him. The Tales are often
the temporal unfolding of what is initially affirmed pictorially, in
the instant of juxtaposition within a Sketch. Three examples of
this will bring into the open the implicit relation between spatial
and temporal contiguity in the *Sketches*. The law of metonymic
correspondence is presupposed as much in the narrative sequence
of the Tales as in the interpretation of the Scenes and Characters
from which these tales emerge. The scenes may present as a
simultaneous tableau a progression which is achieved by a single
individual only through a long period of his life. The presence
in a single instant of more than one stage of such a progression
strongly persuades the reader of the inevitability of the sequence.

One such scene is Boz's glimpse of two young girls, sisters, the
elder defiant, the younger weeping bitterly, being taken from the
Bow Street police station to the prisoners' van which will convey
them to jail:

These two girls had been thrown upon London streets, their vices and
debauchery, by a sordid and rapacious mother. What the younger girl
was then, the elder sister had been once; and what the elder then was,
the younger must soon become. A melancholy prospect, but how surely
to be realised; a tragic drama, but how often acted! ... The progress
of these girls in crime will be as rapid as the flight of a pestilence
(*SB*, 274).

Another such text makes explicit once more the way the physical
objects Boz encounters in London contain folded up in themselves a multitude of tales. Again there appears the motif of the
"progress" frozen into a series of juxtaposed vignettes. The object
contains, immobilized in an instant, the temporal history of the
men and women who have used it: "What an interesting book a
hackney-coach might produce, if it could carry as much in its

head as it does in its body! . . . How many stories might be related of the different people it had conveyed on matters of business or profit—pleasure or pain! And how many melancholy tales of the same people at different periods! The country-girl—the showy, over-dressed woman—the drunken prostitute! The raw apprentice —the dissipated spendthrift—the thief!" (SB, 84). The final example appears in "The Pawnbroker's Shop." Three women side by side in the shop constitute three stages from shabby genteel respectability to destitution and misery:

Who shall say how soon these women may change places? The last has but two more stages—the hospital and the grave. How many females situated as her two companions are, and as she may have been once, have terminated the same wretched course, in the same wretched manner! One is already tracing her footsteps with frightful rapidity. How soon may the other follow her example! How many have done the same! (SB, 195) .

Here are three excellent demonstrations of the metonymic basis of realistic narrative. Such narrative places in temporal sequence what can also be seen as spatially contiguous. The diachronic sequence has the same irresistible coercion as the synchronic law which says that between a man and his door knocker there will inevitably be some degree of resemblance and sympathy.

*

Tales like "The Drunkard's Death," in the final ordering of the *Sketches*, seem to emerge as linear narrative out of the static poses of the earlier Scenes and Characters. They also anticipate the grimmer side of Dickens's later fiction, for example the slow deaths of those destroyed by the Court of Chancery in *Bleak House*. Stories in this mode, however, by no means make up the majority of the Tales, nor of the briefer narratives interpolated in the earlier Sketches. Most of the Tales are comic or farcical stories. They anticipate more Sairey Gamp or Mr. Pecksniff than the career of Jonas Chuzzlewit. The comic Tales are also anticipated in the more journalistic Scenes, for example in the admirable account of "Aggerawatin Bill," the omnibus cad (SB, 146-151), or in the description of the visit of a bourgeois family to Astley's

(*SB*, 104-106). What interpretation of the comedy of the *Sketches* can be made?

To account for the comic aspect of the *Sketches* is one path (there are others) which leads to a recognition that the analysis of them so far undertaken here has been a good example of the way a literary text may contain the invitation to its radical misreading. We have been inveigled into taking as *mimesis* solidly based on an extra-literary world a work which is in fact fiction and which contains the linguistic clues allowing the reader to recognize that it is fiction. Moreover, this accounting for its status as literature takes place in a way especially appropriate to narrative fiction, by a reciprocity between the Scenes, Characters, and Tales themselves, and the implications of Dickens's "representation" of them.

The theme of deception, play-acting, illusion, baseless convention pervades the *Sketches*, and Boz repeatedly performs what may be defined as an act of demystification. As a detached spectator he sees that the pretense is pretense and shows it as such to the reader, but for the most part the characters remain trapped in their illusions. This theme takes a number of different forms in the *Sketches*. One recurrent motif is the imitation of the upper class by the middle or lower class. Boz sees the speech, dress, and behavior of the aristocracy as conventions based on no substantial worth. They are justified by no supernatural models, no "divine right." The apprentices of London, however, in "Thoughts about People," or the *nouveaux riches* of "The Tuggses at Ramsgate," take the shadow for the substance. The four apprentices who go out for a Sunday stroll adorned "like so many bridegrooms" are said to be "the faint reflection of higher lights." In their good humor and innocent self-deception they seem to Boz "more tolerable" than the aristocracy they imitate, "precocious puppyism in the Quadrant, whiskered dandyism in Regent Street and Pall Mall, or gallantry in its dotage anywhere" (*SB*, 219). Mr. Tuggs in "The Tuggses at Ramsgate" is a London grocer who inherits a fortune and straightway leaves for Ramsgate. The story which ensues is the traditional one of the social climbers who are in their naiveté defrauded by a dishonest couple whom they take to be authentic members of the social class they wish to join. Mr. Frederick Malderton, in "Horatio Sparkins," was a young man "who always dressed according to the fashions of the months; who went up the water twice a week in the season; and who actually had an intimate friend who once knew a gentleman who formerly lived in the Albany" (*SB*, 358). His family "affected fashion, taste, and many other fooleries, in imitation of their betters, and had a very decided and becoming horror of anything which could, by possibility, be considered *low*" (*SB*, 356). The story turns on the way the Malderton family take Horatio Sparkins to be a nobleman in disguise and then discover that he is actually an assistant in a linen-draper's shop in the Tottenham Court Road.

If the theme of the inauthentic imitation by the lower middle class of an upper class without authenticity in itself runs through the *Sketches*, an even more pervasive theme is theatrical imitation as such. Critics from the earliest reviewers to present-day commentators have noted the importance of this in the *Sketches*. Dickens was already at this time of his life deeply involved in the theater, both as an amateur actor and as a novice playwright. During the period he was revising the *Sketches* he was at work on a burlesque, *O'Thello*, and on a farce, *The Strange Gentleman*, based on one of the Sketches, "The Great Winglebury Duel." The theater returns so often in the *Sketches* that London in this book comes to seem a place where everyone is in one way or another engaged not in productive work but in performing or witnessing scenic representations. They watch others pretend to be what they are not or play roles themselves. Certainly the attention paid to the theater and to musical performance is disproportionate. It constitutes a deformation in Boz's mirroring of the "real" London. In spite of the importance drama undoubtedly had in the culture of early Victorian London, it seems unlikely that quite so large a proportion of its people were obsessed with it, involved in it in one way or another, or allowed their life styles, attitudes, dress, speech, and gesture to be determined by it. The theatrical theme is also a good example of the way a topic frequently appears in the early journalistic Sketches and then is picked up as the background for a more frankly "fictional" treatment in the Characters or Tales.

Among the Scenes is the admirable sketch of "Astley's." This includes not only a description of the circus part of the performance but also a reference to the farces and melodramas which accompany the circus and a description of the hangers-on around the stage-doors of minor theaters. Central in "Greenwich Fair" is the description of "Richardson's," "where you have a melo-drama (with three murders and a ghost), a pantomime, a comic song, an overture, and some incidental music, all done in five-and-twenty minutes" (SB, 115). This is followed by an amusing paragraph describing the action of the melodrama. Next comes an important Sketch of "Private Theatres," then a description of "Vauxhall Gardens by Day." The theatrical or musical theme appears in several of the Characters: in "The Mistaken Milliner. A Tale of Ambition," which tells how a little milliner is persuaded to take voice lessons and then fails miserably at her first concert; in "The Dancing Academy"; in the visit to the theater in "Making a Night of It"; in the concert and vaudeville in the suburbs in "Miss Evans and the Eagle." Among the Tales there are musical performances aboard ship in "The Steam Excursion" and a return to the theme of private theatricals in "Mrs. Joseph Porter."

Throughout the *Sketches* characters are introduced whose lives are determined by the theater, for example a man seen "lounging up Drury Lane" in "Shabby-Genteel People": "The 'harmonic meetings' at some fourth-rate public-house, or the purlieus of a private theatre, are his chosen haunts; he entertains a rooted antipathy to any kind of work, and is on familiar terms with several pantomime men at the large houses" (SB, 262-263). Another example is prefatory to a description of the brokers' shops in the neighborhood of Drury Lane and Covent Garden:

This is essentially a theatrical neighbourhood. There is not a potboy in the vicinity who is not, to a greater or less extent, a dramatic character. The errand-boys and chandler's-shop-keepers' sons are all stage-struck: they "gets up" plays in back kitchens hired for the purpose, and will stand before a shop-window for hours, contemplating a great staring portrait of Mr. Somebody or other, of the Royal Coburg Theatre, "as he appeared in the character of Tongo the Denounced." The consequence is, that there is not a marine-store shop in the neighbourhood, which does not exhibit for sale some faded articles of dramatic finery (SB, 179).

"All the minor theatres in London," says Boz, "especially the lowest, constitute the centre of a little stage-struck neighbourhood" (*SB*, 120).

The two most extended treatments of this theme of fascination by the drama are the descriptions of amateur theatricals in "Private Theatres" and in the Tale called "Mrs. Joseph Porter." A passage in the last paragraph of the periodical version of "Astley's," later omitted, anticipates the topic which is treated with great circumstantiality and verve in "Private Theatres":

It is to us matter of positive wonder and astonishment that the infectious disease commonly known by the name of "stage-struck," has never been eradicated, unless people really believe that the privilege of wearing velvet and feathers for an hour or two at night, is sufficient compensation for a life of wretchedness and misery. It is stranger still, that the denizens of attorneys' offices, merchants' counting-houses, haberdashers' shops, and coal sheds, should squander their own resources to enrich some wily vagabond by paying—actually paying, and dearly too—to make unmitigated and unqualified asses of themselves at a Private Theatre.[24]

"Mrs. Joseph Porter" is probably based on "Dickens's amateur production of *Clari* at Bentinck Street on 27 Apr. 1833; it may also bear some relation to his burlesque *O'Thello*, written about this time."[25] The Tale describes an amateur performance of *Othello* by a Clapham family all "infected with the mania for Private Theatricals" (*SB*, 421). From the near-slum areas where the private theaters flourish to the well-to-do suburbs like Clapham, from the edges of poverty to the upper middle class,[26] all Boz's London seems to have caught the disease of theatrical representation.

*

The theater permeates the *Sketches* in still another way, a way that will allow a more precise identification of its significance. If there are many characters in the *Sketches* who are actually involved in the theater, the theater is also one of Boz's major sources of metaphorical language. This language is used to describe even those characters who have no direct connection with the theater. Along with the people in Boz's London who either play a role or watch others play one there are many other char-

---

[24] Cited in *Dickens at Work*, p. 45.

[25] *Ibid.*, p. 47.

[26] The head of the family in "Mrs. Joseph Porter" is "a stock-broker in especially comfortable circumstances" (*SB*, 421).

acters who unwittingly behave, dress, or speak in ways that make
them like characters in a melodrama or farce. A pretty young lady,
for example, "[goes] through various ... serio-pantomimic fas-
cinations, which forcibly [remind] Mr. John Dounce of the first
time he courted his first wife" (*SB*, 248). Another character is
shown "standing up with his arms a-kimbo, expressing defiance
melodramatically" (*SB*, 269). Another is "one of those young men,
who are in society what walking gentlemen are on the stage, only
infinitely worse skilled in his vocation than the most indifferent
artist" (*SB*, 278) . This man wears "a maroon-coloured dress-coat,
with a velvet collar and cuffs of the same tint—very like that which
usually invests the form of the distinguished unknown who con-
descends to play the 'swell' in the pantomime at 'Richardson's
Show' " (*SB*, 281) . Another person goes through "an admirable
bit of serious pantomime" (*SB*, 279), speaks in "a stage whisper"
(*SB*, 282), and appears later at a staircase window "like the ghost
of Queen Anne in the tent scene in Richard" (*SB*, 306). Mr.
Septimus Hicks, in the same story, speaks "very tremulously, in a
voice like a Punch with a cold" (*SB*, 285). A few moments later
he has an "expression of countenance" more discomposed than
"Hamlet's, when he sees his father's ghost" (*SB*, 285). A maid
dresses "like a disguised Columbine" (*SB*, 295) , and the "manners and appearance" of an Irishman "[remind] one of Orson"
(*SB*, 298). Another character bursts out of a back drawing-room
"like the dragon at Astley's" (*SB*, 309). A series of such metaphors
punctuate the Tale called "Sentiment": a spoiled child is shown
"looking like a robber in a melodrama, seen through a diminish-
ing glass" (*SB*, 325), and his face looks "like a capital O in a red-
lettered play-bill" (*SB*, 326) . Boz makes self-conscious use in this
story of the language of advertisements for dramatic performances:
"Preparations, to make use of theatrical phraseology, 'on a scale
of magnitude never before attempted,' were incessantly made"
(*SB*, 327), and a group of "fat mammas" look "like the stout
people who come on in pantomimes for the sole purpose of being
knocked down" (*SB*, 329). In another story, "The Bloomsbury
Christening," Mr. Dumps speaks "in a voice like Desdemona with
the pillow over her mouth" (*SB*, 478) and later rises from his
chair "like the ghost in Don Juan" (*SB*, 481).

Whenever Boz wants to find a picturesque way to describe one of his characters he is apt to use some simile or metaphor drawn from a range of theatrical reference extending all the way from Punch to *Hamlet*. The characters are not aware of the similarity of their gestures to those of pantomime, melodrama, or farce, but Boz is aware and makes his readers share his insight. Such metaphors present the characters as unwittingly imitative of something which exists in the social world shared by Dickens and his readers. This social reality, however, is openly factitious, illusory. Unconsciously theatrical gestures or speech are the signs not of a plenitude but of an absence. They have the hollowness of a mask. They refer not to the solidity of physical reality but to the fictions of a highly stylized theater. Such reference is one of the chief sources of comedy in the *Sketches*. This comedy presents people not as victims of coercive social "forces," as seems the case in stories like "The Drunkard's Death," but as consciously or unconsciously frauds. Character after character in the *Sketches* is shown pretending to be what he is not. A man in one story displays ostentatiously "an immense key, which belonged to the street-door, but which, for the sake of appearances, occasionally did duty in an imaginary wine-cellar" (*SB*, 433). Another character looks like "a bad 'portrait of a gentleman' in the Somerset House exhibition" (*SB*, 369). Another person's face lights up with "something like a bad imitation of animation" (*SB*, 438). A coach in the same story draws up before "a cardboard-looking house with disguised chimneys, and a lawn like a large sheet of green letter-paper" (*SB*, 436). Everything in the *Sketches* seems to be what it is not, and Boz's chief work is not objective description but the uncovering of fraud.

The theme of disillusionment runs all through the *Sketches*, as in the description of the decay of May Day celebrations in "The First of May," or in Boz's confession that he is no longer enraptured by Astley's as he used to be and finds more interest in watching the audience than in watching the performance, or in that exercise in disenchantment, "Vauxhall Gardens by Day":

We bent our steps to the firework-ground; there, at least, we should not be disappointed. We reached it, and stood rooted to the spot with mortification and astonishment. *That* the Moorish tower—that wooden shed with a door in the centre, and daubs of crimson and yellow all round, like a gigantic watch-case! *That* the place where night after night we had beheld the undaunted Mr. Blackmore make his terrific

ascent, surrounded by flames of fire, and peals of artillery, and where
the white garments of Madame Somebody (we forget even her name
now), who nobly devoted her life to the manufacture of fireworks,
had so often been seen fluttering in the wind, as she called up a red,
blue, or parti-coloured light to illumine her temple! (*SB*, 127).

Such an uncovering of the sordid reality behind a beguiling
surface is the essential movement of the *Sketches*. The drama is
important to Boz not because he is taken in by the theatrical, as
are his characters, but because the theatrical metaphor expresses
perfectly the process whereby Boz sees behind the scenes and
leads his readers to see behind them too. Boz is the man who
knows that behind the stage set is the cobwebby disorder back-
stage. Behind each mask he sees the shabby performer.

In this context it is possible to identify the somewhat surprising function in the *Sketches* of a character who anticipates Scrooge
in hating children and dogs, and in refusing to participate in the
social fictions which make life bearable for others. This bachelor
figure, "life-hater" as Robert Browning calls him,[27] is not so much
rejected by Dickens in the two Sketches in which he appears
("Mr. Minns and His Cousin" and "The Bloomsbury Christening") as he is a surrogate for Boz himself. Like Boz he is a detached
spectator able to see through the falseness of social life. Mr. Minns
is the point of view from which the reader sees the absurdity and
vulgarity of the cousin's dinner party in his little cottage "in the
vicinity of Stamford Hill" (*SB*, 312), and Mr. Nicodemus Dumps,
who "adored King Herod for his massacre of the innocents; and
if he hated one thing more than another, it was a child" (*SB*, 467),
is the reader's perspective in "The Bloomsbury Christening."
Mr. Dumps is granted the honor of using a style of metaphor
peculiarly Boz's own. He describes the baby about to be christened
as looking "like one of those little carved representations that
one sometimes sees blowing a trumpet on a tombstone" (*SB*, 476).
When Boz himself describes the child's arm and fist as "about
the size and shape of the leg of a fowl cleanly picked" (*SB*, 479), it
is clear that Boz (and Dickens) shared some of Dumps's distaste
for babies and for the fuss that is made over them.

Boz's uncovering of the fictive nature of society by way of the

---

[27] *Dickens and the Twentieth Century*, p. 28.

metaphorical use of other fictions is not performed in the name
of some possible authentic way of living. Each way of living imitates another way which is itself not solid or authentic. Each
character lives as a sign referring not to substance but to another
sign. This emphasis on playacting and on the factitious calls the
reader's attention to the fact that English society as a whole is
based on arbitrary conventions, on the fictional ascription of
value and significance to the stones, paper, glass, cloth of which
the buildings, streets, clothes, and utensils of London are made.
This giving of meaning is an act of interpretation creating a
culture, generating those signs which Boz the speculative pedestrian must then interpret. Such ascription of meaning is not free.
The imprisonment of the human spirit in its conferring of
meaning is a fundamental theme of the *Sketches*. The collective
creation of meaning and value is enclosed rigidly within conventions, modes of language, institutions, ways of behaving and judg-
ing, which have been inherited from the past. People in the
Sketches are trapped not by social forces but by human fabrica-
tions already there within which they must live their lives. They
live not in free creativity but as stale repetitions of what has gone
before. The world of the *Sketches* is caught in the copying of
what preceded it. Each new form is a paler imitation of the past.
Each person is confined in the tawdry imitation of stale gestures.
The reader of the *Sketches* receives a powerful sense not only of
the comic vitality of Dickens's earliest creations, but of their enclosure, the narrowness of their lives, their spiritual poverty. They
are pathetically without awareness that their cheapness is pathetic,
hopelessly imprisoned within the cells of a fraudulent culture.

The comedy of the *Sketches* arises from the juxtaposition of
Boz's knowledge of this situation against the blindness of the
characters to it. They are blind either in the sense that they are
not aware that their gestures have the stiff, conventional quality
of pantomimic movements, or in the sense that they perform the
imitation consciously but in the mistaken belief that what they
are imitating has absolute value or substance, as the apprentices
of London are beguiled by the dress and swagger of the Pall Mall
dandies. The comedy of the *Sketches* depends on the innocence
of the objects of our laughter and on the opposing presence of a

spectator who sees the insubstantiality of the spectacle he beholds. At the same time Boz mimes the foolishness of the people he sees, creating it anew in a constant hyperbole which translates it into the linguistic acrobatics of his discourse. The pathos of Boz's characters lies in the fact that their spiritual energy is determined in its expressions by the objects within which they live, or rather by their acceptance of the meaning collectively ascribed by their culture to those objects. These objects are the residue of the culture they have inherited and have coercive force not as physical energies but as signs, habits of interpretation, forms. Such inherited forms constitute a world in which nothing is what it is, but everything is the arrow pointing towards something else. This world of the presence of an absence channels and confines the spirit in a metonymic determination of contained by container, vital energy by environment. In this sense the latter can indeed be taken by the attentive spectator as the index of the former.

*

The theme of inauthentic repetition persists in Dickens's later work and forms one of its most important continuities. Examples are the motif of theatricality in *Nicholas Nickleby* and the treatment in *Great Expectations* of Pip's snobbish imitation of the manners of the gentility when he is living in London. The use of the motif of repetition in *Oliver Twist* is of special interest here, however, not only because *Oliver Twist* is with *Sketches by Boz* one of the two works by Dickens illustrated by George Cruikshank, but also because *Oliver Twist* both in its comic and in its melodramatic aspects grows naturally out of the *Sketches*. The latter anticipate the former in so many stylistic and thematic motifs that *Oliver Twist* might almost be described as the last and longest of the Tales from the *Sketches*. The murder of Nancy, the last night in the condemned cell, the juxtaposition of the respectable girl and the prostitute, the description of a crowd of juvenile pickpockets, the labyrinthine disorder of London's streets, the contiguous presentation of comic and melodramatic stretches of narrative, the comic aspect of a parish beadle, the explicit references to stage melodrama—all are already present in the *Sketches* and are given what might be called their definitive form in *Oliver Twist*.

Oliver Twist dramatizes a covert struggle between two kinds of repetition, kinds which might be associated with two grand antagonists in the history of philosophy: Plato and Nietzsche. In Platonic imitation there exists a substantial model for the act of copying, and the imitation itself is spontaneous. In obedience to this paradigm of imitation, Oliver has no inkling of who he is and nevertheless behaves instinctively according to his God-given "nature." He is incorruptibly good, that is, modeled on his father. Ultimately Mr. Brownlow adopts Oliver "as his own son"[28] and goes on, "from day to day, filling the mind of his adopted child with stores of knowledge, and becoming attached to him, more and more, as his nature develop[s] itself, and [shows] the thriving seeds of all he wishe[s] him to become . . . He trace[s] in him new traits of his early friend, that awaken[s] in his own bosom old remembrances, melancholy and yet sweet and soothing" (*OT*, 367-368). Oliver ends his life as a copy of his father.

Shadowily set against this, its mirror image and yet its deadly opposite, as the sophist in Plato is the dangerous simulacrum of the philosopher, is another kind of repetition. This other kind is present in *Oliver Twist* as a secret possibility which puts in question the credibility of the happy ending. It also puts in question the status of the novel as "realism" or as "history." This alternative form of copying brings into the open the inauthenticity of what is imitated. It is based on difference rather than on similarity. For it there is no eternal realm of archetypal models, no divine center.[29]

Dickens affirms the first kind of repetition and rejects the second, but the hidden energy behind the novel is the tension between the two. This tension is present in the opposition between those passages which confess that the model for the novel's structure is not the real world but popular melodrama, and those passages which affirm, perhaps a bit too emphatically, the historical verisimilitude of the novel. On the one hand, the narrator calls

---

28 Charles Dickens, *Oliver Twist,* The Clarendon Dickens, ed. Kathleen Tillotson (Oxford: Oxford University Press, 1966) , p. 365. Further quotations from this text will be identified as *OT*, followed by the page number.

29 For a discussion of the opposition between these two kinds of copying, see Gilles Deleuze, "Platon et le simulacre," *Logique du sens* (Paris: Les Éditions de Minuit, 1969) , pp. 292-307.

attention to the fact that *Oliver Twist* is structured according
to stage conventions and, like "all good, murderous melodramas,"
"present[s] the tragic and the comic scenes, in as regular alternation, as the layers of red and white in a side of streaky, well-cured
bacon" (*OT*, 105). On the other hand, Dickens, in the preface
to the third edition of 1841, argues of his presentation of Nancy
that "it is useless to discuss whether the conduct and character
of the girl seems natural or unnatural, probable or improbable,
right or wrong. IT IS TRUE" (*OT*, lxv). Dickens seems to have
been at least partly aware of the similarity between the two forms
of imitation in conflict here and of the threat that one poses to
the other. Fagin's hidden society of thieves bears a sinister resemblance to the good bourgeois world of Mr. Brownlow. The
unsettling similarity of the community of outlaws to the community of the good puts the validity of the latter in question.
The moment when this similarity is brought most dramatically
into the open is the moment, it may be, when Oliver is in greatest
danger of losing his birthright by betraying the conditions of his
father's will. This moment comes in the scene in which Fagin
enacts the role Mr. Brownlow is going to play in the following
chapter, the chapter in which Oliver is arrested for the supposed
picking of Mr. Brownlow's pocket as he stands at a bookstall:

When the breakfast was cleared away, the merry old gentleman
and the two boys played at a very curious and uncommon game, which
was performed in this way: The merry old gentleman: placing a
snuff-box in one pocket of his trousers, a note-case in the other, and
a watch in his waist-coat-pocket: with a guard-chain round his neck:
and sticking a mock diamond pin in his shirt: buttoned his coat tight
round him, and putting his spectacle-case and handkerchief in his
pockets, trotted up and down the room with a stick, in imitation of
the manner in which old gentlemen walk about the streets any hour
in the day. Sometimes he stopped at the fire-place, and sometimes at
the door; making belief that he was staring with all his might into
shop-windows. At such times, he would look constantly round him,
for fear of thieves; and keep slapping all his pockets in turn, to see
that he hadn't lost anything; in such a very funny and natural manner,
that Oliver laughed till the tears ran down his face (*OT*, 54).

As the reader laughs with Oliver at Fagin's performance of
the role of the good man, he may realize that Mr. Brownlow himself exists as Dickens's imitation of him. The act of role-playing,
whether within the novel or as its generative source, comes to

seem far from innocent. Its danger lies not so much in the way it is factitious in itself as in the way it leads the reader to suspect that what is imitated may be factitious too. This suspicion is reinforced a few paragraphs later when Fagin exhorts Oliver, apropos of the Dodger and his friend: "Make 'em your models, my dear. Make 'em your models . . . ; do everything they bid you, and take their advice in all matters: especially the Dodger's, my dear. He'll be a great man himself; and will make you one too, if you take pattern by him" (*OT*, 55). The Dodger, his dead father—these two models are presented to Oliver as patterns for his imitation. He must choose which to copy. What is the difference between imitating the one and imitating the other? Does it lie only in the fact that in one case the imitation is deliberate and in the other case spontaneous, based on what Oliver "naturally" is? Which form of imitation is *Oliver Twist* itself? The fundamental question in this novel is whether anyone can break the iron chain of metonymy whereby a person is inevitably like his environment. The determining pressure of what is around them dooms Fagin, Sikes, Nancy, and the Dodger. Oliver escapes this chain only to be bound by another, the form of copying which says, "like father, like son." The strength of *Oliver Twist* is its oblique suggestion that the two forms of imitation may be the same, though it is only in Dickens's much later novels, for example in *Great Expectations* or in *Our Mutual Friend*, that this dark truth is brought more clearly into the open.

*

My discussion of repetition in *Oliver Twist* has suggested that the thematic polarity of the represented action in this novel has the strange effect of raising questions about the status of the novel itself as a form of representation. Does this also happen in the *Sketches by Boz*, or should they be interpreted as a false society mirrored truly by an objective narrator? One way to see that the *Sketches* do put their own status in question is to return to the theatrical metaphors which appear in them so frequently. These work in a radically ambiguous way which contains in miniature the linguistic movement essential to the *Sketches*. This movement challenges the authenticity of what is represented while what is represented in its turn undermines the apparent solidity of the

Sketches as an innocent act of representational mirroring. This reversal between two elements facing one another within the text is basic to the mode of existence of a work of literature and constitutes it as a literary use of language. In this fluctuation the figurative becomes the literal only to be transformed into the figurative again by a corresponding change of what it faces from the one into the other. In this subtle movement nothing moves but the interpretative act, but this movement may be stilled only at the peril of a necessary misreading. Such a hermeneutical wavering is like that egg mentioned by Yeats which turns inside out without breaking its shell, or it is like those Gestaltist diagrams which change configuration bewilderingly before the viewer's eyes. When Boz describes a character as having a "melodramatic expression of horror" (*SB*, 397), or another character as "going through a threatening piece of pantomime with [a] stick" [*SB*, 415), the first effect of this is to present a coolly analytical spectator confronting a real world whose factitiousness he uncovers by comparing it to the conventions of drama. In the second movement of the reader's interpretation, he recognizes that the characters have no existence outside the language Dickens has invented to describe them. Dickens has modeled them on the popular drama of his day. What had seemed "realistic" comes to be seen as figurative, and the radically fictive quality of the *Sketches* as a whole comes into the open. Back and forth between these two interpretations the reader oscillates. Neither takes precedence over the other, but the meaning of the text is generated by the mirage of alternation between them.

When the reader has broken through to seeing local fragments of the text inside out, as it were, as well as outside in, then he recognizes that the *Sketches* from beginning to end are open to being read in this way. The *Sketches* are not *mimesis* of an externally existing reality, but the interpretation of that reality according to highly artificial schemas inherited from the past. They came into existence through the imposition of fictitious patterns rather than through the discovery of patterns "really there." Though this double reading of the *Sketches* would be valid whether it was asserted explicitly or not in the text, it happens that there are abundant clues informing the reader that

the *Sketches* are fiction rather than *mimesis*. These clues identify
the main sources of the fictional patterns according to which Boz
interprets the appearances he confronts when he walks through
London. One of these is the drama, as I have shown. The other
two are the conventions of previous fiction and the conventions
of graphic representation. There are almost as many explicit references to these last as to the theater. If people in the *Sketches*
are often seen as like characters in a pantomime or melodrama,
they are also often presented as like characters in a novel or in a
print. A "little coquette with a large bustle" looks "like a French
lithograph" (*SB*, 480). Another character "with his white dress-
stock, blue coat, bright buttons, and red watch-ribbon, strongly
resemble[s] the portrait of that interesting but rash young gentleman, George Barnwell" (*SB*, 357), and a "young gentleman with
. . . green spectacles, in nankeen inexplicables, with a ditto waistcoat and bright buttons" is dressed "like the pictures of Paul—
not the saint, but he of Virginia notoriety" (*SB*, 392). The reference here is to the illustrations in *Paul et Virginie*. In another
place a character is described as having "looked something like
a vignette to one of Richardson's novels, and [having] had a
clean-cravatish formality of manner, and kitchen-pokerness of
carriage, which Sir Charles Grandison himself might have en-
vied" (*SB*, 431). In another Sketch there is an explicit reference
to Hogarth, whom Dickens much admired and who is mentioned
again in the preface of 1841 to *Oliver Twist*. In the latter, Hogarth
is invoked as an excuse for the presentation of "low" characters
and is defined as "the moralist, and censor of his age—in whose
great works the times in which he lived, and the characters of
every time, will never cease to be reflected" (*OT*, lxiv). In the
Sketches Boz abandons the attempt to describe in language what
could only be represented by a great artist like Hogarth: "It
would require the pencil of Hogarth to illustrate—our feeble
pen is inadequate to describe—the expression which the countenances of Mr. Calton and Mr. Septimus Hicks respectively assumed, at this unexpected announcement" (*SB*, 289). The effect
of this is to invite the reader to imagine the scene as if it were
schematized according to the conventions of Hogarth's prints. If
the reader has this reference in mind he may note, for example,

that the juxtaposition of three women at different stages on the road to degradation in "The Pawnbroker's Shop" is as much modeled on the eighteenth-century pictorial convention of the "Progress" as it is on any observation of the real London of Dickens's day. The "real London," here, is presented according to forms borrowed from *A Harlot's Progress*.

In other Sketches Boz's imagination is controlled by literary rather than by theatrical or graphic conventions. In the examples already given of references to Richardson and to *Paul et Virginie* the allusion (significantly from the point of view of the interpretation I shall suggest of the relation between the *Sketches* and the illustrations for them by Cruikshank) is not to the texts of the novels but to their illustrations. These seem to have stuck in Dickens's mind as much as the stories themselves. There are, however, many explicit references to literary texts. The fare in a cab is "as carefully boxed up behind two glazed calico curtains as any mysterious picture in any one of Mrs. Radcliffe's castles" (*SB*, 471). There are several ironic references to the artificial conventions of fiction or journalism: "Like those paragons of perfection, advertising footmen out of place, he was always 'willing to make himself generally useful'" (*SB*, 382); "Then, as standard novelists expressively inform us—'all was a blank!'" (*SB*, 270); "We are not about to adopt the licence of novel-writers, and to let 'years roll on'" (*SB*, 284); "A troublesome form, and an arbitrary custom, however, prescribe that a story should have a conclusion, in addition to a commencement; we have therefore no alternative" (*SB*, 354); "'We will draw a veil,' as novel-writers say, over the scene that ensued" (*SB*, 369). Even the name Boz, as Dickens later revealed, was an allusion to *The Vicar of Wakefield*. It was a corruption of "Moses," a name in the novel, and was the nickname Dickens gave to one of his younger brothers.

Side by side with the realistic way of seeing the *Sketches* as the discovery by Boz of true stories hidden behind the objects he encounters in his walks through London, there is another way which involves the same elements but with reverse polarity, as the ghost of the other way, its "negative," in which black becomes white, white black. To see the *Sketches* in this new way is to recognize that metonymy is as much a fiction as metaphor. Both are the assertion of a false identity or of a false causal connection. The metonymic associations which Boz makes are fancies rather than facts, impositions on the signs he sees of stock conventions, not mirroring but interpretation, which is to say, lie. A man's doorknocker is no necessary indication of his personality. It only seems so to the imagining mind of the inimitable Boz. An excellent example of this importation of the fictive into the real is the "Meditations in Monmouth Street," which seemed, according to my first reading of it, such a perfect case of the linguistic act whereby metonymy is employed as a decoding of the hidden significance of the real. The row of old clothes which Boz sees in Monmouth Street gives rise, however, to a wholly conventional narrative, the story of the idle apprentice. This story has many antecedents in eighteenth-century fiction, drama, and graphic representation. To remember this is to see that the theme in the *Sketches* of the irresistible coercion of social forces, the motif which seemed to be a fundamental part of their representation of urban life, is not "truth" but literary fiction, perhaps no more than a sentimental lie. If the *Sketches* unmask their characters and show them to be living in terms of theatrical gestures, they also turn at crucial moments on their own conventions and expose these as fictions too. The stories which rise from the doorknockers, the old clothes, the objects in the pawnshop are Boz's inventions, not objective facts. Moreover, far from being the free creations of his imagination they are as much bound by forms inherited from the past as the gestures and speech of the characters within the *Sketches*. The movement from Scene to Character to Tale is not the metonymic process authenticating realistic representation but a movement deeper and deeper into the conventional, the concocted, the schematic.

Nor is Boz unaware of this. In several places he gives the reader the information he needs to free himself from a realistic interpretation of the *Sketches*. To be so freed is to perceive that throughout the *Sketches*, in the phrase I have taken from "The Drunkard's Death" as an epigraph for this essay, "the illusion [is] reality itself" (*SB*, 493). In "Meditations in Monmouth Street" Boz says, in a clause allowed to pass without question in my "realistic" reading of this Sketch, that he fits the old clothes

"upon some being of [his] own conjuring up" (*SB*, 75). Later in
the same Sketch, when Boz is in the midst of his invention of a
new version of the story of the idle apprentice, he says, "we felt
... much sorrow when we saw, or fancied we saw—it makes no
difference which—the change that began to take place now" (*SB*,
76). It makes no difference which because the seeing of Boz is all
imaginary rather than real, made out of the whole cloth of those
old suits. In another Sketch Boz says that "the sudden moving of
a taper" seen in the window of a hospital "is enough to awaken
a whole crowd of reflections" (*SB*, 240). He then proceeds to narrate the story of a girl beaten to death by her ruffian lover which
anticipates the murder of Nancy by Sikes in *Oliver Twist*. In
another place Boz demystifies his childhood enslavement to literary convention when he says: "We remember, in our young
days, a little sweep about our own age, with curly hair and white
teeth, whom we devoutly and sincerely believed to be the lost
son and heir of some illustrious personage" (*SB*, 171). To believe
this was to be the victim of the fairy tale patterns of children's
literature, but the adult Boz has been disillusioned, or, at any
rate, one part of his mind has been disillusioned. The other part
used this same story of the workhouse son of the "illustrious
personage" as the basis of *Oliver Twist*. The *Sketches by Boz*, like
Oliver Twist, express both the illusion and its deconstruction,
just as the critic's interpretation of them must hover between
realistic and figurative readings.

Perhaps the best example of a text explicitly calling attention
to the fictive quality of the *Sketches* is a curious paragraph in
which the failure of Boz's habitual processes of imagination brings
into the open the laws by which it usually operates. Boz has been
left alone in the parlor of "an old, quiet, decent public-house"
(*SB*, 235) near the City Road in the east of London:

> If we had followed the established precedent in all such instances,
> we should have fallen into a fit of musing, without delay. The ancient
> appearance of the room—the old panelling of the wall—the chimney
> blackened with smoke and age—would have carried us back a hundred
> years at least, and we should have gone dreaming on, until the pewter-
> pot on the table, or the little beer-chiller on the fire, had started into
> life, and addressed to us a long story of days gone by. But, by some
> means or other, we were not in a romantic humour; and although we

tried very hard to invest the furniture with vitality, it remained perfectly unmoved, obstinate, and sullen *(SB, 239)*.

Here the inability of Boz's romantic imagination to follow the established precedent brings to the surface the precariously fictive quality of that imagination. The pewter pot and the little beer-chiller are characteristic examples of utensils which in other *Sketches* are read as metonymic signs of the life which has been lived in their vicinity. In their failure to start into life there is a revelation of the fact that the vitality of such objects does not belong in reality to them. It is invested in them by Boz, and it is invested according to patterns of interpretation taken from traditional literary forms. In such moments the *Sketches* make problematical their mimetic function. In doing so they fulfill, in a way appropriate to narrative fiction, the definition of literature as a use of language which exposes its own rhetorical devices and assumptions.

*

This uncovering of the fictitiousness of the fictive is not performed, however, in the name of some "true" language for which a space is cleared through the rejection of the fictive. Behind each fiction there is another fiction, and this new fiction is sustained in its turn by the counterpart phantom of a beguiling literal reading. Once more this is easiest to see in its mirroring within the lives of the characters in the *Sketches*. This mirroring corresponds rigorously to the mode of existence of the *Sketches* themselves. In the *Sketches* the liberated characters are not those who escape from conventional behavior. No one can escape. Liberation is possible only to those who, like Aggerawatin Bill, the omnibus cad, play their roles to the hilt, perform their part with such abandon that this hyperbolic verve constitutes a kind of freedom. It is a paradoxical freedom which both accepts the role (any action in the world of the *Sketches* is a role of some sort) and, at the same time, reveals in the excess with which the part is played that it is a part, that it could be otherwise. Any behavior is incommensurate with the vitality which gives energy to it. The heroes of the *Sketches* are such characters as Bill Barker, the "cad," or his counterpart in the same Sketch, the red-cab-driver. The latter knocks down a gentleman who protests the way he is treated, and then "call[s] the police to take himself into custody, with all the civility in the world" (*SB*, 146).

Such admirable displays of deliberately outrageous behavior are exactly parallel to the function of hyperbole in Dickens's own playing of the role of Boz, the speculative pedestrian. In the incongruous metaphors, in the pervasive facetious irony, in a constant play of language which calls attention to its own clichés in ways which destroy their innocent existence as nominal turns of language, Boz liberates himself in the only way one can be liberated through language. He does not substitute true language for false, nor does he copy true models. Neither true language nor true models exist for Boz. Like Bill Barker, he must tell lies, employ fictions, in ways which expose the fact that they are lies. The use of clichés, in ways that reveal their reliance on metaphors which have come to be taken literally and which thereby have become the support of social fictions, contains this linguistic resource of the *Sketches* in miniature. An example is Boz's play with the phrase "coming out" in "The Mistaken Milliner. A Tale of Ambition":

Now, "coming out," either in acting, or singing, or society, or facetiousness, or anything else, is all very well, and remarkably pleasant to the individual principally concerned, if he or she can but manage to come out with a burst, and being out to keep out, and not go in again; but it does unfortunately happen that both consummations are extremely difficult to accomplish, and that the difficulties of getting out at all in the first instance, and if you surmount them, of keeping out in the second, are pretty much on a par, and no slight ones either—and so Miss Amelia Martin shortly discovered (*SB*, 254).

If the real world is a fiction and the reflection of it in literature a fiction too, what of the interpretation of the relation between them expressed by the critic? Can criticism formulate without equivocation the truth which the creative writer can only convey indirectly and in such a way that it will inevitably be misunderstood by his readers? No, the critic is caught in exactly the same predicament as the creative writer or as the man living in the real world. To formulate the relation between reader, text, and world assumed here will guard against misunderstanding what I have been saying as the return to a traditional polarity between seeing literature as realistic representation, on the one hand, and seeing it, on the other, as the creation of a self-contained subjective realm. The view of literary language I am presupposing would not see a work of literature as able ever to be self-contained, self-sustaining, hermetically sealed in its self-referential purity. A work of literature is rather a link in a chain of transformations and substitutions. To identify its ambiguous relation to the links in either direction is one way to articulate the incessant displacement of figurative by literal and of literal by figurative which takes place within a text in its transactions with the social world and with its readers. In one direction there is the social world which the *Sketches* "describe." This world is not a collection of hard facts. It is itself interpretation, based on other texts, of the matter of which London is made. In the other direction is the critic. His reading of the text, the connections he makes between one part of it and another, the pattern he establishes as his commentary on the whole, is interpretation in its turn. He asserts similarities and configurations which are not asserted as such in the text itself. He creates a pattern of meaning nowhere explicitly articulated. The fiction of the *Sketches* inserts itself as a text among other fictional texts, those within which the characters of the *Sketches* are shown to live. The critic's interpretation is fiction too. The *Sketches* are not a mirror of reality, but interpretation of interpretation, and the critic's discourse about the *Sketches* may be defined as interpretation of interpretation of interpretation. This chain of substitutions and transformations creates illusion out of illusion and the appearance of reality out of illusion, in a play of language without beginning, end, or extra-linguistic foundation.

A glimpse of this reciprocity is provided by the story of the young Dickens's visit in his capacity as journalist to review a new farce at the Adelphi Theater. The new play, he found, was a blatant plagiarism from one of his Sketches already published, "The Bloomsbury Christening." If his *Sketches* owed much to the theatrical part of the already existent culture, they entered themselves into that culture as one of its aspects. Dickens's interpretation of Victorian England is part of English history.

Now it is possible to see what is misleading in the formulation of Roman Jakobson which gave my interpretative journey its initial impetus. The distinction between romantic or symbolist

poetry, based on metaphor, in which the set of language is toward
itself, and "realistic" texts, based on metonymy, in which the set
of language tends to be "primarily upon referent,"[30] cannot be
made a diametrical opposition. Any literary text is both self-
referential and extra-referential, or rather it is open to being not
seen as the former and mistakenly taken as the latter. All language
is figurative, displaced. All language is beside itself. There is no
"true" sign for the thing. Even proper names, as linguists and
ethnologists have come to see, are figurative.[31] The true word,
the hidden Logos, always slips away, is always a matter of somewhere else or of some other time. Both metonymy and metaphor
are versions of the same "fundamental of language," the fiction
of identity. The lie which says A equals B (metaphor) is no more
"poetic" than the lie which says A leads to B (metonymy). Both
are naming one thing with the name of another, in a constant
stepping aside which constitutes the life of language. Both metaphor and metonymy are open to a correct interpretation in which
the figurative is seen as figurative. Both invite the misinterpreta-
tion which takes as substantial what are in fact only linguistic
fictions. All poetry, however strongly based on metaphor, is liable
to be read literally, and all realistic narrative, however metonymic
in texture, is open to a correct figurative reading which sees it as
fiction rather than *mimesis*. One might in fact argue that metonymic displacement, in its movement from presence to absence,
is even more fundamental than metaphorical transference or
superimposition. Metaphor could as easily be described as a special case of metonymy as metonymy a special case of metaphor.
In any case, it is misleading to suggest that they are polar opposites, either as synchronic rhetorical fact giving rise to two distinct
forms of literature or as the basis of literary history, for example
the development from romanticism to realism to symbolism. All
these historically located forms of literature are versions of the
fundamental structure of a figurative language open to misread-

30 *Fundamentals of Language*, p. 81.
31 See Jacques Derrida's discussion of the problematic of proper names in Lévi-
Strauss's *Tristes tropiques*: "La guerre des noms propres," *De la grammatologie*
(Paris: Les Éditions de Minuit, 1967), pp. 157-173, and see also Roland Barthes,
"Proust et les noms," *To Honor Roman Jakobson* (The Hague: Mouton, 1967),
pp. 150-158.

ing as literal. All are open to similar procedures of correct interpretation.

In support of this view of language could be cited Nietzsche, Heidegger, Wittgenstein, Freud, or Jacques Lacan. Nietzsche in *The Will to Power* sees all cultural forms—art, science, metaphysics, religion—as "fictions," "lies," "interpretations." All are based on the mistake of "making similar, equal" what is "always something new"; "Form, species, law, idea, purpose—in all these cases the same error is made of giving a false reality to a fiction, as if events were in some way obedient to something." "No, facts is precisely what there is not," says Nietzsche, "only interpretations." "We can comprehend only a world that we ourselves have made," and *"we cease to think when we refuse to do so under the constraint of language,"* for *"rational thought is interpretation according to a scheme that we cannot throw off."*[32] Heidegger in *Sein und Zeit* argues that naming something always means naming it *as* something. To do this assimilates the thing into the network of names and functions which incorporates it into the already existing human world. At the same time, this naming hides the thing by making it available only "as" something other than it is. Even the most authentic poetry is simultaneously revelation and covering up, disclosure and veiling.[33] In paragraphs 50 through 56 of *The Brown Book,* Wittgenstein assimilates the "narration of past events," that is, precisely the form of language which is the basis of realistic fiction, into the category of "language games." The telling of a story about the past becomes one more case in point in Wittgenstein's subtle demonstration of the impossibility of measuring the validity of any form of language by its one-to-one correspondence to some external structure of objects or events.[34] Freud identifies the two forms of dreamwork, condensation and displacement, in ways that Jaques Lacan, in his

---

[32] Friedrich Nietzsche, *The Will to Power,* paragraphs 515, 521, 481, 495, and 522. I have cited the translation by Walter Kaufmann and R. J. Hollingdale (New York: Vintage Books, 1968) .

[33] See the crucial sections on language and the hermeneutical circle in Martin Heidegger, *Sein und Zeit,* eleventh ed. (Tübingen: Max Niemeyer, 1967) , sections 7, B, and 32-37, pp. 32-34, 148-175.

[34] Ludwig Wittgenstein, *The Blue and Brown Books,* Harper Torchbooks (New York: Harper & Row, 1965) , pp. 104-109.

interpretation of Freud in the light of modern linguistics, can recognize as corresponding closely to metaphor and metonymy. Both figures are modes of that activity of naming which is always shifted aside and can never rest in a happy correspondence of name and thing.[35] This collective recognition of man's inescapable dependence on linguistic fictions constitutes a primary theme in recent developments in the arts of interpretation. Metaphor and metonymy are labels which may be given to two important categories of such fictions, but they are brothers rather than opposites, as Goethe recognized in a striking phrase cited by Jakobson: "Alles Vergängliche ist nur ein Gleichnis." This Jakobson interprets as meaning that "anything sequent is a simile," so that "In poetry where similarity is superinduced upon contiguity, any metonymy is slightly metaphorical and any metaphor has a metonymical tint."[36] Jakobson here comes close to formulating the covert identity of metonymy and metaphor as two versions of the necessary displacement involved in all language. This displacement is the basis of the interplay between literal and figurative understandings of language which is the foundation of literature.

*

So far in this essay I have concentrated on the language of the *Sketches by Boz* and on the way analysis of that language may

---

[35] See Sigmund Freud, *Die Traumdeutung,* ninth ed. (Vienna, 1950), and Jacques Lacan, "L'instance de la lettre dans l'Inconscient," *Écrits* (Paris: Éditions du Seuil, 1966). A footnote in the French translation of Jakobson's "Two Aspects of Language and Two Types of Aphasic Disturbances," from *Fundamentals of Language,* notes a difference between Lacan and Jakobson in their interpretation of Freud. Jakobson identifies metonymy with both the "displacement" and the "condensation" of Freud, while he sees metaphor as the basis of Freud's "identification and symbolism" *(Fundamentals of Language,* p. 81). "On remarquera," says Jakobson's translator, Nicolas Ruwet, "que ce rapprochement ne coïncide pas avec celui fait par J. Lacan...; celui-ci identifie, respectivement, condensation et métaphore, et déplacement et métonymie. Roman Jakobson, à qui nous en avons fait la remarque, pense que la divergence s'explique par l'imprécision du concept de condensation, qui, chez Freud, semble recouvrir à la fois des cas de métaphore et des cas de synecdoque" (Roman Jakobson, *Essais de linguistique générale,* trans. N. Ruwet [Paris: Les Éditions de Minuit, 1963], p. 66). It would seem rather that Jakobson's exaggerated emphasis on the "polar" opposition between metaphor and metonymy has led him astray in his understanding of Freud. Lacan's interpretation is perhaps truer to Freud's insight into the dependence of both forms of dreamwork on the basic linguistic act of naming one thing with the name of another.

[36] *Style in Language,* p. 370.

help bring into the open what I have called "the fiction of realism." What role in the meaning of the *Sketches* and of *Oliver Twist* is played by the admirable illustrations for them by George Cruikshank? To ask this raises the complex aesthetic question of the meaning of the fact that novels have traditionally been illustrated, sometimes by crude woodcuts, sometimes by etchings or engravings, sometimes by sumptuous colored plates, sometimes, in more recent years, as in the case of James, Meredith, or Hardy, by photographs. What is the relation between text and illustration in a work of fiction? Both Flaubert and Mallarmé, for example, were hostile to the convention of illustrating works of literature. "Je suis pour—aucune illustration," said Mallarmé in 1898, "tout ce qu'évoque un livre devant se passer dans l'esprit du lecteur."[37] Nevertheless, many novels (as well as other works) have been illustrated by distinguished artists, and the illustrations must be accepted as in some sense part of the texts they illustrate. Does the existence of illustrated books mean that there is something language cannot do or can only do imperfectly, so that in the picture we can see more exactly what a character or scene "really looked like"? To say this is to assume implicitly not that the illustration represents in pictorial terms something described in verbal terms in the text but that both text and illustration stand side by side as imitations in different media of a third entity, some "reality," whether ideal, psychological, or material, which exists independently outside both and needs neither words nor pictures to continue in existence. Certainly the first effect of illustrations in a work of fiction is to reinforce those mimetic assumptions which are, as I have shown, so problematical. To encounter, in a picture, people or scenes one has already encountered in the text is to be invited to assent to their authenticity and to say, "Ah, that's how he really looked at that moment, then!" The illustrations may take precedence over the text as affirmations of the presence and appearance of the characters. I have called attention to the fact that Dickens in the *Sketches by Boz* refers more to the illustrations of eighteenth-century novels than to their words, so that Sir Charles Grandison apparently

---

[37] Stéphane Mallarmé, *Oeuvres complètes,* éd. de la Pléiade (Paris: Gallimard, 1965) , p. 878.

existed for him as the pictures rather than as Richardson's text. Dickens was the victim of the same kind of response. For many readers Fagin, Sikes, Nancy, Oliver, Mr. Brownlow, and Rose Maylie live even more in Cruikshank's etchings than in Dickens's words.

The most celebrated reader for whom this was so was, of course, Henry James. *Oliver Twist*, says James in *A Small Boy and Others*, "perhaps even seemed to me more Cruikshank's than Dickens's; it was a thing of such vividly terrible images, and all marked with that peculiarity of Cruikshank that the offered flowers of goodnesses, the scenes and figures intended to comfort and cheer, present themselves under his hand as but more subtly sinister, or more suggestively queer, than the frank badnesses and horrors. The nice people and the happy moments, in the plates, frightened me almost as much as the low and the awkward."[38] If the response to Dickens's language of a reader as sensitive to the power of words as James could be so overwhelmed and effaced by his response to the great Cruikshank illustrations, then the critic must be willing to consider those illustrations as perhaps an integral part of their texts.

To do this, however, creates a host of problems. What happens, for example, to the integrity of the literary text, its organic wholeness as an integument of words establishing its own meaning and the rules by which it is to be read? To allow a non-verbal element full rights within this structure of meaning is no longer to be able to maintain a now traditional view of the self-enclosed unity of the literary work. Moreover, if the illustrations are as much a part of the text as any of its verbal elements, which has priority over the other in the case of a discrepancy? Which is the "origin" of the other? Which illustrates which? There is more than paranoia, pathological lying, or professional jealousy in the claims the aged George Cruikshank made to have originated both the *Sketches* and *Oliver Twist*. As Jane R. Cohen shows in the most recent detailed study of the relation between the two,[39] there is little evidence to support Cruikshank's claim that he first

---

[38] Henry James, *Autobiography*, ed. Frederick W. Dupee (New York, 1956) . p. 169.
[39] " 'All-of-a-Twist': the Relationship of George Cruikshank and Charles Dickens," *Harvard Library Bulletin*, XVII, 2, 3 (April, July 1969) , 169-194, 320-342.

drew pictures for which Dickens supplied the text, even though it is clear that Cruikshank made many suggestions to Dickens during the writing of *Oliver Twist*. Nevertheless, one might argue that within the atemporal realm of the finished works Cruikshank's drawings seem prior, originating. They appear to be the radiant source beside which Dickens's words are secondary, from which they appear to have derived. It will be remembered that *Pickwick Papers* was at first planned as pictures by a well-known artist, Robert Seymour, to be "illustrated" by Dickens's letter-press. I have shown that there are frequent references in the *Sketches* to the graphic arts or to pictorial effects. As their title after all suggests, the *Sketches* are often self-consciously visual. They strive for effects which have already been achieved in the other medium, or they are written so that they might be illustrated. The degree to which this is so is indicated by the correspondence between Dickens and Cruikshank.[40] It is true that Dickens kept the upper hand with his "illustrious" illustrator, rejected plates of which he disapproved, and often specified in detail what should be illustrated. At the same time, it is also evident that he wrote *Oliver Twist* in order that it might be illustrated by Cruikshank. He kept in mind as he wrote the necessity of having something suitable for illustration in each number, and, of course, he knew Cruikshank's earlier work just as he knew that of Hogarth. Cruikshank's work was part of that tradition of graphic illustration which is so important an ingredient in establishing the conventions of the *Sketches* and *Oliver Twist*.

The relation between text and illustration is clearly reciprocal. Each refers to the other. Each illustrates the other, in a continual back and forth movement which is incarnated in the experience of the reader as his eyes move from words to picture and back again, juxtaposing the two in a mutual establishment of meaning. Illustrations in a work of fiction displace the sign-referent relationship assumed in a mimetic reading and replace it by a complex and problematic reference between two radically different kinds of sign, the linguistic and the graphic. Illustrations establish a relation between elements within the work which shortcircuits the apparent reference of the literary text to some real world

---

[40] This is recapitulated and commented on in detail by Mrs. Cohen.

outside. This is true even if the illustrations are photographs of the "original" scenes in the novel, as in the case of photographs in the Wessex and Anniversary editions of Thomas Hardy's novels. Such an intrinsic relation between text and picture sets up an oscillation or shimmering of meaning in which neither element can be said to be prior. The pictures are about the text; the text is about the pictures, in another form of metaphoric superimposition or metonymic juxtaposition which may move in a spectrum all the way from the formal painting which is verbalized only with a descriptive title, through those intermediate cases, poised between *pictura* and *poesis*, like the paintings of Klee, which have their witty or inscrutable poetic titles as intrinsic parts of themselves, or the cartoons in *Punch*, which are meaningless without the lines of dialogue pendant beneath. At the other extreme, a long novel may be "illustrated" only with a bare sketch for a frontispiece, as in the case of the Cheap Edition of Dickens's novels.

The *Sketches by Boz* and *Oliver Twist* are obviously nearer the equal balance between picture and text. A further understanding of the significance of Cruikshank's illustrations for these may come by investigating them as significances in themselves. Of what may they be said to be the signs, or the indications, or the images? There are four incompatible entities or regions to which Cruikshank's illustrations refer. Since my investigations so far have focused chiefly on the *Sketches by Boz*, I shall center my discussion on the forty splendid etchings Cruikshank produced for that text.

*

Just as critics from the publication of the first collected volumes of the *Sketches* until today have emphasized the representational accuracy of Dickens's description of London, so the Cruikshank illustrations are often valued for the authenticity of their mirroring of London in the 'thirties. It seems that Seven Dials did in fact look as it does in Cruikshank's etching. The apparatus for providing a street breakfast shown in the admirable illustration for "The Streets—Morning" has archaeological accuracy. The claustrophobic middle-class interiors, with somber carpets, heavy furniture, and dark curtains, with statues of Cupid under glass on little shelves on the wall, as in "Mr. Watkins Tottle and Miss

Lillerton," show the way bourgeois drawing rooms did look at this time. The costumes of the ladies and gentlemen in "Steam Excursion (I) " (Plate I) [41] may be trusted as accurate copies of the fashions of the day. The fireplace and its equipment in an old-fashioned pub did look as Cruikshank shows them in "Scotland Yard." Portraits of Dickens himself are included in several of the illustrations (the Frontispiece, "Early Coaches," "Making a Night of It," "Public Dinners" [which also contains a picture of Cruikshank], and "A Pickpocket in Custody"). This reinforces the journalistic aspect of the illustrations. Cruikshank shows Boz, that is, a man recognizably Dickens himself, engaged in the activities described in the first person by the narrator of the *Sketches*. Taken all together the forty illustrations for the *Sketches* constitute in another medium the same kind of authoritative representation of middle-class and lower-middle-class life in London in the eighteen-thirties as do Dickens's *Sketches* themselves. Mrs. Cohen asserts the validity of this aspect of Cruikshank's art:

The artist's illustrations [for the *Sketches*] were also characteristic of [Cruikshank's] work in their accuracy. . . . Cruikshank, as Sacheverell Sitwell has observed, was among the first English artists "to attempt historical accuracy in their reconstruction of the past." He was so painstaking with certain fine points of his accessories that historians still find his plates authoritative. "The Last Cabdriver," for example, depicts an obsolete form of the cabriolet with the driver seated over the right wheel, while "The Parish Engine" commemorates the kind

---

41 The five plates accompanying this essay are reproductions of original drawings by Cruikshank of illustrations for the *Sketches by Boz*. They are in the Harry Elkins Widener Collection in the Harvard College Library, and I am most grateful for permission to reproduce them. I wish to thank especially Miss Caroline Jakeman for her many courtesies to me during my study of these and other drawings by Cruikshank from the Widener Collection. Three of the sketches reproduced here ("The Gin Shop," "Sentiment," and "The First of May") are original pencil drawings for these three etchings. The other two ("Steam Excursion [I]" and "Steam Excursion [II]") are original sketches, in color, with numerous studies in the margin, in Dickens's own copy of the 1839 edition of the *Sketches by Boz*. The five plates are versions of the illustrations for the *Sketches* which have not before, to my knowledge, been reproduced. In my discussion of Cruikshank's etchings I am assuming that readers will have available copies of the final plates as published in the edition of 1839. These are reproduced in the Oxford Illustrated *Sketches by Boz* or in the Nonesuch edition of the *Sketches*. The Oxford Illustrated edition omits the etching for "Making a Night of It," while it restores the plate called "A Harmonic Meeting" (originally "The Free and Easy") which was for some reason omitted from the parts edition of 1839. The titles given to the plates in the Oxford Illustrated edition differ in some cases from the titles in the early editions. I have used the Oxford Illustrated titles.

Plate I: Steam Excursion (I)

of fire-extinguisher then in use. His costumes were also meticulously accurate.[42]

If Cruikshank, like Dickens, was a man fascinated by the haunts and neighborhoods of London, if he was a man who, like Dickens, often stayed out all night walking the streets and visiting taverns, and if his illustrations for the *Sketches*, like the *Sketches* themselves, were based on first-hand experience, nevertheless it must be said that this representation of London was mediated rather than direct. It was mediated by the words of Dickens's text. In the case of the *Sketches* the texts unequivocally precede their illustration, since almost all of them had been published in various periodicals before John Macrone, the publisher, suggested that they might be collected in a book and illustrated by Cruikshank. Thirteen of the illustrations were not completed until the publication in 1837-1839 of the edition in twenty monthly parts by Chapman and Hall. Moreover, in spite of the trivial discrepancies noted by F. G. Kitton and Mrs. Cohen,[43] Cruikshank, for the most part, scrupulously follows Dickens's text. There is precedent in the words for everything, or almost everything, that appears in the pictures: gesture, furniture, clothes, décor, Here the verbal text has clear priority over its illustration in another medium. Cruikshank, it appears, created his etchings not by going directly to the London he knew so well, but by representing that London as it was already represented in Dickens's language. His images refer to that language rather than directly to the scenes and objects the language imitates.

Cruikshank's illustrations indicate, however, still another region, one perhaps more difficult to identify, but unmistakably present. I mean Cruikshank's unique sensibility or angle of vision on the world, what Charles Baudelaire, in his brief remarks on Cruikshank, calls "ce je ne sais quoi qui distingue toujours un artiste d'un autre, quelque intime que soit en apparence leur

---

[42] "All-of-a-Twist," p. 174. The quotation from Sacheverell Sitwell is from *Narrative Pictures: A Survey of English Genre and Its Painters* (London, 1937), p. 20. In her remarks about "The Last Cabdriver" and "The Parish Engine" Mrs. Cohen is following the notations of Frederic G. Kitton in *Dickens and His Illustrators* (London, 1899), p. 6.

[43] *Dickens and His Illustrators*, pp. 7-8; "All-of-a-Twist," p. 175.

parenté."[44] This "fugitive et impalpable" "sentiment" distinguishes Cruikshank from all other artists before and after him in
his tradition. It may be partly a matter of habitual ways of composing a picture or of placing the figures against a background,
and I shall try to identify these below. Or it may be a matter of
the unifying mood which is communicated by the illustrations,
that elusive quality which makes it possible to distinguish a
Cruikshank from a Gillray or a "Phiz." It was this pervasive
quality, peculiar to Cruikshank's pictures, which Henry James
was describing in the passage quoted above. The same effect of
frightening meanness and enclosure is described in another well-
known passage, this one by G. K. Chesterton. The illustrations
for *Oliver Twist* seemed to Chesterton "dark and detestable," the
drawing "mean" and "morbid." "In the doubled-up figure and
frightful eyes of Fagin in the condemned cell," said Chesterton,
"there is not only a baseness of subject, but there is a kind of
baseness in the very technique of it. It is not drawn with the free
lines of a free man; it has the half-witted secrecies of a hunted
thief. It does not look merely like a picture of Fagin; it looks like
a picture by Fagin."[45] Here is one way to talk about the self-
expressive aspect of Cruikshank's art. It imitates not the real
London and not the imaginary world created by Dickens's words,
but the special quality of Cruikshank's mind or vision of things.
Chesterton, it happens, was intuitively right, for according to a
well-known anecdote, Cruikshank is supposed to have told Henry
Mayhew that Fagin was copied from a mirrored image of himself
crouching in bed, with his hand to his mouth, meditating despair-
ingly on the difficulty of drawing Fagin in the condemned cell. In
his later years Cruikshank came increasingly to identify himself
with Fagin and to like to play the role of his most famous illustration. In the same way, the preliminary sketches for his illustrations are often marginally decorated with miniature self-portraits.
The narcissistic image of Cruikshank drawing his own mirrored
face seems an appropriate emblem for the way his art is not copied
from the external world or from the literary texts it is supposed

---

44 Charles Baudelaire, *Oeuvres complètes*, éd. de la Pléiade (Paris: Gallimard,
1958) , p. 751.
45 G. K. Chesterton, *Charles Dickens: A Critical Study* (New York, 1935) , p. 112.

to illustrate but is projected outward from his own inner world.

To these three incompatible referents must be added a fourth. In spite of the undeniable existence of special qualities, both technical and more intangible, distinguishing Cruikshank's art from all other art, even so, Cruikshank's work is in many ways related to an elaborate tradition and may be fully understood only in terms of its references to the conventions of that tradition. The tradition in this case is that of caricature, whether political or comic, drawing, etching, or woodcut. Cruikshank's place in this tradition means that his work must be read in terms of its relationship to the work of his father, Isaac Cruikshank, to the work of Seymour, Gillray, Rowlandson, and, of course, Hogarth, as well as to younger artists like Hablot K. Browne. E. H. Gombrich has shown how any tradition of graphic representation involves complex conventions whereby three-dimensional objects are signified by marks on a flat surface. These conventions are in no sense realistic but come to be taken for granted as adequate mirrorings of reality by artists and viewers of art who dwell within the conventions.[46] The system of conventions on which Cruikshank's art depends is only now beginning to be studied in detail. There is new work on Hogarth, Gillray, Rowlandson, and others, as well as on Cruikshank himself.[47] Much remains to be done along these lines, but one may expect that just as Richard A. Vogler can argue that all the figures in Cruikshank's illustrations for *Oliver Twist* (Fagin, Sikes, Nancy, Bumble, and the rest) are based on prototypes appearing in Cruikshank's earlier work,[48] so scarcely an aspect of a given picture by Cruikshank, figure, pose, background, composition, but will turn out to have antecedents

---

[46] See E. H. Gombrich, *Art and Illusion: A Study in the Psychology of Pictorial Representation* (Princeton, N. J.: Princeton University Press, 1969) ; *Meditations on a Hobby Horse and Other Essays on the Theory of Art* (London: Phaidon Press, 1965); "The Evidence of Images," *Interpretation: Theory and Practice*, ed. Charles S. Singleton (Baltimore: The Johns Hopkins Press, 1969) , pp. 35-104.

[47] In addition to the essays by Gombrich, "The Experiment of Caricature," *Art and Illusion*, pp. 330-358, and "The Cartoonist's Armoury," *Meditations on a Hobby Horse*, pp. 127-142, there is the work by Robert Wark on Rowlandson, a forthcoming comprehensive critical biography of Hogarth by Ronald Paulson, and John Harvey's new book, *Victorian Novelists and Their Illustrators* (New York: New York University Press, 1970), as well as the essays by Robert Patten and Michael Steig cited below. I have not yet been able to see John Harvey's book.

[48] See his essay *An "Oliver Twist" Exhibition: A Memento for the Dickens Centennial 1970* (University Research Library, University of California, Los Angeles, 1970) .

within the tradition to which he belongs. Mrs. Cohen, for example, has observed a number of parallels between the illustrations for *Oliver Twist* and certain works by Hogarth.[49] Even
Cruikshank's Fagin, in the etching showing Fagin welcoming
Oliver back after he is recaptured ("Oliver's reception by Fagin
and the boys"), matches almost exactly Hogarth's Jewish pedlar
in the second plate of the "Election" series. Hogarth's Jew is in
turn based on a specific tradition of representing Ashkenazic
faces in this way.[50] Far from being a self-portrait, Cruikshank's
Fagin is one of a long line of similar figures by various artists,
each one referring back to earlier similar ones, and no one identifiable as the "archetype." Just as Dickens's *Sketches* contain many
references to graphic, theatrical, and literary traditions, and just
as they cannot be understood unless they are seen as repetitions
with a difference of elements in those traditions, so Cruikshank's
illustrations are based on complex conventions which include not
only modes of graphic representation, but also the stereotyped
poses of melodrama and pantomime, so clearly alluded to, for
example, in the lively illustration for "The Tuggses at Ramsgate."
Rather than imitating some extra-artistic realm, Cruikshank's
pictures draw their meaning from their relation to other works
of art to which they implicitly refer and on which they depend
for the creation of their own significance.

To investigate a given illustration by Cruikshank on the assumption that it is a "sign" pointing to some reality outside itself
is to discover that each illustration is the meeting point of a set
of incompatible references—the "real" London, Dickens's text,

---

[49] "All-of-a-Twist," p. 184.

[50] See Israel Solomons, "Satirical and Political Prints on the Jews' Naturalisation
Bill, 1753," *Transactions of the Jewish Historical Society of England,* VI (1908-10) ,
205-233; Thomas Whipple Perry, *Public Opinion, Propaganda, and Politics in
Eighteenth-Century England: a study of the Jew bill of 1753* (Cambridge, Mass.:
Harvard University Press, 1962) ; and Ronald Paulson's forthcoming biography of
Hogarth. According to Perry, Ashkenazic pedlars "spoke but little English, and that
with an unfamiliar accent; in an age of clean shaving, they wore beards; their hair
was worn long, and their dress was often both ragged and unorthodox" (p. 8) . The
Ashkenazic figure who is the prototype for Fagin also occurs in three Rowlandson
etchings, *Jews at a Luncheon,* BM Sat. 8536; another called *Traffic* (evidently not in
BM Sat.) , which shows two Jewish pedlars trying to sell a pair of trousers with a huge
hole in the seat; and as a detail in another Rowlandson, BM Sat. 9546. I owe thanks
to Ronald Paulson for calling these to my attention.

Cruikshank's "sensibility," and the tradition of caricature. It is difficult to see how a single work could refer to all these realms at once, especially since each context makes claims not on a part of a picture but on its totality as a single complex emblem. Under the pressure of these mutually annihilating references the picture dissolves, explodes, and vanishes. It cannot mean, so it would seem, all these things at once. The multiple lines of reference tend to cancel one another out, and the beholder is left face to face with the bare ink marks on the page, marks which, it may be, constitute their own intrinsic meaning. They may establish such a self-sufficient meaning within the ruins left by the discovery of overdetermination involved in any attempt at a complete "mimetic" reading. What may be said of the etchings when they are seen as if they had been cut free from their connections to the various entities outside themselves to which they seem so clearly to refer? Such intrinsic interpretation, it should be noted, does not mean reading each illustration separately. It means rather setting a group of plates, in this case the illustrations for the *Sketches by Boz*, side by side. The investigation moves back and forth from one plate to another in an attempt to identify the motifs and structuring forms which recur from one picture to another.

*

Almost all the illustrations for the *Sketches by Boz* have strongly centered, centripetal, circular compositions. They spiral inward toward a point. In this they may be opposed, for example, to Gillray's characteristic composition. Gillray's pictures are explosive, centrifugal, with objects or figures which seem about to fall off the edge of the page. In Cruikshank's case there is almost always something at the middle on which everything is focused and around which everything turns. Sometimes this is a vertical line, sometimes a spot. An example is "Horatio Sparkins," which is strongly centered on the hat of the lady in the middle whose back is to the viewer, or "Mr. Minns and His Cousin," which is organized around the urn in the middle of the table, or "The Boarding-House (II)," which is centered on the candle flame and on the point on the face of the organ from which lines in the woodwork radiate outward like rays from a sun, or "The Danc-

Plate II: The Gin Shop

ing Academy," in which all attention is drawn to the little boy dancing alone in the middle, or "Mr. John Dounce at the Oyster-Shop," in which the portly figure of John Dounce himself constitutes the central line. This kind of composition occurs so universally in these illustrations that it may be called one of their fundamental laws. It is varied only in those pictures which may have two circular forms, one a little behind the other and echoing it, as in "Theodosius Introduced to the New Pupil," or several compositional lines may move around the same center in the form of concentric circles.

Such a concentration of all energy on a central point is responsible in part for that sense of enclosure, even of suffocation, which critics have felt in looking at Cruikshank's plates. It seems as if everything were moving toward that point or were drawn toward it. This centripetal effect is reinforced by the fact that Cruikshank's plates are not only usually dark but are also overshadowed by ponderous architectural overhangings—arches, pediments, or ceilings—or by somber, heavy curtains. Such weights impending from above occur again and again in the illustrations, sometimes in the form of external architectural elements, as in "The Election for Beadle," or in "Vauxhall Gardens by Day," or in the heavy overhanging outdoor lamps in "Seven Dials"[51] and "A Pickpocket in Custody," sometimes in the form of interior furnishings, perhaps most strikingly in the enormous barrels of gin which overshadow the patrons in "The Gin Shop" (Plate II). In some cases the effect of ominous overshadowing is achieved by the emphasis on heavy ceiling beams, as in "Private Theatres," or, more simply, on the corner of the ceiling in an interior scene, as in "The Tuggses at Ramsgate" or "Mr. Watkins Tottle and Miss Lillerton." In other plates, for example in "Under Restraint" or "The Boarding-House (I)," the sense of enclosure in interior scenes is emphasized by doors which are firmly closed. The doors and windows are almost always shut in these pictures. The curtains are always drawn. It seems that it might be impos-

---

[51] These were real enough, as may be seen by their presence in another contemporary representation of Seven Dials, by Gustave Doré, reproduced from his *London* in Angus Wilson, *The World of Charles Dickens*, p. 88. Doré's plate, however, does not give the lamps the threatening weight and size, as if they were giant lamps or the people pigmies, which they have in Cruikshank's etching.

Plate III: Steam Excursion (II)

sible to escape or even to see beyond the confined place in which the inhabitants are trapped. Whatever the combination of these elements, each illustration contains some mixture of them. Their joint effect is to create a world in which even the outdoor scenes are enclosed, confined, hemmed in, and in which the human figures seem dwarfed and threatened by enormous masses of over-hanging cloth or masonry poised above to close them in and imprison them tightly. The terrifying claustrophobia of "Fagin in the condemned Cell" is also characteristic to a lesser degree of the illustrations for *Sketches by Boz.*

Surrounded and belittled by these heavy pressures, driven in toward some focus of attention at the center, Cruikshank's op-pressed human figures perform their little dramas. Charles Baude-laire has identified with great insight the form these dramas take. "Le mérite spécial de George Cruikshank," says Baudelaire ". . . est une abondance inépuisable dans le grotesque. . . . Le gro-tesque coule incessamment et inévitablement de la pointe de Cruikshank, comme les rimes riches de la plume des poëtes naturels. Le grotesque est son habitude."[52] What characterizes Cruikshank's particular form of the grotesque? "Ce qui constitue surtout le grotesque de Cruikshank, c'est la violence extravagante du geste et du mouvement, et l'explosion dans l'expression. Tous ses petits personnages miment avec fureur et turbulence comme des acteurs de pantomime."[53] Baudelaire's analysis here is admir-ably exact. A grotesque comedy constituted by pantomimic vio-lence of gesture, expression, and movement on the part of tiny figures each of whom "se culbute, s'agite et se mêle avec une pétulance indicible" in his "monde minuscule"[54]—these are the essential characteristics of the actions performed in Cruikshank's pictures.

Each illustration takes a fleeting moment in the continuous action described in Dickens's text and concentrates on it to the exclusion of all else. The characters are represented in a moment of surprise in which they are so caught up in what is going on before their eyes that they forget past and future. They give

---

[52] *Oeuvres complètes,* p. 751.
[53] *Ibid.*
[54] *Ibid.,* pp. 751-752.

Plate IV: The First of May

themselves wholly to the excitement of the moment. Their responses to this moment are expressed in the gestures of open-mouthed, wide-eyed amazement which recur so often, as in "The Boarding-House (II)," "The Tuggses at Ramsgate," "Mr. Minns and His Cousin," and in many others, for example, in that queasy representation of universal seasickness, "Steam Excursion (II)," in which the decorum and elegance of "Steam Excursion (I)" has given way to swirling disorder (Plate III). Such absorption in the present moment is also imaged in the fact that the characters are often caught frozen in unstable gestures or in poses which could be held for only a fleeting second as a transition from one posture to another. Mr. Minns, in "Mr. Minns and His Cousin," is half-way up from his chair. The outraged husband, in "The Tuggses at Ramsgate," balances on one leg with the other foot raised high in the air. Samuel Wilkins, in even so relatively calm an illustration as "Samuel Wilkins and the Evanses," is poised with his weight resting in unstable equilibrium on one elegantly shod toe. In each such picture Cruikshank catches a moment in which people are driven by the violence of their reactions to adopt without hindsight or foresight a gesture or pose that could last only an instant and then would pass, never to return. Everything is in lively motion, a motion which necessarily prefigures its own end. Sometimes this evanescence may be imaged in a gesture of eating or drinking, as in "Mr. John Dounce at the Oyster-Shop," "The Gin Shop," or "The Streets—Morning," or in the splendid illustration for "The Poor Clerk." The characters are stopped with the food or drink halfway to their mouths. Sometimes the fleeting instant may be given an emblem in the clouds of smoke, white places in the picture, areas on the etching plate not touched by the acid, as in "A Harmonic Meeting," in "London Recreations—The 'Tea-Gardens,'" or in "Greenwich Fair." The smoke will hold one shape for an instant only, an instant captured forever in the representation of it.

If the pictures seem to dissolve under the pressure of the various incompatible realities they are meant to represent, or if Cruikshank's little people seem in danger of being overwhelmed by the weight of their surroundings, this vanishing away is pictured in the gestures and actions of the people themselves. The

Plate V: Theodosius Introduced to the New Pupil (Sentiment)

theme of Cruikshank's illustrations could without exaggeration
be said to be time, or, better, the present instant in its fugacity.
So great is the effect of various centripetal forces on the frail and
over-sensitive figures at the center that freedom, it seems, could
only be obtained by vanishing altogether—disappearing into a
cloud of smoke, a burst of laughter, an exclamation of surprise.
This vanishing seems about to occur. One is tempted to follow
a given illustration not from preliminary sketch to finished etching, but backward, from completed etching, perhaps in the brightly
watercolored form in which Cruikshank sometimes prepared
them, back to the black and white etching, behind that to the
careful tracing for transfer to the etching plate, back behind that
to the finished pencil drawing, and behind that again, finally, to
the initial sketch, mere ephemeral indications of the pencil on
the paper, tentative, hesitant, experimental, an illustration more
in possibility than in actuality, as in the preliminary drawing
below the more finished sketch for "The First of May" (Plate IV).
These preliminary drawings, it may be, are the most direct expressions of Cruikshank's genius at catching the elusive moment
in its actuality. In their evanescence they are closest to the instant where presence becomes absence.

*

This aspect of Cruikshank's illustrations for the *Sketches* is
countered by another motif which also occurs repeatedly. If the
characters at the center are caught up in a moment so surprising,
so violent, so all-absorbing that they live only in the vanishing
present, such figures are overlooked by another sort of personage,
a spectator who belongs to time and memory. This witness possesses a cool detachment, a power to see the moment in the perspective of what comes before and after. Such a figure corresponds
to the viewer of the illustration. We see each plate in the light
of the other illustrations, in the light of the tradition of caricature
to which it belongs, and in the light of the diachronic text it
illustrates. The spectator of "The Streets—Morning" or of "The
Tuggses at Ramsgate" sees what is present there in the perspective
of the series of events narrated in Dickens's description of the
gradual awakening to life of London in the early morning or in
relation to his story of the confidence trick played on the innocent

Tuggses. This spectator also corresponds to the narrator of the *Sketches*, to Boz as the "amateur vagrant" wandering the streets and watching everything with a sharp eye. Such a figure appears in a number of the illustrations, sometimes in the form of an actual portrait of Dickens as Boz, the "speculative pedestrian," as in "Making a Night of It" and "A Pickpocket in Custody." Sometimes this detached spectator is represented by someone on the sidelines who happens to be passing by and who is not caught up in the violent action which takes up the center of the picture. Examples are the figures on the edge of the scene watching the street fight in "Seven Dials."

The most important and pervasive versions of this motif are the portraits which hang on the walls of so many of Cruikshank's interiors. Variants of this are the busts or statues in a number of the interiors. There are portraits on the walls in "The Broker's Man," in "The Pawnbroker's Shop," in "Samuel Wilkins and the Evanses," in "The Boarding-House (II)," in "Mr. Minns and His Cousin," in "Theodosius Introduced to the New Pupil" (Plate V), in "The Tuggses at Ramsgate," in "Under Restraint," in "Mr. Watkins Tottle and Miss Lillerton," and in "The Blooms-bury Christening." No doubt, Victorian bourgeois households did in fact have portraits on their walls. This motif is part of the "realistic" texture of Cruikshank's recording of the London of his time. The function of these portraits, however, is more than mimetic. They are not allegorical or allusive. The allegorical use of pictures or other details appears more often in illustrations by Phiz, as Michael Steig has shown.[55] In Cruikshank's work such details appear occasionally, as in the picture of the Good Samaritan on the wall of Mr. Brownlow's house in "Oliver recovering from the fever."[56] Such allegorical details never appear at all in the forty illustrations for the *Sketches by Boz*, except perhaps in attenuated form in the statue of Cupid under a glass bell in "Mr. Watkins Tottle and Miss Lillerton." (The pose of

---

[55] "Dickens, Hablôt Browne, and the Tradition of English Caricature," *Criticism*, XI, 3 (Summer 1969), 219-233. See also Robert L. Patten, "The Art of *Pickwick's* Interpolated Tales," *ELH*, XXXIV (1967), 349-366.

[56] This has been noted by Robert L. Patten, review of the Clarendon edition of *Oliver Twist*, in *Dickens Studies*, III (1967), p. 165, by Jane R. Cohen, "All-of-a-Twist," p. 180, and by F. G. Kitton, *Dickens and His Illustrators*, p. ii.

the statue echoes that of the coy Miss Lillerton.) The portraits
on the walls in these plates are merely portraits. They do not
allude to any iconographical tradition. They have no identifiable
meaning as signs of something other than themselves. They are
painted faces hung on the walls—impassive, serene, detached, dead.
They are explicitly drawn in such a way that they appear to be
paying no attention to the violent actions being performed by
the "live" people in the center of the picture. Their expressions
and gestures are exactly the opposite of the grotesque violence
of the live figures. This contrast is emphasized by the striking
similarity between the faces on the walls and the faces of the
living actors. The two drawings on the wall in "Theodosius Introduced to the New Pupil" match exactly the faces of Theodosius
and Miss Brook Dingwall, though one pair of faces is distorted
with surprise and emotion, the other in static repose. The little
bust on the mantelpiece in "Samuel Wilkins and the Evanses"
echoes exactly the face of Samuel Wilkins himself, but one face
is animated, the other has a marble fixity. Part of the comedy in
the illustration for "The Bloomsbury Christening" lies in the fact
that there is a portrait on the wall either of the cross-eyed father,
Mr. Kitterbell, or perhaps of *his* father. If the latter is the case,
then there are, including the baby, three generations of cross-eyed
Kitterbells in the illustration. Mr. Dumps's mock horror as he
exclaims, "Good God, how small he is! . . . *remarkably* small indeed" (*SB*, 475), is given a further twist by Cruikshank's illustration. In the plate, Dumps's horror appears to be his discovery
that still another cross-eyed male has been added to the long line
of Kitterbells. In "The Pawnbroker's Shop" Cruikshank has picked
up Dickens's point by making the faces of the three women (the
old prostitute, the young one in her finery, and the respectable
girl who may be driven to the streets) all resemble one another
closely. He has added, however, in the portrait on the wall in the
background, a fourth woman who looks like the other three. This
face is a figure from the past who has perhaps lived through the
whole sequence represented in the living women and now has
achieved the peace of death. All the portraits in this group of
illustrations appear to be of ancestors, calm faces from the past
looking down on the ephemeral violence of the present moment.

"As we were once you are now," they seem to be saying, "and you too will someday be what we are now, only portraits on the wall."

The structure of the Cruikshank etchings for the *Sketches* is a double one. If the action at the center represents immediacy, life, self-forgetful engagement in the present moment, the portraits, like the spectator figures in other plates, represent time as duration, time as memory and anticipation, human temporality as detached self-possession. This double structure is exactly that ascribed by Baudelaire to the "absolute comic." For Baudelaire "le comique absolu" is comedy based on the grotesque, and in the passage cited earlier he describes Cruikshank as "un artiste doué de riches facultés comiques."[57] The comedy of Cruikshank's plates, however, lies not in the grotesque violence of gesture and expression of his "prestigieuses petites créatures" (751), but in the copresence of that violence and the spectator of it. "Le comique, la puissance du rire," says Baudelaire in "De l'essence du rire," "est dans le rieur et nullement dans l'objet du rire" (717).[58] This means that "pour qu'il y ait comique, c'est-à-dire émanation, explosion, dégagement de comique, il faut qu'il ait deux êtres en présence" (727). An example of this is the absolute comic in Hoffmann's stories, *Daucus Carota, the King of the Carrots,* or in *The Princess Brambilla.* "Il est bien vrai qu'il le sait," says Baudelaire of Hoffmann, "mais il sait aussi que l'essence de ce comique est de paraître s'ignorer lui-même et de développer chez le spectateur, ou plutôt chez le lecteur, la joie de sa propre supériorité et la joie de la supériorité de l'homme sur la nature. Les artistes créent le comique; ayant étudié et rassemblé les éléments du comique, ils savent que tel être est comique, et qu'il ne l'est qu'à la condition d'ignorer sa nature" (728).

Baudelaire reserves his highest admiration for a comic structure which corresponds closely to the one I have identified in Cruikshank's illustrations. The perfection of the absolute comic is the combination in a single consciousness or structure of both

---

[57] *Oeuvres complètes,* pp. 721, 752. Further quotations from Baudelaire will be identified by page numbers from this edition in parentheses after the quotations.

[58] See Paul de Man's discussion of *De l'essence du rire* in "The Rhetoric of Temporality," *Interpretation: Theory and Practice,* ed. Charles S. Singleton (Baltimore: Johns Hopkins Press, 1969), pp. 194-199.

the laugher and the object of his laughter. The personage so
caught up in the moment that he has ceased to be fully human
and has become the victim of a fall into nature is integrated into
a single system of awareness with the laughing witness of this fall.
"Ce n'est point l'homme qui tombe qui rit de sa propre chute,"
says Baudelaire, "à moins qu'il ne soit un philosophe, un homme
qui ait acquis, par habitude, la force de se dédoubler rapidement
et d'assister comme spectateur désintéressé aux phénomènes de son
moi. Mais le cas est rare" (717). To the rare self-doubling of the
philosopher must be added the similar self-division of the great
comic artists, "les hommes qui ont fait métier de développer en
eux le sentiment du comique et de le tirer d'eux-mêmes pour le
divertissement de leurs semblables" (727-728). The development of
this feeling for the comic depends, argues Baudelaire, on a single
all-important factor in man, "l'existence d'une dualité permanente,
la puissance d'être à la fois soi et un autre" (728). Every great
artist is only an artist "à la condition d'être double et de n'ignorer
aucun phénomène de sa double nature" (728). Baudelaire has
here described exactly, though without specific reference to Cruikshank, the comic pattern in Cruikshank's illustrations for the
Sketches by Boz. Their comedy depends on the copresence, within
the picture, of the comic personages and the witness of their comic
antics. Cruikshank's etchings are divided within themselves. They
contain both the moment and duration, both unself-conscious
violence of engagement in action and the disinterested spectator
of that violence, both the comic being and the detached witness
in whom laughter resides.

*

There is more to be said about this double structure. This
more will expose the homology between the pattern of meaning
in Cruikshank's plates and the pattern I identified above in the
text of the *Sketches*. The internal structure of the illustrations is
a temporal pattern combining duration and the instant in an
ambiguous tension. Such a doubling also constitutes a tension between *mimesis* and fiction. The portraits on the wall are mimetic,
copies of faces which once existed in the real world. They are also
pictures within pictures. As in all such cases, the picture within

a picture calls the spectator's attention to the problem of representation. The action at the center of the picture is not "real life." It is, like the portraits themselves, a picture of real life, a representation. It is something derived and secondary, fixed and dead. To the doubling constituted by the presence of a picture within the picture could be applied the formula from Walter Benjamin used at the beginning of this essay to describe the doubling within the text of the *Sketches*. The portraits on the wall underline the relation of the represented action to the action signified by the fact itself of representation.

The play between the portraits and the foreground scene initiates an oscillation in which the location of authenticity changes place bewilderingly. The pictures on the wall are dead representations. As such they put the action at the center in question by reminding the viewer that however vital and explosive it seems it is only *mimesis* too. It is a picture of a moment of life and not that life itself. The "living" figures are as motionless, as mute and dead, as the figures in the portraits. Both exist as marks on the pages, scratches on the etcher's copper. The representative aspect, as in all great art, tends to dissolve before the spectator's recognition of the primacy of the medium in its meaninglessness. As a sculpture is stone, a painting paint, so an etching is ink on paper, or perhaps, as in the case of the clouds of smoke in several of the plates for the *Sketches,* the represented object exists not even as ink, but as a blank place on the paper.

On the other hand, the portraits in the illustrations represent, paradoxically, life as it is copied in art. The paradox lies in the fact that the central action is apparently life itself, though actually art masquerading as life, therefore deceptive. The portraits in their obvious stiffness and immobility are more honest. They openly reveal the inauthenticity of all art, its irremediable distance from life, the fact that it is the copy of the thing, not the thing itself. But, to turn to the other side of the coin once more, if the portraits exemplify the counterfeit quality of mimetic art, the grotesque comic figures, in their ephemeral violence, if they are seen as free from any mimetic relationships, manifest the authenticity of true art. This authenticity exists as the withdrawal from nature, as the transformation of natural objects, the paper, the ink, into signs. Such signs are freed from their inherence in the causal web of nature and have created a realm of fiction. This realm belongs neither to natural duration nor to the natural instant. It is the place of that time out of time created within art by the reference of each fiction to the near nothingness of other fictions. Such fictional representation of the moment remains, while the moment passes.

Here another hint in the brief passage by Baudelaire on Cruikshank may be followed as a clue to the fictional nature of his illustrations. "Tous ses petits personnages miment avec fureur et turbulence," says Baudelaire, "comme des acteurs de pantomime." The allusion to pantomime is correct. Cruikshank, like Dickens, much admired the popular theater. Just as allusions to pantomimic gestures and theatrical expressions are fundamental in the text of the *Sketches,* so the poses of Cruikshank's figures are often borrowed from melodrama or pantomime. An example is the admirable tableau of "The Tuggses at Ramsgate." The English pantomime tradition also plays a fundamental role in Baudelaire's definition of the absolute comic in "De l'essence du rire." Central in that essay is Baudelaire's description of a performance he witnessed in Paris in 1842 of an English pantomime which probably included in the cast the famous English clown Tom Matthews. Baudelaire's description of this emphasizes, as does his commentary on Cruikshank, the violence of the performance. The pantomimic actors seemed to be seized suddenly by a great wind of extravagant madness which carried them into that dizzy realm of hyperbole, the absolute comic. "Il m'a semblé que le signe distinctif de ce genre de comique était la violence. . . . Le Pierrot anglais arrivait comme la tempête, tombait comme un ballot, et quand il riait, son rire faisait trembler la salle; ce rire ressemblait à un joyeux tonnerre. . . . Et toutes choses s'exprimaient ainsi dans cette singulière pièce, avec emportement; c'était le vertige de l'hyperbole" (723-724). The essence of comedy is this hyperbolic vertigo, an extravagance of gesture which transfigures the actors, puts them beyond what Baudelaire calls "la frontière du merveilleux" (725) and makes them into purely conventional figures. They are then no longer people playing the role of someone else, but men and women "introduits de force dans une existence nouvelle" (725). This existence is that realm of pure fiction which belongs neither to the moment nor to duration and which is not mimetic, for it imitates nothing, and yet not autonomous either. The more free, spontaneous, extravagant, hyperbolic the gestures or expressions of pantomimic actors or of the figures of Cruikshank's plates become, the more conventional, melodramatic, repetitive, fictive they are. They allude not to anything outside art, but to other fictive entities, as Cruikshank's illustrations for the *Sketches* echo one another in faces, figures, gestures, and compositions, and then repeat earlier Cruikshanks, and behind that earlier figures in the pantomimic and graphic tradition.

Not Baudelaire, but Mallarmé, in a passage called "Mimique" in *Crayonné au théatre*,[59] identifies most exactly the power of the hyperbolic gestures of the mime to abolish both any representational element and any link to a falsely naturalistic sense of the living present. Such abolition replaces representation and the presence of the present with a contradictory realm of fiction. This fictional space exists in the perpetual allusion of the present sign to a past and a future which it is both married to and separated from by an unbreakable glass. This glass is the "hymen" of the failure of the fictive gestures of pantomime, of literature, or of caricature to perform any action whatsoever in the real world. Mallarmé's text describes the performance of the mime Paul Margueritte of the pantomime "Pierrot Assassin de sa Femme." In this performance, of course, there is no wife, and she is not killed. "La scène n'illustre que l'idée, pas une action effective, dans un hymen (d'où procède le Rêve), vicieux mais sacré, entre le désir et l'accomplissement, la perpétration et son souvenir; ici devançant, là remémorant, au futur, au passé, *sous une apparence fausse de présent*."[60] A false appearance of the present which establishes a realm of pure fiction, by its allusions to a past and to a future which never did and never will take place except as fictions in their turn—this describes perfectly the strange reality brought before our eyes by Cruikshank's best works. This reality is glimpsed at the vanishing point of that oscillation between

[59] See Jacques Derrida's subtle interpretation of this text in "La double séance," cited in footnote 2, above.
[60] *Oeuvres complètes*, p. 310.

mimetic and figurative readings of the illustrations which initiates the vibration leading to the "vertige de l'hyperbole." In this oscillation, most easily identifiable in the interpretation the viewer makes of the portraits in their relation to the living figures, the values of each change place before his eyes. What seemed inauthentic, the portraits, becomes authentic. What seemed authentic becomes a fiction. The violent action the portrait figures so serenely behold seems at first to have the genuine quality of life in the immediate present. Then it comes to be seen as inauthentic, because these unself-conscious figures fail to see the instant in the perspective of its end, in the perspective of death. Then the central figures appear authentic again when they are recognized as constituting the fictive mobility and allusiveness of true art. Back and forth between representation and fiction the illustrations move, as does the text by Dickens which Cruikshank's pictures illustrate. In both cases this wavering is the life and meaning of the works and of our activity of interpreting them. For both Dickens's *Sketches* and Cruikshank's illustrations the validity of the fictive reading cannot be reached unless we are tempted into accepting and exploring the representational reading.

To raise the question of what it means to have an illustrated book, to set Cruikshank's etchings and Dickens's *Sketches* side by side,[61] or to investigate either separately, as I have done in this study, is to encounter a contradictory vibration between a mimetic reading sustained by reference to something extra-artistic and a reading which sees both the literary text and its illustrations as fictions. The meaning of such fictions is constituted and maintained only by their reference to other equally fictional entities. This reciprocally sustaining, reciprocally destroying vacillation between literal and figurative interpretations is crucial to the process of explicating both graphic and literary works.

---

[61] As Dickens did in one of his proposed titles for the first volume of the *Sketches:* "Sketches by Boz and Cuts by Cruikshank" (Letter to Macrone, Pilgrim edition of *The Letters of Charles Dickens,* I, 82).

The Dickens Drama:
Mr. Dombey

IAN MILNER

THERE ARE VARIOUS WAYS of looking at Mr. Dombey. He is Pride going before a fall on a Jonsonian stage. He is mercantile man, rich, self-sufficient, domineering, in a trading empire on which the sun never sets. He is alienated man, shut within himself by nature and the illusory power of wealth, robbed of his only son, self-isolated from his daughter. He is man redeemed when in the end, pride broken and fortune gone, Florence brings him by love and tears into "the community of feeling." He has been seen as suffering and remorseful man, "a character of tragic stature." [1] He is also, for a time, domestic man: husband of a woman whose will he cannot subdue and whose strong sensual presence fascinates and baffles him.

In the "outline" of his "immediate intentions" Dickens makes it plain that "Dombey and Son" is merely the necessary prelude to the central theme of "Dombey and Daughter": "I purpose changing his feeling of indifference and uneasiness towards his daughter into a positive hatred. . . . At the same time I shall change *her* feeling towards *him* for one of a greater desire to love him, and to be loved by him. . . ." [2] We are to witness the fall of worldly Pride in Dombey's ruin. But the dramatic potential is located in his inner conflict, to be resolved by the final reconciliation: "For the struggle with himself, which goes on in all such obstinate natures, will have ended then; and the sense of his injustice, which you may be sure has never quitted him, will have at last a gentler office than that of only making him more harshly unjust." Dickens's primary interest in the inner moral drama is evident from his "apologia" in the preface to the 1867 edition of the novel: "Mr. Dombey undergoes

---

[1] Kathleen Tillotson, *Novels of the Eighteen-Forties* (Oxford, 1954), p. 170.
[2] John Forster, *The Life of Charles Dickens*, ed. J. W. T. Ley (London, 1928), p. 472.

no violent change, either in this book, or in real life. A sense of
his injustice is within him, all along. The more he represses it, the
more unjust he necessarily is. Internal shame and external circumstances may bring the contest to a close in a week, or a day; but, it
has been a contest for years, and is only fought out after a long
balance of victory." The extended treatment given to the com-
plicating triangle of emotional forces arising from Dombey's second marriage, and the entry of Carker into that field of tension,
indicates how far Dickens became absorbed, as the novel pro-
gressed, in the personal theme.

The role of Mr. Dombey is therefore something of a test case for
Dickens's art. Henry James, reviewing *Our Mutual Friend,* found
that Dickens was incapable of effectively treating the inner life: "it
is one of the chief conditions of his genius not to see beneath the
surface of things. . . . He has created nothing but figures. He has
added nothing to our understanding of human character." [3]
Recently the thesis has been elaborated that Dickens's peculiar
gift, and limitation, was for "theatrical art" in which "the primary
object of our attention is the artist himself, on the stage of his own
theatre, performing his brilliant routines. The characters he "creates" on this stage will come to us, and be consistently known to
us, as the embodiments of his brilliant gift for *mimicry*." [4] Dickens
is accordingly disqualified as a practitioner of what is called "serious art": "he did not ever learn to practise the mode of moral
drama which is the norm for serious art, that mode which consists
of the dramatization of moral choice in the inner life of the individual human consciousness." [5]

Concerning the presentation of the inner life, if Dickens is
judged by Jamesian criteria he is naturally found wanting. He does
not deal in the "finer consciousness" and its nuances nor is he concerned with intellectual inquiry, self-analysis, and debate. G. H.
Lewes complained, with some reason considering his own phreno-
logical bumps, that "Dickens sees and feels, but the logic of feeling
seems the only logic he can manage. Thought is strangely absent
from his works." [6] *Thought* is a tricky word. We know Mr. Casau-

[3] *The House of Fiction: Essays on the Novel,* ed. Leon Edel (London, 1957), pp.
256–57.
[4] Robert Garis, *The Dickens Theatre: A Reassessment of the Novels* (Oxford,
1965), p. 54 (emphasis as in original).
[5] Ibid., pp. 253–54.
[6] "Dickens in Relation to Criticism," *Fortnightly Review* (Feb. 1872), rptd. in

bon's thoughts; we know Strether's. Mr. Dombey also has his thoughts, simpler and at an appropriately conventional level. But what Dickens is concerned with are the dominant elements in Dombey's motivation: the nature of his inner conflict and its development: the "passions" that "spin the plot."

As to method we are not usually shown Dombey reflecting about himself. Nor does Dickens much analyze his state of mind, although both authorial comment and *style indirect libre* are used as supplementary means with fine effect. Dickens's primary mode is to show us Dombey, and Edith, at a series of nodal points in the action. These points have been selected so as to provide the dramatic intensity and vividness of focus needed for the most effective illumination of personality. What Dombey says or does at such a point offers a sudden and peculiarly revealing vision of his inner self and its motivations. Character is shown in action; the mode is kinetic. And it is impressionistic. Character, and inner growth, is evoked and suggested by the discontinuous, selective "picturing" of high points of experience. There is not the linear sense of character development depending on the knowledge and insights derived from continuous authorial or other mediation. Rather an intermittent series of dramatic illuminations imply and suggest instead of interpreting and defining. But the impressionism is cumulative in its effect. We come to know, or sense, a great deal about Dombey's inner life and the less conscious and submerged impulses involved in its primary conflict as we pass from one nodal point to another.

We meet Mr. Dombey, and son, in the opening chapter. Curiously little is said, descriptively, about him: "Dombey was about eight-and-forty years of age . . . , rather bald, rather red, and though a handsome well-made man, too stern and pompous in appearance, to be prepossessing." What he does suggests the kind of person he is: "Dombey, exulting in the long-looked-for event, jingled and jingled the heavy gold watch-chain that depended from below his trim blue coat, whereof the buttons sparkled phosphorescently in the feeble rays of the distant fire." The jingling of the watch chain, heavy gold, is no mere externalized mannerism like the pantings and chokings that always signalize Major Bagstock. It has here a metonymic quality; it fixes on our senses the potentate presence of

The Dickens Critics, ed. George H. Ford and Lauriat Lane, Jr., (Ithaca, N.Y., 1961), p. 69.

its wearer and his euphoric pride. And what is then *said* rounds out
the picture, deftly and economically suggesting the kind of husband
the watch chain jingler is: " 'The house will once again, Mrs.
Dombey,' said Mr. Dombey, 'be not only in name but in fact
Dombey and Son; Dom-bey and Son!' The words had such a softening influence, that he appended a term of endearment to Mrs.
Dombey's name (though not without some hesitation, as being a
man but little used to that form of address): and said, 'Mrs. Dombey, my-my dear.' "

The rhetoric of the first chapter is exuberant, the irony heavily
marked. But the mind of Mr. Dombey is not a finer consciousness. And it is his mind that we here see ticking as clearly as we
hear his "very loud ticking watch." Very little has been authorially
said about him. But his personality has been exposed to the reader
as sharply focused as it appeared, through a child's eyes, to Florence: "the blue coat and stiff white cravat, which, with a pair of
creaking boots and a very loud ticking watch, embodied her idea of
a father." The initial picture may be that appropriate to a comedy
of humors. But it is extremely alive, economical, and objective.
There is no Manager of the Performance getting in between us
and Mr. Dombey. Dombey himself is out at the center of the stage
from the start. With a minimum of stage directions (such as the
familiar irony of "the earth was made for Dombey and Son to trade
in, and the sun and moon were made to give them light") his
actions and his words, heightened by the precise dramatic context,
show us the man.

The death of Paul sets the stage for the central drama of Dombey
and Florence. A key chapter in this development is 18, entitled
"Father and Daughter," an admirable instance of Dickens's skill
in dramatic composition, particularly of his ability to use scene to
suggest inner qualities. There are six interlinked scenes arranged
in tonal contrast. First the funeral procession and church service.
Nothing is authorially said about Dombey's thoughts, scarcely anything of his looks. There is only the little incident, presented in
dialogue, in which his inscription for the grave ("beloved and only
child") has to be corrected. Suddenly we see the vein of pathos in
Dombey's obsessive pride in his son and heir. Without a word of
analysis, commentary, or *erlebte Rede*, Dickens "shows" Dombey
in a new light.

There follows the conversation between Mrs. Chick, Miss Tox,

and Florence about his desire to be left to himself and his decision
to go away to the country. Florence's lonely sad reverie then leads
into the contrasting "fairy-tale" mode of "the rosy children" playing with their father in the house opposite. Then the brief intermezzo in somber tones of Florence's nightly visits to her father's
always closed door, anticipating the tragic encounter at the close.
Comic relief intervenes in the shape of Mr. Toots and Diogenes,
the dog who serves as a "sort of keepsake" for Paul, followed by
another brief intermezzo in which Susan Nipper informs Florence
that her father is to leave the next morning (she has not even seen
him since the funeral). Again making her nightly visit Florence
finds the door slightly open. There is a special significance in this
chance detail. Florence is the estranged child of humanity crying
to be let into the house of love and community; but "the door was
ever closed, and he shut up within." [7] Seeing him now in his "utter
loneliness," she speaks to him:

> He started at her voice, and leaped up from his seat. She was close
> before him, with extended arms, but he fell back. "What is the mat-
> ter?" he said, sternly. "Why do you come here? What has frightened
> you?"
> If anything had frightened her, it was the face he turned upon her.
> The glowing love within the breast of his young daughter froze before
> it, and she stood and looked at him as if stricken into stone.
> There was not one touch of tenderness or pity in it. There was not
> one gleam of interest, parental recognition, or relenting in it. There
> was a change in it, but not of that kind. The old indifference and cold
> restraint had given place to something: what, she never thought and
> did not dare to think, and yet she felt it in its force, and knew it well
> without a name: that as it looked upon her, seemed to cast a shadow on
> her head.

It is characteristic of Dickens that he does not offer at this dramatic point any analysis or interpretation of that "something" in
her father's face. There is the string of accompanying questions, on
a "Jamesian" reading crudely intrusive rhetorical questions suggesting possible motives: Florence as his "successful rival" in Paul's
affection, a kind of "mad jealousy," the "gall" of seeing her "in

---

[7] Images of immurement recur throughout the novel: Dombey is "shut up within
himself" (chap. 20), he would (with Paul) "shut out all the world as with a double
door of gold" (chap. 20), he is "shut up in his supremacy" (chap. 51), he lives
"encased" in "the cold hard armour of pride" (chap. 40); Florence is "shut out"
and "lost" (chap. 18), she "stand[s] without, with a bar across the door" (chap. 24),
she is "shut up" in the lonely house (chap. 23 and chap. 28).

her beauty and her promise" while his son is dead. The questions are Dickens's way of indicating that Dombey is himself not yet conscious of the motives for and extent of his new darker feelings toward his daughter. What the reader is given is the intuitive shock of recognition of that change on Florence's part, and, with the insight and command of great art, the conflicting impulses and genuine suffering of Mr. Dombey. Even at this point he is, in his way, compassionate, taking her by the arm (though his hand is "cold, and loose") and saying she must be tired: "I will remain here to light you up the stairs. The whole house is yours above there," says the father slowly. "You are its mistress now. Good night!" The chilling irony of this property grant ("Dombey and Son had often dealt in hides, but never in hearts") is lost on the father. Then with a natural simplicity of means Dickens reveals another side to Dombey's cold indifference:

The last time he had watched her, from the same place, winding up those stairs, she had had her brother in her arms. It did not move his heart towards her now, it steeled it: but he went into his room, and locked his door, and sat down in his chair, and cried for his lost boy.

The cadence and finely achieved tragic insight of this final sentence prove Dickens in command of resources that might easily in such a context have slipped into facile pathos. The chapter as a whole shows the hand not of any "theatrical" manipulator of externalized characters but that of the born dramatist who matches control of stage and scene with searching insight into basic human motivations.

The drama of father-daughter tension is now both diversified and intensified by the "external circumstances" of Dombey's second marriage. Dickens offers a preview of the direction the tension will take. Carker comes to Leamington to consult Dombey and mentions casually, immediately after being told about Edith, that he has "seen Miss Dombey." The father has no comment nor apparent interest, but "there was a sudden rush of blood to Mr. Dombey's face." It is a small touch but deliberate and expressive. The earlier cold hostility toward his daughter has given way to something so blood-suffusing as to suggest hate. During the train journey from London he had formed the homicidal thought that he could have lost Florence "without a pang" if only Paul had been spared. And in the "rush of blood" there is also implied an element of sexual frustration and resentment. While informing Carker much later on (chap. 42) of Edith's insubordination (and remembering the encounter in her apartment where her sexual allure was most evident), Dombey feels "the blood rush to his own face." In regard to Florence, the deepening of his resentment into hate is overtly linked with her transition from girl to young woman. He suddenly becomes possessive. The night he returns home from his "honeymoon" in Paris, he sits alone with Florence secretly watching her "in her beauty, almost changed into a woman without his knowledge." For a moment he relents and is on the point of calling her to him when Edith enters. He observes without illusion the affection that exists between them and from then on his attitude to Florence is overlaid by sexual jealousy fed by his own inability to subdue Edith's will.

Dombey's motivation in regard to wife and daughter is partly expressed scenically. The dramatic mode works to a climax with Edith's elopement. As he rushes from her dressing-room where he found "in a costly mass upon the ground" every ornament and dress Edith had possessed, Dombey has the "frantic idea of finding her yet . . . and beating all trace of beauty out of the triumphant face with his bare hand" (chap. 47). When a little later Florence approaches him to offer her sympathy, he tells her what Edith was, and bids "her follow her, since they had always been in league" and strikes her so heavily on the breast (it remained not merely figuratively "bruised") that she falls to the marble floor. She sees him "murdering that fond idea" of gaining his affection; she sees his "cruelty, neglect, and hatred dominant above it, and stamping it down" (chap. 47). The suddenly unleashed violence and savage energy of act and mood, and the particular direction his impulses take in each instance, make this a revealing dramatization of Dombey's interlocked sexual frustration, jealousy, and rage.

Dickens does not rely on the dramatic mode alone. In chapter 40, titled with cool irony "Domestic Relations," Dombey's ambivalent attitude toward Florence, linked with that toward his wife, is indicated in a blend of authorial interpretation and *style indirect libre:*

In his sullen and unwholesome brooding, the unhappy man, with a dull perception of his alienation from all hearts, and a vague yearning for what he had all his life repelled, made a distorted picture of his rights and wrongs, and justified himself with it against her [Florence]. The worthier she promised to be of him, the greater claim he was disposed to ante-date upon her duty and submission. When had she ever shown him duty and submission? Did she grace his life—or Edith's? Had her attractions been manifested first to him—or Edith? Why, he and she had never been, from her birth, like father and child! They had always been estranged. She had crossed him every way and everywhere. She was leagued against him now. Her very beauty softened natures that were obdurate to him, and insulted him with an unnatural triumph.

Such a passage (by no means the only one of its kind in this novel) indicates how effectively Dickens uses on occasion a mode so characteristic of George Eliot when treating the inner life of her characters.[8] The sudden, natural shift away from the authorial stance ("When had she ever shown him duty and submission?") brings all the advantages of dramatic immediacy and authentic expression of Dombey's tortured rationalizing. The "insulted him with an *unnatural* triumph" suggests the sexual element in his frustration which is made overt in the immediately following scene with Edith.

The distinctive use of scene to suggest phases of character and motivation is well displayed when Dombey confronts his wife, late at night in her own apartment, with his "ultimatum" that she show him more obedience. Edith is of course "melodramatic"; she makes her way in the novel accompanied by a mounting array of rhetorical cliché (flashing eye, haughty brow, scornfully curled lip). But her melodramatic aspect is insisted upon much more heavily after her flight with Carker. As she defies her husband in this scene in her "brilliant dress," her "white arms" folded "upon her swelling breast," there is a good deal more than the simplified motivations of melodrama in the rendering:

---

[8] *Dombey and Son* offers a wider and more varied use of *erlebte Rede* than has been recognized; see, however, Lisa Glauser, *Die erlebte Rede im englischen Roman des 19. Jahrhunderts* (Bern, 1948), pp. 34–35. In addition to instances of a kind of *erlebte Rede* authorially stylized to heighten dramatic effect, as Glauser suggests, there are transitions to genuine *style indirect libre*, e.g., the very effective registration of Dombey's homicidal state of mind during the train journey to Leamington: "Because he knew full well, in his own breast, as he stood there, tinging the scene of transition before him with the morbid colours of his own mind, and making it a ruin and a picture of decay.... that life had quite as much to do with his complainings as death. One child was gone, and one child left. Why was the object of his hope removed instead of her?" (chap. 20)

If she had been less handsome, and less stately in her cold composure, she might not have had the power of impressing him with the sense of disadvantage that penetrated through his utmost pride. But she had the power, and he felt it keenly. He glanced round the room: saw how the splendid means of personal adornment, and the luxuries of dress, were scattered here and there, and disregarded; not in mere caprice and carelessness (or so he thought), but in a steadfast haughty disregard of costly things: and felt it more and more. . . . The very diamonds—a marriage gift—that rose and fell impatiently upon her bosom, seemed to pant to break the chain that clasped them round her neck, and roll down on the floor where she might tread upon them.

He felt his disadvantage, and he showed it. Solemn and strange among this wealth of colour and voluptuous glitter, strange and constrained towards its haughty mistress, whose repellent beauty it repeated, and presented all around him, as in so many fragments of a mirror, he was conscious of embarrassment and awkwardness.

The atmospheric and suggestive power of the narration here enables Dickens to present the conflict between husband and wife as more complex than the clash oß strong wills or the resentment of a "purchased" wife against husbandly domination. We are made aware of the sexual undercurrent on both sides. Dombey is embarrassed and constrained face to face with Edith's beauty and the "voluptuous glitter" in which she moves. In the same chapter she reveals in high rhetorical color the passionate potential under her officially "cold" self. At Dombey's mention of Carker who, she knows, is well aware of her real nature, her face and bosom glow "as if the red light of an angry sunset had been flung upon them." Characteristically Dickens uses a visual detail, in this instance a compulsive mannerism, to complement and vivify the narrative. As the tension mounts between them she sits—"still looking at him fixedly—turning a bracelet round and round upon her arm; not winding it about with a light, womanly touch, but pressing and dragging it over the smooth skin, until the white limb showed a bar of red." The image here is at the level of poetic metaphor. In that "bar of red" on the smooth skin we see, in a flash of rare insight that fuses the personal and the social elements, Edith Dombey's divided and tortured nature: her need, and capacity, for love, her scorn, and the passionate self-contempt she had herself voiced in an earlier conversation with her mother: "There is no slave in a market; there is no horse in a fair: so shown and offered and examined and paraded, mother, as I have been, for ten shameful years" (chap. 27).

Dickens has been criticized for contriving his denouement too summarily: "The year was out, and the great House was down" (chap. 58). Ironically for those who see him as a writer of "external" life, he here skimps the treatment of his social framework in order to concentrate on the inner life. His finale is centered on the last agonized stage of Dombey's self-conflict and its resolution. Those who find the redemption a purely stage-managed surrender to Florence's all-too-consistent Angel of Mercy mission should in all fairness not ignore the registration of Dombey's preceding mood. Bankrupt and "shut up" (again this image of alienation) in the rooms of his house now given over to creditors, disgraced by his wife and abandoned by his daughter, he turns his back, still proud, on the world. The savage contest between "pride" (and all that emotionally repressive mechanism that we have seen at work in his relations with daughter and wife) and remorse drive him—we are made to feel it—to the verge of madness and suicide.

The means used to represent the intensity of his suffering are varied. If there is for many readers the melodramatic dross of the invocation, reiterated from chapter 18, "Let him remember it in that room, years to come!" there is dramatic gold as well. Alone at night he thinks of the spoliation of his house, and life, in terms of the innumerable footsteps of the furniture removers and creditors' agents:

Of all the footmarks there, making them as common as the common street, there was not one, he thought, but had seemed at the time to set itself upon his brain while he had kept close, listening. . . . He began to fear that all this intricacy in his brain would drive him mad; and that his thoughts already lost coherence as the footprints did, and were pieced on to one another, with the same trackless involutions, and varieties of indistinct shapes.

If it is "theatre," then it is effective theatre when in the end he watches, doppelgänger fashion, his image in the mirror, a separated and impersonal thing: "Now it rose and walked about; now passed into the next room, and came back with something from the dressing-table in its breast."

The highly wrought tension here may seem suspect in view of the miraculously timed coup de theatre of Florence's kneeling before the would-be suicide and praying for forgiveness. But the overriding impression, created by the finely controlled blend of scenic

presentation, authorial interpretation, and *erlebte Rede,* is of the
father's suffering—and of the slow changes forced on him by experience: the death of Paul, remarriage, the relations of Edith and
Florence, Edith's willfulness and adultery (in spirit; Dombey
thinks of her as "sunk into a polluted creature"), Carker's treach-
ery, Florence's flight and marriage, his own disgrace and financial
ruin. The nerve-shattered aging man whom Florence rescues has
come a long way from the "handsome well-made" Dombey who
jingled his heavy gold watch chain in pride at his son's birth. And
Dickens has so vividly caught the "felt life" of that human journey
that the reader accepts at the end the portrayal of the breaking of
Dombey's pride not as theatrical manipulation but as the objective revelation of great art.

Dickens's Attitudes in
A Tale of Two Cities

SYLVÈRE MONOD

STUDIES OF THE AUTHOR-READER RELATIONSHIP are easy enough to conduct in the case of writers who, like Thackeray, George Eliot, or Charlotte Brontë, address their readers. It was an examination of *Jane Eyre* that first attracted my attention to this problem a few years ago; the reader of that book is apostrophized on some thirty occasions, and the author's attitude to him or her can be inferred with tolerable clarity from the relevant passages, as can the mental image Charlotte Brontë—or is it Jane Eyre?—has formed of this elusive person. Dickens—and especially the later Dickens—presents more difficult problems. As I note elsewhere, in *Bleak House,* for instance, very little visible attempt is made to establish any kind of specific relationship with the reader.[1] And in *A Tale of Two Cities* there seems to be even less than in *Bleak House.* Yet, as has often been remarked, no novel is written in a complete vacuum; every work of literature meant for publication, and preeminently every work of fiction by Charles Dickens, was originally written for the reader and is thus in some sense addressed *to* the reader. The relationship may, and indeed most of the time does, remain implicit, but it is present, inevitably, in the writer's consciousness. It ought to be possible to infer its varying nature from the study of other types of relationship occurring at more visible levels; the reader is addressed by the writer through several channels, such as narrator or narrators and characters.

This discussion is an attempt to analyze and sort out a complex of relationships involving the author, the narrators, the characters, and the readers of *A Tale of Two Cities.* I must from the outset make it clear that it is not my purpose to sit in judg-

---

[1] "Esther Summerson, Charles Dickens, and the Reader in *Bleak House*," *Dis* 5 (May 1969): 5–25.

ment on the attitudes and procedures adopted by Dickens but merely to describe them and define their consequences. It is my present belief—and I tend to think it is also a simple, perhaps a platitudinous, truth—that no attitude on the part of a novelist is intrinsically better than another. The words "omniscience" and "author intrusion" are often used disparagingly nowadays. When I disclaim any judicial or magisterial connotation of these words which I am inevitably using many times, I mean that the only justified adverse criticism would be against deviations from the convention initially adopted or against destruction of credibility.

Author and Narrators

In a lecture delivered at Lausanne in 1959 Angus Wilson made some useful comments on the division of labor while a novel is being written between the novelist, the narrator, and the remainder of the writer's personality. He said: "I have found in the course of ten years' writing that three personalities or separate wills exist during the making of a book—the narrator, the craftsman, and the residue"; he went on to add: "The three exist in perpetual warfare—to the detriment I may say of the physical and nervous health of the whole—and their warfare is an eighteenth-century one of evershifting alliances to maintain the balance of power." [2]

This theory seemed to me illuminating when I heard the lecture in which it was put forward, and I have continued to regard it as valid and to use it in my teaching and in the critical analysis of various novelists. I am tempted, however, to introduce a slight modification of emphasis in the use of Wilson's distinctions. Not being an experienced novelist myself, I would hesitate to describe any part of Dickens's personality, however nonauthorial or nonnarrating, as a mere residue. On the other hand the more traditional opposition between author and narrator which Wilson was not interested in discussing remains in my eyes important and useful, whereas his own pair of narrator and craftsman are possibly more perceptible to the practicing artist— he says that his natural aptitude as a novelist is "for narration rather than for craft"—than to the external observer and the

[2] "The Novelist and the Narrator," *English Studies Today*, 2d ser., ed. G. A. Bonnard (Bern, 1961) pp. 43–50; quotations from pp. 44–45.

critic. Yet on the whole Angus Wilson's suggestion of an at least threefold division of the novelist's personality is immensely helpful. The private man (what he calls the residue) goes on with his private life, holds the pen physically, lights an occasional cigarette, answers the telephone or decides to ignore its call but is nevertheless disturbed by it, goes out for a meal, falls asleep; inevitably this private man conditions or interferes with the progress of the narrative, if only through temporary reluctance or unfitness, but sometimes through more positive impulses. Of the other two, those properly concerned with the narrative work itself, one—the "author" or "novelist"—is like the architect, the other—the narrator—like the foreman. The former conceives the general plan, invents the story and the characters, and issues orders in consequence; the latter has to carry out those orders, to transmute them into the descriptions, the narrative, and the dialogues of the book.

This delegation of part of the author's creative function to a subordinate persona is crystal clear in the case of all first-person narratives. David Copperfield is Dickens's narrative persona, so is Pip, and Jane Eyre is Charlotte Brontë's. But the delegation also exists, though less visibly, in third-person narratives. It does not merely assume the form of "point of view"; it also involves the adoption of a specific style and tone, of a certain set of habits and beliefs, of a certain store of general knowledge and specific information. Obviously we are not to take *all* the statements made in a third-person narrative as representing the author's permanent views; we can often form some idea of the narrator's personality as distinct from the author's. I believe that it is, at a lower level, a fairly common experience with most of us. We may adopt a lecturing tone and a writing tone and vary them in accordance with the particular audience we are addressing, the specific periodical we are writing for; we may even when writing letters assume a distinct persona for each correspondent or at least class of correspondents. A writer like Dickens, whose letters show how much he liked disguise and parody, would alter his manner not only from David to Esther to Pip but also from the narrator of *Pickwick* to that of *Oliver Twist* or *Nicholas Nickleby*. And like the writers of epistolary novels or like himself in *Bleak House*, he would also vary his stance from chapter to chapter or from episode to episode in some of his books.

In the case of *A Tale of Two Cities* it is obvious that there was an exceptionally close link between the book and the author, between the narrative and the man Charles Dickens, who asserted in his brief but striking preface that "throughout its execution, it has had complete possession of me" and significantly added: "I have so far verified what is done and suffered in these pages, as that I have certainly done and suffered it all myself." Even while making allowance for the writer's habitual overemphasis of his own emotional attitudes, his statements must be borne in mind; they imply that the usual distance or detachment from characters and tale could not be preserved entirely and even that the normal delegation from author to narrator could hardly be maintained throughout.

The bulk of the narrative, with the exceptions that must be called "intrusive," is delegated not to one but to several narrators, that is, to the teller of the tale or narrator proper, to a historian, and to a polemicist. The narrator occupies the position and exerts the privileges of omniscience, with some minor reservations as we shall see, but on the whole comfortably and unashamedly; he knows all that there is to be known about the characters and their thoughts and the course of events. The historian takes over whenever the knowledge required is not of private circumstances and fictional persons but of the real fate of two countries through a quarter of a century or more. A clear case of this substitution of the historian for the narrator occurs in book 1, chapter 5,[3] after the description of the wine-cask episode in the Paris suburb of Saint-Antoine. The street lamps in that area are said—presumably by such a contemporary observer as the narrator—to be swinging "in a sickly manner overhead, as if they were at sea." The very next sentence states, "Indeed they were at sea, and the ship and crew were in peril of tempest," a broader view of things and one that implies knowledge of the future as well as the present.

As for our third man, the polemicist, he is not so easily to be distinguished from the historian, for there is a satirical way of giving historical information that serves the purposes of both. The "Monseigneur" chapter (2.7) is neither straightforward narrative nor straightforward history; it is a kind of personalized

---

[3] The numbers given after each quotation hereafter in my text likewise refer to book and chapter numbers of the *Tale*.

satire that seems to rest on fragmentary or warped historical documentation. The aside about the Old Bailey and Bedlam (2.2) is satire in the guise of information; the allusion to "the last Louis but one, of the line that was never to break—the fourteenth Louis" (2.9) is again polemical history. What the three narrators have in common is their undisguised omniscience, even though it varies in degree, as does the distance between them and the tale or the characters.

OMNISCIENCE

The omniscient convention is not popular with modern critics, especially in France since Jean-Paul Sartre's onslaught on François Mauriac;[4] Sartre argued that Mauriac—in *La Fin de la nuit* —had made himself guilty of claiming to know more about his fictional characters than they could know about themselves and thereby limiting their freedom. Yet it is obvious that Sartre's own practice as a novelist derives from a different convention— except when he forgets about it—but that it is just as conventional and artificial as any other. So does that of our "nouveaux romanciers"—no one can reproduce life in its entirety; it is probable that books by authors who attempted to do that and no more would be extremely confused and dull, as life often is, and that most people read novels in the hope of finding in them a sifting and interpretation of the raw materials of life. It is probable also that life can no more be translated into words than painting, or music, or even poetry can be translated into prose. A novel therefore inevitably implies a process of selection and rejection on the part of the author. The most deliberately patternless novels ever written are far more patterned than reality, and the pattern has had to be imposed from the outside by the author's act; the most impressive transcript-of-life novel—Joyce's *Ulysses*—is also the most ingeniously patterned. The omniscient convention thus appears not only to be traditional, to have often been applied successfully and delightfully, but also to be entirely legitimate in itself. In any case Dickens happily belonged to a pre-Sartrian era when omniscience created no problems, when it was used by everyone with a clear conscience, when it was *the* available and accepted novelistic convention. *A Tale of Two Cities* is thus quite blithely told by omniscient narrators.

[4] "M. François Mauriac et la liberté," *NRF* 52 (1939): 212–32, and again in "Qu'est-ce que la littérature?" *Situations* 2 (Paris, 1948): 55–330.

Blithely, but not quite uniformly or simply.

The narrator occasionally affects not to be quite sure of what he asserts and qualifies some of his statements with an inserted "perhaps" or "probably." In a few cases he goes so far as to deny that he possesses complete knowledge of the facts he is expounding. Yet on the whole, omniscience is practiced by the narrator for the *Tale* to the full. The use of dramatic irony inevitably implies omniscience since its purpose is to share with the reader knowledge not possessed by at least one of the characters on the stage. There are many cases here. Several references to Miss Pross's illusions about her brother Solomon (e.g., as the fittest bridegroom for Lucie [2.18] and several warnings as to the course of some revolutionary actions, of which the characters are in temporary ignorance, provide examples: "Troubled as the future was, it was the unknown future, and in its obscurity there was ignorant hope" (3.1) is the clearest, made clearer still in the next sentence (about Charles Darnay in Paris): "The horrible massacre, days and nights long, which, within a few rounds of the clock, was to set a great mark of blood ... was as far out of his knowledge as if it had been a hundred thousand years away." Here great play is made with words like "unknown," "ignorance," and "out of his knowledge." But the examples of ordinary, straightforward, omniscient statements are far more numerous still; things like "Monsieur Defarge ... feigned not to notice the two strangers" (1.5) show that the narrator sees inside the characters and reads their thoughts and hidden purposes. When the Doctor describes his past experiences and asks his daughter, "Can you follow me, Lucie? Hardly, I think? I doubt you must have been a solitary prisoner to understand these perplexed distinctions" (2.17) the narrator seems to claim that he himself is miraculously or intuitively possessed of that understanding which neither Lucie nor the reader can acquire. Otherwise the proper narrative use of omniscience consists in knowing more than can be observed from the point of view temporarily adopted. When Mr. Lorry calls on Stryver, he finds him—and we move into Stryver's house with Mr. Lorry—"among a quantity of books and papers, littered out for the purpose" (2.12); Mr. Lorry could not know that it was "for the purpose," but the narrator can, because he can stand—omnisciently—within the consciousness of two or more persons at the same time. Similarly what Miss Pross does not recognize about her brother's history has come to the knowledge of Mr. Lorry, as we are told twice (in 2.6, where it is most acceptable, as his possession of such information conditions the manner in which he receives Miss Pross's speech, and again in 3.8). Every summary of a career (e.g., Stryver's at the beginning of 2.5) or of a scene ("The sweet scents of the summer night rose all around him, and rose, as the rain falls, impartially, on the rusty, ragged, and toil-worn group at the fountain not far away" [2.8]) also omnisciently expands the scope of the narrative in time or in space.

Of course the historical narrator has to practice omniscience almost permanently on the broadest scale: "They hanged at Tyburn in those days . . ." (2.2); "The new era began; the King was tried, doomed and beheaded . . ." (3.4). In one case the nature of narrative, historical, and polemical omniscience is asserted with particular clarity: "He looked at them and saw in them, without knowing it, the slow sure filing down of misery-worn face and figure, that was to make the meagreness of Frenchmen an English superstition which should survive the truth through the best part of a hundred years" (2.8). Similar devices can be used to impart to the text not ironical pungency alone but also prophetic solemnity or even cosmic magnitude. A sentence like "There were few buildings then, north of the Oxford-road, and forest-trees flourished . . . in the now vanished fields" (1.6) is there to show us, naturally enough, that the narrator has a wide stretch of time at his fingers' ends, "then" as well as "now," that he moves in his characters' as well as his readers' time and thus acts as a link between the two. Of this privileged position he takes advantage to project the readers' present (or any intermediate period) into the past in the guise of prophecy: "The time was to come, when that wine too [BLOOD] would be spilled on the streetstones" (1.5); the acme of that procedure is reached at the very end of the book when Carton is about to die and, because "he looked sublime and prophetic," is credited—hypothetically it is true ("If he had given utterance to his [thoughts]; and they were prophetic. . . .")—with a hyperprophetic vision extending presumably even beyond the readers' present, beyond 1859 (or 1970): "I see a beautiful city and a brilliant people rising from this abyss. . . ." As for space, his command extends to the whole earth ("all the wide dominions of sleep" [2.17]) and even beyond to a point whence "the feeble shining of this earth of ours" is seen only as "a twinkling star" (2.16) and beyond that again to the remotest bodies of the cosmos, "so remote from this little earth that the learned tell us it is doubtful whether their rays have even yet discovered it, as a point in space where anything is suffered or done" (1.6). Here we have omniscience with a vengeance when the narrator takes us away with him into "the arch of unmoved and eternal lights."

On the whole, then, the narrators, though they occasionally choose not to show it, know between them everything. What they give the reader is the truth, the facts, not just conjectures or suggestions. They treat the reader as a person who has to be informed about private events and general history, therefore as a person inferior to them.

NARRATORS AND NARRATIVE

The narrators' attitude to the story ought to be relatively simple; the narrative is their job, is what they have to relate—it is their *raison d'être*. Yet within this general program there are interesting variations in the way the things described or reported are seen or heard; the variations are mainly concerned with distance and point of view and with the narrators' degree of personal involvement.

The first element that varies is the distance between the narrator and his narrative, between the storyteller and the events described. And it varies quite spectacularly from the very beginning of the book. At the end of the first chapter there is a sudden focusing of the attention, a kind of "zooming" effect. The body of the chapter is a general picture of England and France in the year 1775, comprising several references to the royal couples in both countries. "All these things, and a thousand like them," the reader is told in the final paragraph, "came to pass in and close upon the dear old year one thousand seven hundred and seventy-five." The last sentence, however, introduces the effect I have alluded to: "Thus did the year one thousand seven hundred and seventy-five conduct their Greatnesses, and myriads of small creatures—the creatures of this chronicle among the rest—along the roads that lay before them." Thus is the way paved for the beginning of the second chapter which runs: "It was the Dover road that lay, on a Friday night late in November, before the first of the persons with whom this history has business." This effective

narrowing of the narrator's field of vision, from "myriads of
creatures," a whole year, and two large countries to a small group
on one English road on a specific night, is all the more interesting
as the reverse process can be observed at a later stage of the novel:
the narrator concerns himself with Monsieur Gabelle's experiences on the night when the Marquis's castle is burnt down (2.23),
then suddenly recedes or zooms back and launches into the
broader view—"Within a hundred miles, and in the light of
other fires, there were other functionaries less fortunate, that night
and other nights."

In these instances the narrator shifts his position but does not
give up his function. In other passages, however, he delegates it
to different persons. In book 2, chapter 3, the reader is informed
of the course of the trial not through the narrator's direct report
but through Jerry Cruncher's imperfect perceptions: "He had
now to attend while Mr. Stryver fitted the prisoner's case on the
jury.... Mr. Cruncher had next to attend while Mr. Attorney-
General...." The satirical value of this method is obvious: legal
language at best, in Dickens's opinion, was confused and confusing; by going through Jerry's dull and ignorant brain, it is made
ten times more so. And in a later chapter (2.14) a similar function
is delegated to young Jerry, who, as a hidden and terrified observer of his father's "honest trade" (conducted at night and in a
churchyard), makes the tale more impressive and mysterious.

The narrator of *A Tale of Two Cities* also practices more
ordinary shiftings of his point of view. In book 2, chapter 6, for
instance, he sees Barsad's visit to the wine shop mostly from
Madame Defarge's point of view; yet on at least two occasions he
takes us inside the visitor's consciousness, thereby implicitly
claiming his freedom to move about from one point of view to
another within the same scene so as to leave no psychological
corner in the dark.

The other element that varies is the degree of the narrator's
personal involvement in the tale. Close to the beginning of the
first book, in chapters 1 and 2, there are a few sentences in which he
depersonalizes himself and uses such conventional and antiquated
forms as "this chronicle" or "this history." But this particular
attitude is given up almost as soon as it has been attempted. The
use of the first person is also more severely restricted than in
almost any other Dickens novel or than in any novel by Thackeray

or George Eliot. There are so few cases that they can all be reviewed briefly at this point. The first person singular—*I*—occurs ten times in the first paragraph of book 1, chapter 3: "A solemn consideration, when I enter a great city by night, that every one of those darkly clustered houses encloses its own secret.... No more can I turn the leaves of this dear book that I loved...." But this is the philosopher's *I* and it is used for general statements, not in order to convey any impression of the narrator as an individual person. "Our booked passenger" (1.2) produces an effect similar to that of "this chronicle," even if it also faintly associates the author or narrator and the reader, like the *us* of "the learned tell us" (1.6). The *you* and *your* at the beginning of book 2, chapter 1, in the description of Tellson's Bank ("If your business necessitated your seeing 'the House,' you were put into a species of Condemned Hold at the back....") and the *you* of "not in shadow so remote but that you could see beyond it into a glare of brightness" are quite impersonal and mean no more than any indefinite pronoun (like *one*) would. The *all of us* and *some of us* of book 3, chapter 6, are more interesting: "In seasons of pestilence, some of us will have a secret inclination to die of it. And all of us have like wonders in our breasts, only needing circumstances to evoke them." Here the author (rather than the narrator) seems to be indulging in introspective analysis under the guise of omniscient generalization. Finally, in chapter 13 of book 3, first-person pronouns are used lavishly for a different purpose; it is during the flight of the English characters from Paris that they occur: "Sometimes, we strike into the stinking mud, to avoid the stones that clatter us and shake us...." This is a clear case of sudden emotional identification with the characters at a critical moment, an impression reinforced by the use of the present tense.[5] On the whole, however, the narrators of the *Tale* do not indulge in personal confidences and the reader cannot form a clear idea of the kinds of persons they are.

AUTHOR AND CHARACTERS

In the division of labor between author and narrator or narrators, the characters of any novel must be taken as conceived by the author and handed over to a narrator to be dealt with accord-

---

[5] This shift to the first person is noticed and adequately commented on by John Gross in his discussion of the *Tale* in *Dickens and the Twentieth Century*, ed. Gross and Gabriel Pearson (London, 1962), pp. 190–91.

ing to fairly specific and strict directions. One can hardly imagine the narrator part of a writer modifying a character in opposition to the author part of him. The author, in this matter as in that of the story, remains the masterbuilder or the taskmaster. I am aware of course that most novelists have claimed at one time or another that their characters often became uncontrollable and flatly refused to act in the way predetermined for them by their creator. But even if one does not—as I must confess I do—take the liberty of doubting the truthfulness of such statements, of discounting them as the mere cant of the trade, as the kind of thing a writer is expected to say if he wishes to be regarded as a powerful artist, it may at most mean that the novelist occasionally discovers the inadequacy or inconsistency of his original purpose concerning his characters, of his arbitrary predeterminations. In any case such fits of irresistible inspiration, such outbreaks of the divine afflatus, can only visit the author, not the narrator. But at this point it is apparent that our distinction between author and narrator, however convenient in a study of the processes of imaginative creation, cannot be regarded as hard and fast. After all, the author and the narrator are parts of the same individual— they work together; the delegation of power by the author to the narrator is incomplete and revocable; the author is always close at hand; the narrator is merely a personality or a persona temporarily assumed for the purposes of story-telling. Attitudes toward the characters, however, bring us more directly in touch with the author than the aspects examined so far in this article. There are several revealing examples in *A Tale of Two Cities*.

Charles Darnay's case is indeed somewhat peculiar. It would be difficult to find a passage in which admiration for him is explicitly expressed or solicited. The story gives him a prominent place, but he occupies it on the whole with modesty. It might be contended that Sidney Carton's sacrifice magnifies the person who is implicitly supposed to be worthy of it or at least to be worth saving at the cost of Carton's life, but Carton's life is obviously sacrificed for Lucie's sake, not for Charles's; it is as Lucie's husband solely, as the sine qua non of her happiness, that he has to be kept alive. Lucie's love for him is not much of an argument in his favor either, partly because it is a dull affair in itself and dully presented, partly because Lucie is not brilliantly attractive. She is loved by two or three men, as other pretty women, however humdrum, have been and will be, but she is on the whole uninteresting. Her husband on the other hand has created an unusually unanimous critical feeling against him.

John Gross writes: "Darnay is, so to speak, the accredited representative of Dickens in the novel, the 'normal' hero for whom a happy ending is still possible. It has been noted, interestingly enough, that he shares his creator's initials—and that is pretty well the only interesting thing about him. Otherwise he is a pasteboard character, completely undeveloped." [6] For K. J. Fielding Darnay is "no more than a shadow." [7] Edgar Johnson finds him "plodding, unimaginative, rather pedestrian, . . . all sobriety and quite incapable of making a joke." [8] Even Mrs. F. S. Boas, who has so much more than other readers to admire in the *Tale,* is unenthusiastic and says that Darnay's "gallant but weakly impulsive nature comes out in all he does." [9] Yet there is a high degree of emotional identification with Darnay on the author's part, as also with Carton of course.[10] And yet both are strikingly different from the author himself. Carton represents tendencies which he might have liked to let loose in himself; he is far more dissolute and eventually far more heroic, far less egotistic than the novelist. The creation of Carton thus appears as an exercise in imaginative, tentative reconstruction and reorganization of the self. Whereas when the novelist identifies himself with Darnay, as he so passionately does, he above all identifies Darnay with himself (rather than the other way round as with Carton), lending him for instance his own leaning toward "the Loadstone Rock" (2.24). The intensity with which Darnay's last hours in his condemned cell are presented makes them quite moving; obviously they were lived by Dickens. Yet Darnay was not given more than .01 percent of Dickens's vitality.

The treatment of Carton is considerably more subtle. Dickens at first studiously refrains from creating any liking for him and then suddenly makes him profoundly pathetic ("he threw himself down in his clothes on a neglected bed, and its pillow was wet with wasted tears" [2.5]), as if to show that a life can be both

---

[6] P. 189.

[7] *Charles Dickens: A Critical Introduction,* 2d ed. (London, 1965), p. 202.

[8] *Charles Dickens: His Tragedy and Triumph* (London, 1953), 2 vols. 2:973.

[9] Intro., *A Tale of Two Cities,* World's Classics ed. (London, 1903), p. xxi.

[10] "As everyone recognizes, he divides himself into two between Carton and Darnay" (Fielding, p. 203).

worthless and thoroughly, movingly unhappy. The chapter ironically called "The Fellow of No Delicacy" (2.13) is far less successful; it is the dreary and impossible chapter in which Sydney calls
on Lucie, not exactly to propose to her but to explain to her
why he cannot do so, why he is "even thankful that it cannot
be." One understands of course why the chapter is there, why it
has to be there: it enables Carton to utter such statements as "In
the hour of my death, I shall hold sacred the one good remembrance," and especially "I would embrace any sacrifice for you
and for those dear to you." Yet it makes one shudder to think
that this chapter must have been dear to Dickens's own heart,
that he must have believed he had made it believable. As for
Carton's death, Edgar Johnson's guarded statement seems to me
acceptable: "There are many readers who are not entirely unjustified in feeling that the death of Sydney Carton is drenched
in overindulged sentiment, with Dickens pulling all the organ-
stops to make it heart-rending." [11] The other readers who feel
that this episode is beautifully and poetically written "are not entirely unjustified" either. The emotion with which it is fraught
may or may not be shared by individual readers and critics, but
there can be no doubt that Dickens's own emotion at this point
was sincere and intense.

The clearest case of a character who made Dickens's blood
boil and caused him to lose whatsoever self-control and detachment he possessed is of course Stryver, who is worth looking at in
some detail from that point of view. Toward Stryver the novelist
has only one attitude, but it results in a variety of devices, from
irony to downright insult. Chapter 11 of book 1 is called "A
Companion Picture"; it is devoted to ponderously stressing the
contrast which had already been made abundantly clear before
between Carton and Stryver, between appearance and reality, between worldly success and personal value. Perhaps the insistent
method used here takes its tone from what Dickens wished to convey about Stryver's coarseness; perhaps coarseness cannot be conveyed light-handedly, yet it is efficiently conveyed through Stryver's
speeches, and I think the reader may well resent Dickens's comment at the end: "The prosperous patronage with which he said
it, made him look twice as big as he was, and four times as offensive." We have heard Stryver talk big and assumed or inferred

---

[11] Intro., *A Tale of Two Cities*, Pocket Library Ed. (New York, 1955), p. xviii.

that he looked as big as he talked, and we must preserve our right to decide just how "offensive" we find him. The same attitude is adhered to throughout the next chapter (2.12), whose top-heavy irony is expressed in the title "The Fellow of Delicacy," delicacy being precisely and all too obviously what Stryver is incapable of. After he has fitly enough married not Lucie but "a florid widow," the novelist's indignation extends itself unfairly to his three stepsons—unfairly, it seems to me, because the boys "who had nothing particularly shining about them but the straight hair of their dumpling heads" (2.21) are not his offspring. The novelist's growing indignation against Stryver then produces a vigorous outburst of moralization and even an appeal to the shortest way with such dissenters from the truth; after telling us that Stryver had so often repeated his lie about Lucie that he believed it himself, the author adds: "which is surely such an incorrigible aggravation of an originally bad offence, as to justify any such offender's being carried off to some suitably retired spot, and there hanged out of the way." There are further insults to Stryver in book 2, chapter 24, where he is called "Bully Stryver" and his sneers are said to be "coarse," needlessly once more, because the man's own speeches had again exposed him quite eloquently; in fact "Bully Dickens" was bullying the reader into detesting "Bully Stryver." The Stryver case therefore shows that the novelist lost his control not over his character—who is superbly alive and almost painfully convincing—but over himself in front of his readers.

AUTHOR AND READER

A relationship with the reader can be established either by the narrator or by the author of a novel. In *Wuthering Heights* different types of relationship are created by Lockwood and by Nelly Dean; in some of Dickens's own first-person narratives the relationship is fairly intimate and the first-person narrator efficiently interposed between author and reader; *David Copperfield, Great Expectations* and *Bleak House* provide interesting cases; so do several shorter stories, like the two "Lirriper" fragments; the only disastrous experiment was the creation of Master Humphrey, because the liveliest of young writers, at twenty-eight, was trying to address the reader from the point of view of a sentimental, sententious, and weary old man. But in most novels the relationship with the reader has to be established by the author himself.

The type of relationship created in *A Tale of Two Cities* can only be inferred from a study of the generalities and other intrusions. I call "intrusions" all the passages that interrupt the progress of the narrative, but I studiously refrain from asserting that they "needlessly" interrupt it, because I have every reason to believe that Dickens knew better than I do what was needful or what he intended to do. Most intrusions are obviously authorial, in other words, represent the author part of the novelist intruding on and temporarily taking over from the narrator part of him.

The preface of the *Tale* states that it was Dickens's purpose "to add something to the popular and picturesque means of understanding" the French Revolution and thus to act as a teacher. That he "remained a moralist and a preacher" is, according to John Gross, "his saving strength." [12] His teaching bears mainly, but not exclusively, on the history of France. As regards the Revolution itself, the lesson taught by Dickens is far from clear because he alternates between sympathy and horror. Briefly—no detailed discussion of that interesting issue can be indulged in at this point—he seems to see the outbreak of violence as inevitable and even justified, for "Monseigneur as a class had, somehow or other, brought things to this" (2.23). When the Marquis's chateau is destroyed by fire, the description of the episode is impressive but tendentious and provides an imaginative interpretation of it as the just punishment of evil, "as if it were the face of the cruel Marquis, burning at the stake and contending with the fire" (2.23). In the early stages of the Revolution the novelist even appears to have felt that it held out a promise of moral improvement: the people who have murdered old Foulon go back to their suppers "innocent of meat, as of most other sauce to wretched bread. Yet, human fellowship infused some nourishment into the flinty viands" (2.22). But the later excesses and the blind, mad cruelties of the revolutionaries are seen as no less inevitable, and the lesson at the end is a warning to England: social injustice must be remedied before it is too late, before the infernal cycle of violence and destruction is let loose, for it will eventually drench in blood the aspiration to human fellowship that causes the rebellion. A revealing analysis of this mechanism is contained in the following reconstruction of a revolutionist's thought processes: "The raggedest nightcap, awry on the wretchedest head, had

---

[12] P. 197.

this crooked significance in it: 'I know how hard it has grown for me, the wearer of this, to support life in myself; but do you know how easy it has grown for me, the wearer of this, to destroy life in you?' " (2.22).

The rest of Dickens's teaching is conducted in the form of intrusive comments. Among the minor intrusions may be counted a number of indiscreet epithets by means of which the writer takes the reader, so to speak, by the hand and tells him what he must think: "odd description" (1.4); "deplorable peculiarity" (1.6); "unconscious insistency" (2.1); "wicked face" (2.16); "cruel knife" and "detested word" (2.21). Irony and satire, and prophecy, are similarly intrusive in many such passages as: "The Marquis . . . as elegantly despondent as he could becomingly be of a country still containing himself, that great means of regeneration" (2.9); Young Jerry's "cunning was fresh with the day, and his qualms were gone with the night—in which particulars it is not improbable that he had compeers in Fleet-Street and the City of London, that fine morning" (2.14); "If a picture of the château as it was to be a few years hence . . . could have been shown to him that night, he might have been at a loss to claim his own from the ghastly, fire-charred, plunder-wrecked ruins" (2.9). On several occasions the reader may feel that his intelligence is being seriously underrated by the author's overinsistence on perfectly clear points. Thus after two pages about the prison of La Force, when a turnkey mentions "the love of Liberty" (3.1), no one needs Dickens's comment that his words "sounded in that place like an inadequate conclusion." Nor do we require to be told in so many words that Solomon is Miss Pross's "by no means affectionate brother" or again that he is "the brother who so little deserved her affection" (3.8). The case of Stryver has already been discussed above, but the same tendency to overexplicitness is evinced on many other occasions. Jerry's embarrassment when he has been found out by Mr. Lorry takes the form of "that peculiar kind of short cough requiring the hollow of a hand before it, which is seldom, if ever, known to be the infirmity attendant on perfect openness of character" (3.9). Generalizations introduced through expansion from a specific incident in the story occur fairly frequently: a waiter watches Mr. Lorry at his meal in the Dover inn "according to the immemorial usage of waiters in all ages" (1.4); Miss Pross's proneness to exaggeration is said to be characteristic of her "as

of some people before her time and since" (2.6), a particularly
otiose and unilluminating comment. There is more vividness
but also more intrusiveness in the author's murderous longing
expressed at the sight of the grindstone scene and the mob with
their "frenzied eyes;—eyes which any unbrutalized beholder
would have given twenty years of life, to petrify with a well
directed gun" (3.2). Unlike Dickens, I am not prepared to answer
for all other beholders, but it seems to me that the particular
beholder he had in mind is sufficiently "brutalized" at that point
to be reminiscent of the Defarges' reaction to the spy's visit, "the
person . . . whom either of them would have shot with the greatest
satisfaction" (2.16).

All the above statements are more or less called for by the
narrative or at least derive from it. But the book is also inter-
spersed with numerous generalities of varying interest and origi-
nality which are still more definitely intrusive. Among the feeblest
may be mentioned the remark about "the calm that must follow
all storms—emblem to humanity, of the rest and silence into
which the storm called Life must hush at last" (1.6); the assertion
that "an emotion of the mind will express itself through any
covering of the body" (2.2); the unsensational announcement
that "from the days when it was always summer in Eden, to these
days when it is mostly winter in fallen latitudes, the world of
man has invariably gone one way . . . the way of the love of a
woman" (2.10); the disquisition on "the moonlight which is always sad, as the light of the sun itself is—as the light called
human life is—at its coming and its going" (2.17);[13] the sentimental view that children will inevitably attach themselves to
their mothers' unrequited lovers (2.21); the revelation that "all
secret men are soon terrified" (3.8); or the hopeful assurance that
"the vigorous tenacity of love" must be "always so much stronger
than hate" (3.14).[14] We do not go to the work of a writer of
Dickens's caliber in order to receive information of that kind.
Other generalities are of greater value: when the author tells us
that "any strongly marked expression of face on the part of a
chief actor in a scene of great interest will be unconsciously

---

[13] This particular example is not merely uncalled for and vapid but also clearly
wrong; neither sunrise nor the birth of a child is intrinsically or usually sad.

[14] This, however, even if it does no more, justifies Edward Wagenknecht's view
that in the Tale "the moral quality of the book is Dickensian in its glorification of
love and hatred of cruelty" (Dickens and the Scandalmongers [Norman, 1965], p. 126).

imitated by the spectators" (2.3), we can take it on trust from
such a shrewd and experienced observer as our novelist; a remark
about the owl is even characteristically and delightfully Dickensian: it "made a noise with very little resemblance in it to the
noise conventionally assigned to the owl by men-poets. But it is
the obstinate custom of such creatures hardly ever to say what is
set down for them" (2.9); and the opening paragraph of chapter 3
of book 2 about the mystery of "every human creature . . . to every
other" is of remarkable interest and modernity.

It is a little difficult and perhaps arbitrary to sort out what is
a mere pointing out of the lessons of the tale from what is by
the way. But in both cases generalizations are intrusive; they are
contributions made by the author in his own real person and in
his capacity as teacher and preacher. Their number makes it apparent that while the narrator knows everything concerning the
events and characters of the story, the author knows everything
about the world, life, and mankind; he knows in short everything
about everything. From this privileged position, Dickens was enabled not to content himself with simply informing his readers'
minds (e.g., about French history). Like the hero of *David Copperfield* (in chapter 48) who resolves to "form" his little wife's mind,
Dickens was out to form his little readers' minds. His treatment
of the reader seems high-handed, sometimes contemptuous, always magisterial.

On the whole the relationships among author, narrators, characters, and reader of *A Tale of Two Cities* are complex because
of the uncertain division of labor between author and narrators
and the frequent shiftings of their respective positions; however,
they are complex rather than subtle.

Until all Dickens's novels have been subjected to an analysis
similar to that attempted here, and from the same point of view,
only provisional and conjectural conclusions can be reached. If
such analyses were to confirm that efforts at establishing intimacy
with the reader became less frequent with each succeeding novel,
it might mean that Dickens gradually evacuated the personal address out of his novels into his periodicals and later into his readings, leaving to the novels themselves the voice of the masterly,
the superb, the imperious artist.

Carlyle and Jerrold into Dickens: A Study of *The Chimes*

MICHAEL SLATER

"B

OZ," REMARKS THE *Christian Remembrancer* in noticing Dickens's second Christmas Book, *The Chimes*, in January 1845, "has taken to Carlyle although he does not own it." The book is indeed written so much in the spirit and occasionally even in the very idiom of Carlyle's social writings that it seems odd that only one review (of the fifty or so that I have seen) should actually mention the fact. Although this influence had already manifested itself in Dickens's work, nothing written previous to *The Chimes* had been conceived and executed in such a thoroughgoing spirit of discipleship. Not surprisingly, Dickens felt Carlyle's presence to be "indispensable" at his prepublication reading of the book.[1]

John Forster tells us that by the time Dickens came to write *The Chimes* he had been "startlingly impressed" by certain aspects of Carlyle's writings,[2] and we learn from J. A. Froude and others that the early 1840s were in general the time of the sudden efflorescence of Carlyle's influence on "the young, the generous . . . , everyone who took life seriously, who wished to make an honourable use of it, and could not be content with sitting down and making money." To such people Carlyle's "words were like the morning reveille"; his unquestionable sincerity, his freedom from the dogma of any particular creed, his glowing faith, his literary genius, his "bold attitude on the traditionary formulas," and the "impressiveness of his personal presence" all combined to make him the intellectual hero of those who, like the young Dickens, nursed "a general hope for the introduction of a new and better

---

[1] John Forster, *Life of Dickens*, ed. J. W. T. Ley (London, 1928), p. 356.
[2] P. 347.

[184]

order of things" and who were "agreed to have done with com-
promise and conventionalities." [3]

From Forster onward writers on Dickens seldom fail to mention
Carlyle's influence though few attempt to assess this influence in
any detail, particularly in the works before *Hard Times*. Mildred
G. Christian's two articles in *The Trollopian* twenty-three years
ago[4] mention *The Chimes* but concentrate mainly on the later
novels; her scope does not allow any detailed study of the Christmas Books but she makes an important point when she states that
although Dickens thought himself a Radical at the time, *The
Chimes* expresses views less Radical than Liberal (which helps to
explain its unpopularity with such Radical organs as *Lloyd's
Weekly London Newspaper*). And it is well to remember her general caveat that since Dickens "quite definitely rejected" certain
elements in Carlyle's social theories, it is sometimes "difficult to
determine when identity of view between Carlyle and Dickens
means influence of the former upon the latter, and when it merely
means coincidence."

The two coincide, for example, in their feeling that some sort
of social apocalypse was imminent. Carlyle's ominous prophecy at
the outset of the essay on "Chartism" (1840)—"if something be
not done [about the condition of England], something will *do* itself one day, and in a fashion that will please nobody" [5]—may be
compared with Dickens's remarks in a letter to Forster in March
1844 in which he affirms his contempt and hatred for "society":
"The more I see of its extraordinary conceit, and its stupendous
ignorance of what is passing out of doors, the more certain I am
that it is approaching the period when, being incapable of reform-
ing itself, it will have to submit to be reformed by others off the
face of the earth." [6]

The phrase about society's "stupendous ignorance" points to
another concern which the two writers shared, alarm at the widen-
ing gulf between the rich and the poor. "Wealth," writes Carlyle

---

[3] Froude, *Thomas Carlyle: A History of His Life in London 1834–1881*, 2 vols.
(London, 1884), 1:2ff. On this point see also the various other testimonies cited by
Kathleen Tillotson in her "Matthew Arnold and Carlyle" (Warton Lecture on
English Poetry), *PBA* 42(1956):136.

[4] 2(March 1947):27–35 and 3(June 1947):11–26.

[5] *The Works of Thomas Carlyle*, Centenary Ed., ed. H. D. Traill, 30 vols. (London,
1896–99), 29:118.

[6] *The Letters of Charles Dickens*, ed. Walter Dexter, Nonesuch Dickens ed., 3
vols. (Bloomsbury [London], 1938), 1:558f.; hereafter cited as *Letters*.

in 1831, "has accumulated itself into masses; and Poverty, also in accumulation enough, lies impassably separated from it; opposed, uncommunicating, like forces in positive and negative poles." [7] And Will Fern, in Trotty's vision in *The Chimes*, admonishes the gentry that the spirit of the laborer "is divided from you at this time." [8] The key to the solution of this problem, in the view of both Carlyle and Dickens, lay in the spread of mutual understanding and sympathy between the classes: "all battle is misunderstanding" declares Carlyle; "did the parties know one another, the battle would cease." [9] Again, in *Past and Present* he writes, "men's hearts ought not to be set against one another . . . [their souls should not be] jaundiced, blinded, twisted all awry by revenge, mutual abhorrence and the like." [10] Repugnant as even such a man as the "adroit" Voltaire might seem, it is nevertheless necessary to try to *understand* him before abusing him: "let us be sure, our enemy is *not* that hateful being we are too apt to paint him." [11] That Dickens was in agreement here we learn from Forster, who writes (with particular regard to *The Chimes*), "to set class against class he never ceased to think as odious as he thought it righteous at all times to help each to a kindlier knowledge of the other," [12] an observation echoed by a reviewer of *American Notes:* "In all the writings of Dickens there is manifested the disposition to promote a better understanding between the upper classes and the lower." [13] The last paragraph of *The Chimes* itself is an urgent plea to its more comfortably-off readers to "endeavour to correct, soften and improve" wherever possible the "stern realities" (of the harsh lot of the poor) of which Dickens tries to make them aware in the book.

Indeed Carlyle's dictum, "without love men cannot endure to be together," [14] might serve as an epigraph for much of Dickens's social writing, his Christmas-all-the-year-round philosophy as it is sometimes called. Yet even if Carlyle had always confined himself to German literature and never written a line about the Condi-

---

[7] *Works*, 28 ("Characteristics"):20.

[8] *Christmas Books*, New Oxford Illus. Ed. (London, 1954), p. 133; unless otherwise specified, page references following quotations from the Christmas books in my text are to this edition.

[9] *Works*, 29:122f.

[10] Ibid., 10:17.

[11] Ibid., 26:405.

[12] P. 348.

[13] *Westminster Rev.* 39 (Feb. 1843):149.

[14] *Works*, 10:272.

tion-of-England Question, it is certain that Dickens would still
have belabored the political economists with their profit-and-loss,
supply-and-demand view of human relationships. But once he had
read such Carlylean onslaughts on the cash-nexus as "We have
profoundly forgotten everywhere that *Cash-payment* is not the
sole link between human beings. We think, nothing doubting,
that *it* absolves and liquidates all engagements of men," [15] Dickens's instinctive distaste for Benthamite theorizing was reinforced
and given a certain *point d'appui*.[16] Sir Joseph Bowley in *The
Chimes* exemplifies the belief that cash payment is indeed the
chief, if not the sole, link between human beings. Every quarter-
day his poor "friends" will be "put in communication with Mr.
Fish" (106). Once they have paid their rent—and been made the
subject of an annual treat by their patron—the relationship between them and him is at an end except that once in his life a
poor tenant of Sir Joseph's "may even perhaps receive—in public,
in the presence of the gentry—a Trifle from a Friend" (106).
When the baronet questions Toby, "You have no bill or demand
upon me . . . of any kind from anybody, have you? . . . If you have,
present it. There is a cheque-book by the side of Mr. Fish. I allow
nothing to be carried into the New Year. Every description of
account is settled in this house at the close of the old one" (104),
the authorial implication is obvious that Bowley ignores obliga-
tions to his fellow men more fundamental than financial ones.
The apotheosis of the rules of cash payment as the whole duty of
man is reached in Bowley's peroration: "We should feel that every
return of so eventful a period in human transactions [i.e., the New
Year] involves a matter of deep moment between a man and his—
and his banker" (105). Bowley (in whose mouth the Carlylean
slogan about the "Dignity of Labour" becomes a mockery) is evidently a close relation of the manufacturer, Plugson of St. Dolly
Undershot, whom we meet in *Past and Present* and whom Carlyle
pictures as saying to his workmen: " 'Noble spinners, this is the

---

[15] Ibid., 10:146.

[16] Cf. Louis F. Cazamian's words in his *Le Roman social en Angleterre (1830–
1850)*: *Dickens, Disraeli, Mrs. Gaskell, Kingsley*, rev. ed., 2 vols. (Paris, 1935):
"D'après Weber . . . Dickens aurait emprunté à Carlyle toutes ses idées sociales et, en
particulier, son antipathie contre l'économie politique. Cette thèse est fort exagérée.
Dickens attaque déjà le dogmatisme économique dans *Olivier Twist* . . . à une
époque ou il ne connait pas Carlyle et ou ce dernier n'a pas encore écrit ses
oeuvres sociales. L'influence de Carlyle a précisé et fortifié ses propres tendances et
leur a souvent donné leurs formules" (1:216).

Hundred Thousand we have gained, wherein I mean to dwell and plant vineyards; the hundred thousand is mine, the three and sixpence daily was yours: adieu, noble spinners; drink my health with this groat each, which I give you over and above!' The entirely unjust Captain of Industry, say I; not Chevalier, but Bucanier! 'Commercial Law' does indeed acquit him; asks, with wide eyes, What else?" [17]

Dickens finds another stick with which to beat the political economists in the contempt which Carlyle pours on the new science of statistics, the "stutterings" that were to perplex poor Sissy Jupe. Carlyle's major onslaught on statistics appears in the second chapter of his essay on Chartism where he quotes a "witty statesman" who says, "you might prove anything by figures." [18] In *The Chimes* Dickens shows Mr. Filer mathematically "proving" that Trotty is a robber because he has eaten some tripe. And Filer's retort to praise of the peasant's lot in the good old days is: "there was scarcely a vegetable in all England for him to put into his mouth. . . . I can prove it, by tables" (96).

Just as Dickens's dislike of political economy was strengthened and sharpened by reading Carlyle, so his contempt for Parliament, based upon his own experience of it as a reporter, was, as Forster points out,[19] reinforced by Carlyle's gibes at the "National Palaver" [20] and at Parliamentary attempts to improve social conditions by such measures as the notoriously inefficient sliding scale for duty on imported wheat, upon which measure Carlyle pours his contempt, remarking that England's governors were " 'sliding,' as on inclined-planes, which every new year they *soap* with new Hansard's-jargon under God's sky, and so are 'sliding,' ever faster, towards a 'scale' and balance-scale whereon is written *Thou art found Wanting.*" [21] Parliament (Bowley is an MP) is

---

[17] *Works*, 10:193.

[18] Ibid., 29:124.

[19] P. 347; see p. 64 for Dickens's attitude toward Parliament during his reporting days.

[20] *Works*, 10:219. In his "Dickens on American Slavery: A Carlylean Slant" (*PMLA* 68 [1952]), Arthur A. Adrian writes: "Whereas Carlyle denounced Parliamentary government as intrinsically bad and incompetent, Dickens felt only an intelligent and educated participation of the middle and working classes could correct the evils of English politics" (315); but Dickens's attitude was much nearer to Carlyle's than this would suggest. Nowhere in his writings, I believe, does he ever sound optimistic about Parliamentary government.

[21] *Works*, 10:273. For the inefficiency of Peel's sliding scale see Élie Halévy, *The Age of Peel and Cobden: A History of the English People 1841–1852*, trans. Edward I. Watkin, ed. Paul Vancher (London, 1947), pp. 11f.

never considered for a moment in *The Chimes* as a likely source
of help. To Trotty it is just a place that is "full of obserwations"
(87) where "they're always a-bringing up some new law or other"
to the detriment of the poor (89). Dickens is reproved by *Lloyd's
Weekly London Newspaper* (29 Dec. 1844) for giving the impression in his book that "the amendment of landlords and con-
current justice to the labouring classes may be safely left to the
exertions of popular writers." In sound Radical vein, *Lloyd's* lead
columnist goes on to stress that Parliament was in fact the only
proper agent for the relief of the poor and urged that it should
speedily look to it.

Carlyle's attitude to Parliament arose from his general objection
to all "mechanical" or rule-of-thumb solutions to the Condition-
of-England Question. In *Signs of the Times* (1829) he complains
that "men are grown mechanical in head and in heart, as well as
in hand," that they think to solve their social and even their spiritual problems by laws and theories similar to those by which
they achieve industrial and scientific advancement; "all our systems and theories," he continues, "are but so many froth-eddies
or sand-banks, which from time to time she [Nature] casts up,
and washes away." [22] Parliamentary legislation is later belabored
(in "Chartism" and in *Past and Present*) as an example of such
mechanical approaches to social problems. Dickens on the other
hand, having started out with his own exasperation with Parliament, seems to have developed this exasperation—under Carlyle's
influence—into a general rejection of all cut-and-dried "practical"
theories. He sets out in *The Chimes* to attack some of the more
prominent contemporary ones; to the delight of the *Dublin Review*, "every species of cant, worldly-mindedness and affectation
of humanity . . . Dickens has set a mark upon." [23]

One species of cant which Dickens set out to stigmatize in *The
Chimes* was Disraeli's Tory splinter group known as "Young England," but on Forster's advice this particular piece of satire sur-
vived into print only in a very vestigial form.[24] In the "youngish
sort of gentlemen" found in the manuscript version of the story,
however, we have perhaps the first example in Dickens's work of

[22] Ibid., 27:63 and 71.

[23] *DubR* 24 (1844) 17:560.

[24] See my article, "Dickens (and Forster) at Work on *The Chimes*," *DiS* 2(1966):
106–40; also "Dickens's Tract for the Times" in the centenary volume, *Dickens 1970*,
to be published by Chapman and Hall under my editorship.

that Carlylean bête noire, the Dilettante. In Carlyle's view the
aristocracy who spend their time preserving their game instead
of fulfilling their traditional responsibilities as governors, the
middle-class idlers who live parasitically upon society, and all
who are guilty of social, artistic, or religious affectation and of
ignoring Schiller's admonition (used by Carlyle as the epigraph
for *Past and Present*), "Ernst ist das Leben," are to be classed as
dilettantes. The succession of flaneurs who appear in Dickens's
later novels—Harthouse, Gowan, Eugene Wrayburn—would seem
to owe something to Carlyle's archetypal figure. One species particularly attacked in *Past and Present* is the dilettante who patron-
izes the past, regarding it as a sort of primitive and picturesque
pageant. After summarizing the world-picture of the twelfth-century Abbot Samson—"he lives in an element of miracle: Heaven's
splendour over his head, Hell's darkness under his feet. A great
Law of Duty, high as these two Infinitudes, dwarfing all else,
annihilating all else"—Carlyle rounds upon his modern readers
with the scathing comment, " 'Rude poetic ages'? The 'primeval
poetic element'? Oh, for God's sake, good reader, talk no more of
all that! It was not a Dilettantism this of Abbot Samson. It was a
Reality, and it is one."

Carlyle's attack upon Dilettantism leads to another favorite
target: "But of our Dilettantisms, and galvanised Dilettantisms;
of Puseyism—O Heavens, what shall we say of Puseyism, in comparison to Twelfth-Century Catholicism?" [25] The Young England
movement, as I have indicated elsewhere, was closely connected
with Puseyism and sprang from precisely the same romantic and
picturesque view of the Middle Ages which Carlyle so deplores
and which the Hon. Mrs. Skewton was shortly to expound so
enthusiastically to an impassive Mr. Dombey. In the extant manuscript of omitted portions of *The Chimes* Dickens's Young England gentleman enthuses languidly over Strutt's book of antique
costumes and declares that even the fires of Smithfield (at this
time a standard symbol for the "bad old days") "were at least
associated with the Glowing and the Picturesque";[26] of Richard
and Meg's intended marriage he observes wistfully, "The nuptials
of these people in the old times would have been a Pastoral thing;

---

[25] *Works*, 10:116f.
[26] Quotations from the manuscript of *The Chimes* in the Forster Coll. are made
by courtesy of the Victoria and Albert Museum.

a subject for the Painter," revealing that his attitude to the past which he professes to admire is in fact mere Dilettantism. Here again, as with his attitude toward the political economists, one feels that Dickens would still have mocked at Young England even had he not been a student of Carlyle, for they shared, though for different reasons, a dislike for this romantic idealization of a past era. At the same time it seems probable that having absorbed Carlyle's concept of Dilettantism, Dickens drew on it when creating his own Young England gentleman.

Carlyle dislikes Young England on historical grounds because it creates a false picture of the Middle Ages, and he dislikes it on social grounds because it seems to him to be a wrong approach to the Condition-of-England Question. But it displeases Dickens simply because, not having yet lost his Victorian faith in progress, he sees the past as a bad time anyway, "ages of darkness, wickedness and violence" wherein "millions uncountable, have suffered, lived and died" to point the way ahead to posterity (123). "The voice of Time" announces the Spirit of the Great Bell to Toby, "cries to man, Advance!" and those who raise "a cry of lamentation for days which have had their trial, and their failure, and have left deep traces of it which the blind may see—a cry that only serves the present time, by showing men how much it needs their help when any ears can listen to regrets for such a past—who does this, does a wrong" (123). Dickens's watchword at this time was "Awake the Present!" [27] and the dummy book-backs later installed at Gad's Hill Place are eloquent enough testimony to his view of (to quote one of the spoof titles) "The Middling Ages." [28]

One of the points at which Dickens and Carlyle part company is highlighted if we compare the latter's description of Gurth, the Saxon swineherd, "born thrall of Cedric the Saxon," with one of the passages deleted from *The Chimes* (we may speculate whether deference to Carlyle played any part in Dickens's decision here). In *Past and Present* Gurth is pictured for us "with the brass collar

---

[27] The opening words of the prologue written by Dickens for Westland Marston's *The Patrician's Daughter* (1842). Marston broke with tradition by giving his five-act blank-verse tragedy a contemporary setting.

[28] See "Dummy Books at Gad's Hill Place," *Dickensian* 54(1958):46–47. It was about this time too that Dickens was composing his *Child's History of England* (published in *Household Words* in 1851) with its emphasis on the brutality and squalor of the past. See his letter to Jerrold, 3 May 1843, *Letters*, 1:517–18.

round his neck, tending Cedric's pigs in the glades of the wood."
He is not, Carlyle admits, "an exemplar of human felicity" but,

Gurth, with the sky above him, with the free air and tinted boscage
and umbrage round him, and in him at least the certainty of supper
and social lodging when he came home; Gurth to me seems happy, in
comparison with many a Lancashire and Buckinghamshire man of
these days, not born thrall of anybody! Gurth's brass collar did not
gall him; Cedric *deserved* to be his master. The pigs were Cedric's, but
Gurth too would get his parings of them. Gurth had the inexpressible
satisfaction of feeling himself related indissolubly, though in a rude
brass-collar way, to his fellow-mortals in this Earth. He had superiors,
inferiors, equals—Gurth is now "emancipated" long since; has what
we call "Liberty." Liberty, I am told, is a divine thing. Liberty when
it becomes the "Liberty to die by starvation" is not so divine!

Carlyle goes on to extol aristocracy, or government by the best
and wisest, of which he takes Cedric's government of Gurth to be
an example. True liberty for any man at any time "were that a
wiser man ... could, by brass collars, or in whatever milder or
sharper way, lay hold of him when he was going wrong, and order
and compel him to go a little righter; ... were it by never such
brass collars, whips and handcuffs, leave me not to walk over
precipices." [29] But Dickens, though he was little more of a believer
in complete social equality than Carlyle, could not contemplate
with equanimity a human neck encircled by a brazen collar. In
this case and at this time at least he was not the "push-over for
Carlyle's bullying, sensational intellectual tone" that Angus Wilson
son finds him always to have been.[30] His glimpse of Negro slavery
in America had sickened him of such matters. We recall the description
of Mark Tapley's encounter in New York with an ex-
slave who had been "shot in the leg; gashed in the arm; ... had
his neck galled with an iron collar, and wore iron rings upon his
wrists and ankles." [31] This passage was written only a few months
before Dickens began *The Chimes,* and we may safely take it that
the brass collars which Trotty sees in the Young England gentleman's dream are no rough-and-ready symbols of government by
the best: "Before one sofa when the youngish sort of gentleman
lay dozing ... a small party were enjoying rustic sports, while an-

---

[29] *Works*, 10:211f.

[30] See Wilson's review of Philip Collins's *Dickens and Crime* (London, 1962) in
Observer, 5 Aug. 1962, p. 14.

[31] *Martin Chuzzlewit*, New Oxford Illus. Ed. (London, 1951), p. 282.

other rather larger party were being hanged on trees in the background and a third were having brazen collars soldered round their necks as the born vassals of an undeniably picturesque Baron."

But despite an inability to follow him in finding anything praiseworthy in the medieval institution of serfdom, Dickens responds enthusiastically in the main to Carlyle's outlook on contemporary society and life in general. The opening of the "Third Quarter" of *The Chimes* is another passage where this can be seen. Though the style, particularly in the first sentence, is too flatulent to be Carlylean (the soft hand of Bulwer-Lytton may be detected here as he himself recognized),[32] the idea—that of man as the symbol of "the Great Mystery," an emblem of the Divine—is certainly traceable to Carlyle. "What is man himself," says Teufelsdröckh, "but a Symbol of God?"[33] One recalls Carlyle's favorite quotation from Novalis, "There is but one temple in the world and that temple is the Body of Man. Nothing is holier than this high Form. Bending before men is a reverence done to this Revelation in the Flesh. We touch Heaven, when we lay our hands on a human Body."[34] So Dickens here, commenting on the return to consciousness after a sleep or a swoon, says, "when, and how, and by what wonderful degrees, each [thought] separates from each, and every sense and object of the mind resumes its usual form and lives again, no man—though every man is every day the casket of this type of the Great Mystery—can tell" (120). The key word is *wonderful*. One of Carlyle's grand objects in *Sartor Resartus* is to help his readers to peer through the "Clothes-screen" of the appearances of things and look, "even for moments, into the region

---

[32] In a letter to Forster (25 Dec. 1844), which is among Lady Hermione Cobbold's collection of Lytton MSS deposited at the County Record Office, Hertford, Bulwer remarks that he is constantly plagiarized unwittingly by Dickens. Referring to *The Chimes* he says, "Compare for instance pp. 92–3 with any part of Zanoni." The passage in question is the opening of the Third Quarter (which the *Christian Remembrancer*, reviewing *The Chimes* in Jan. 1845, thought to be "among the most turgid and absurd" pieces of writing ever perpetrated by Dickens). It certainly has the true Bulwerian ring; there is the same shallow mystification, the same foggy and inflated language characterized by a liberal use of abstract nouns and capitals ("The Sea of Thought," etc.), the same straining after lofty "poetic" utterance that we find throughout the Rosicrucian romance of *Zanoni* (published 1842). In fairness to Bulwer one ought perhaps to add that Northrop Frye calls this particular passage in *The Chimes* "very eloquent" ("Dickens and the Comedy of Humors," in *Experience in the Novel*, ed. Roy Harvey Pearce [New York, 1968], p. 73).

[33] *Works*, 1:175.

[34] Ibid., 1:190f.; see also 10:124 and 27:39.

of the Wonderful," and see and feel that "daily life is girt with
Wonder, and based on Wonder, and [their] very blankets and
breeches are Miracles." [35] One scarcely imagines that such exhor-
tations would not affect so eager a disciple as Dickens, and the
mystical note that he strikes in the opening of the Third Quarter
of *The Chimes* is surely evidence that he responds to them.

We have noticed that, although Dickens's meditation on a return to consciousness may owe something to Carlyle in conception,
it is yet not couched in "Carlylese"—it lacks the rugged ejacula-
tory tone that Macaulay deplores when he describes Carlyle's
writing as "a series of epileptic fits." But the speech of the Goblin
of the Great Bell, despite its too stately rhythm, does have some
Carlylean echoes—"Who seeks to turn him [Mankind] back, or
stay him on his course, arrests a mighty engine which will strike
the meddler dead; and be the fiercer and the wilder, ever, for its
momentary check!" (123).[36] That isolated last clause with its exclamation mark is a very Carlylean touch. Compare, for example,
this chapter-ending from *Sartor:* "Thus does Teufelsdröckh . . .
confound the old authentic Presbyterian Witchfinder with a new,
spurious, imaginary Historian of the *Britische Journalistik;* and
so stumble on perhaps the most egregious blunder in Modern
Literature!" [37] Later in the Goblin's speech the phrase "the many-
sorrowed throng" seems more typical of Carlyle than of Dickens.
Such fleeting stylistic echoes are scattered through *The Chimes*
though hardly enough to justify the *Christian Remembrancer*'s
charge (in the review cited at the beginning of this article) that
"a good deal of the diction is a palpable borrowing from Carlyle."
There is one paragraph, however, where Carlyle's voice sounds
loud, clear, and unmistakable. It comes when Dickens apostro-
phizes Cute after the Alderman learns of Deedles's suicide:

What, Alderman! No word of Putting Down? Remember, Justice, your
high moral boast and pride. Come, Alderman! Balance those scales.
Throw me into this, the empty one, no dinner, and Nature's founts in
some poor woman, dried by starving misery and rendered obdurate to
claims for which her offspring *has* authority in holy mother Eve. Weigh

---

[35] Ibid., 1:215.

[36] Carlyle would not, however, have agreed with the Great Bell's sentiments. Far
from holding that Time was for man's "greater happiness" he denies, in *Sartor*,
that man has any right to expect happiness: "Foolish soul! What Act of Legislature
was there that *thou* shouldst be Happy?" (*Works*, 1:153).

[37] *Works*, 1:35.

me the two, you Daniel, going to judgment, when your day shall come!
Weigh them, in the eyes of suffering thousands, audience (not unmind-
ful) of the grim farce you play. Or supposing that you strayed from
your five wits—it's not so far to go, but that it might be—and laid
hands upon that throat of yours, warning your fellows (if you have a
fellow) how they croak their comfortable wickedness to raving heads
and stricken hearts. What then? (129–30)

These words, says Dickens, "rose up in Trotty's breast, as if they
had been spoken by some other voice within him" (130). Contemporary readers could surely have had little difficulty in identifying whose voice it was. Even more than certain paragraphs in
Chuzzlewit this whole passage might have been penned by Carlyle
—though he would almost certainly have employed the old second
person singular. The barking imperatives, the obsolete ethic da-
tive, the parentheses, the *not un-* construction, the resounding
phrase ("holy mother Eve," etc.), the Shakespearean allusion, the
savagely crude gibes at the subject of the passage, and the violent
imagery of "croaking" and "raving heads and stricken hearts"—
all these tricks are part of the stock-in-trade of Carlylean prose. In
such *Chuzzlewit* passages as "Oh, moralists, who treat of happiness
and self-respect" and "Oh, late-remembered, much-forgotten,
mouthing, braggart duty," [38] Dickens's proneness to slip at rhetorical moments into blank verse (especially after an exclamatory
"Oh!") tends to water down the "Carlylese," but here it is un-
diluted.

Dickens has too strongly individual a style, however, for it to
be more than momentarily submerged beneath that of his mentor.
It is rather to the general outlook revealed in *The Chimes* and
to its particular incidents that we must look when seeking to trace
Carlyle's enormous influence on it. The effect on its general outlook we have already considered, but when we turn to its incidents
we find signs just as unmistakable.

For example, Dickens shows us Trotty reading in his newspaper
an account of a case of infanticide among the poor, a crime "so
revolting to his soul . . . that he let the journal drop and fell back
in his chair appalled! 'Unnatural and cruel!' Toby cried. 'Unnatural and cruel! None but people who were bad at heart, born
bad, who had no business on the earth, could do such deeds'"
(117). Except that Trotty is hardly an "idle reader" and is there-

―――――――――
[38] Pp. 224, 497f.

fore less casual in his reaction, this scene is remarkably similar to one which Carlyle presents to his readers at the outset of *Past and Present*. He recalls a case at Stockport Assizes in 1841 in which a poverty-stricken couple were found guilty of poisoning three of their children "to defraud a 'burial-society' of some £3 8s. due on the death of each child." Carlyle observes:

"Brutal savages, degraded Irish," mutters the idle reader of Newspapers; hardly lingering on this incident. Yet it is an incident worth lingering on; the depravity, savagery and degraded Irishism being never so well admitted. In the British land, a human Mother and Father, of white skin and professing the Christian religion, had done this thing; they, with their Irishism and necessity and savagery, had been driven to do it.[39]

Later on in the same book Carlyle makes great play with the Irish widow in Edinburgh who

went forth with her three children, bare of all resource, to solicit help from the Charitable Establishments of that City. At this Charitable Establishment and then at that she was refused; referred from one to the other, helped by none;—till she had exhausted them all; till her strength and heart failed her: she sank down in typhus-fever; died, and infected her Lane with fever, so that "seventeen other persons" died of fever there in consequence.[40]

This episode is echoed in *The Chimes* when Meg and her baby go in search of public charity:

She mingled with an abject crowd, who tarried in the snow, until it pleased some officer appointed to dispense the public charity (the lawful charity; not that once preached upon a Mount), to call them in, and question them, and say to this one, "Go to such a place," to that one, "Come next week"; to make a football of another wretch, and pass him here and there, from hand to hand, from house to house, until he wearied and lay down to die (148).

The shadow of Carlyle appears again when Cute hears of Deedles's suicide; the horrified Alderman is made to harp on the dead man's respectability (he mentions it four times) as though this quality should have proved a charm against all misery and distress. Like Cant and Dilettantism, Respectability "with its

---

[39] *Works*, 10:4.
[40] Ibid., p. 149 (see also p. 211).

thousand gigs" is yet another of those words that are anathema to Carlyle: "Mammon," he thunders, "in never such gigs and flunky 'respectabilities' is not the alone God." [41] And here Dickens gives a striking instance of this false god disastrously failing his "respectable" devotee, the banker.

Another favorite theme of Carlyle's is to lament that "the word *Soul* with us, as in some Slavonic dialects, seems to be synonymous with Stomach." [42] Castigation of this popular confusion of soul and stomach occurs frequently in Carlyle's social writings, and it is perhaps not altogether fanciful (bearing in mind how greatly his influence pervades *The Chimes*) to see in the character of Tugby an attempt by Dickens to picture a man whose soul is indeed his stomach. *Parker's London Magazine* might have seen Tugby as a mere feeble reworking of Old Weller in *Pickwick* and Joe Willet senior in *Barnaby Rudge*,[43] but the resemblance is only a superficial one. Sam's amiably convivial father is certainly not lacking in Soul, as his magnanimous gesture to Mr. Pickwick amply demonstrates, and even the pig-headed Mr. Willet is not shown in a totally unsympathetic light; as mine host of that nonpareil of inns, the Maypole, he has ever an aura of rosy warmth about him. Tugby, however, is sketched in with a few strokes as the epitome of sordid selfishness. As he gloats swinishly over his buttered muffins, his delight is increased by thoughts of the discomfort that people abroad in the wind and sleet must be suffering; he furtively robs his kindly wife's till while she is occupied in relating Meg's moving story to the doctor; his only concern about the dying lodger is to get him to a workhouse before he dies upon the premises; and his ejection of Meg and baby is done with an underhanded meanness. His obesity, on which Dickens lays particular stress, is evidently not a jovial sign of a pleasantly convivial life as in the case of Mr. Weller or Old Joe Willet; it is rather to be taken as the mark of a brutally selfish man, a man whose Soul, in Carlylean terms, has in good earnest become his Stomach.

Carlyle's influence may be found in the general outlook that informs *The Chimes*, in its language occasionally, and in certain in-

---

[41] Ibid., 10:276.

[42] Ibid., p. 154.

[43] This judgment appears in an extremely interesting article, "Boz versus Dickens," published in the journal (a short-lived monthly) in Feb. 1845, pp. 123ff.

cidents and characters. But when we turn to consider the overall *tone* of the book—and it was this above all which distressed so many contemporary readers—another voice makes itself heard. Many reviewers took exception to the unmitigated ferocity of the book's attack upon the rich and its almost total lack of Dickens's usual geniality (of which *A Christmas Carol* is brimful). The *Illustrated London News*, reviewing one of the stage adaptations, comments on 21 December 1844: "The dialogue was forcible, but there appeared to us to be less kindliness in its intent than we have been accustomed to admire in Mr. Dickens's work." A year later Elizabeth Barrett notices that the next Christmas Book, *The Cricket on the Hearth,* is "quite free from what was reproached as bitterness and one-sidedness last year." [44] The *Illustrated London News,* also referring to the *Cricket,* rejoices at Dickens's discovery that "his popularity was founded in pourtraying the amenities of life, and [that] it will not be extended by sharpening its asperities or exaggerating its enormities." [45]

Now this un-Dickensian bitterness detected by readers of *The Chimes* cannot be ascribed to Carlyle. Before the publication of his *Latter-Day Pamphlets* at least, Carlyle was not thought of as a bitter man. The cry of "aloes! aloes!" struck a chord then more recognizable in the writings of another of Dickens's close literary friends, the passionate Radical, Douglas Jerrold.[46] After fluctuating success as a dramatist and journalist, Jerrold had in 1841 at last found his true métier in writing for *Punch.* His contributions to this turbulent new journal—usually over the signature "Q"—are mainly a succession of barbed and acid squibs directed against the aristocracy, the prosperous, the magistracy (the City aldermen being among his favorite butts)—all those, in short, who in his view oppress or neglect the poor and needy. When the *Christian Remembrancer* says that the part of the diction of *The Chimes* not borrowed from Carlyle most resembles "the higher portions of 'Punch,'" it is Jerrold's contributions that are meant.

Jerrold's technique is very different from Carlyle's. The latter

---

[44] *The Letters of Robert Browning and Elizabeth Barrett: 1845–1846,* ed. R. W. B. Browning, 2 vols. (London, 1899), 1:345.

[45] 27 Dec. 1845, p. 406, col. 2.

[46] Cf. Jerrold's complaint in the preface written for *St. Giles and St. James* when it was published as vol. 1 of *The Writings of Douglas Jerrold,* 8 vols. (London, 1851–54): " 'bitter' has, I think, a little too often been the ready word when critics have condescended to bend their eyes upon my page: so ready, that were my ink redolent of myrrh and frankincense, I well know the sort of ready-made criticism that would cry, with a denouncing shiver, 'aloes; aloes.' "

would take a fictitious representative of a certain group or class, give him some grotesque name—Pandarus Dogdraught, Aristides Rigmarole, Bobus Higgins of Houndsditch, and so on—and inflate him into a figure of gigantic and joyous absurdity like a character in Rabelais, eventually blowing him off the scene with a salvo of rollicking abuse. A certain geniality informs the whole process; there is admitted to be some good even in Bobus. We should recall that Herbert Paul feels that Froude's biography does not give an adequate idea of Carlyle's essential humorousness:

When he was letting himself go, and indulging freely in the most lurid denunciations of all and sundry, he would give a peculiar and most significant chuckle which cannot be put into print. It was a warning not to take him literally, which has too often passed unheeded. He has been compared with Swift, but he was not really a misanthropist, and no man loved laughter more, or could excite more uproarious merriment in others.[47]

Jerrold, however, while no misanthrope, goes a different way to work. In *Punch* he attacks individuals by name, wittily and mercilessly exposing their incompetence, vanity, petty tyrannies, and neglect of their social duties. Occasionally he does use a technique more reminiscent of Carlyle. In December 1841, for example, he has a short piece in *Punch* entitled, "How Mr. Chokepear keeps a merry Christmas," in which he describes the "respectable" Chokepear and his family indulging in a "Christmas of the belly." Their churchgoing (to hear Dr. Mannamouth preach) is the merest formality, and they display an entire lack of charity toward the poor while gorging themselves with luxurious repasts; "If the human animal were all stomach—all one large paunch—" Jerrold remarks, "we should agree with CHOKEPEAR that he *had* passed a merry Christmas." The piece lacks Carlyle's gusto, however; instead of the uproarious denunciation of a grotesque fictitious representative of a certain group or type, we get a much thinner, rather nagging little diatribe, coconuts hurled at a very cardboard

---

[47] *Life of Froude* (London, 1905), p. 425. The value that Carlyle himself placed on humor is often made explicit in his works. In *Sartor*, e.g., he declares, "no man who has once heartily and wholly laughed can be altogether irreclaimably bad. How much lies in Laughter; the cipher-key, wherewith we decipher the whole man!" (*Works*, 1:26). Coleridge, he feels, is "deficient in laughter" (*Works*, 11:57), and also Ebenezer Elliott, whom he much admires, but whose worst fault is that "he has little or no Humour. Without Humour of character he cannot well be; but it has not yet got to utterance. Thus, where he has mean things to deal with, he knows not how to deal with them" (*Works*, 28:154).

Aunt Sally. What a figure would Carlyle have made of Dr. Mannamouth! Jerrold is at his waspish best not in an exercise like this but
in such pieces as the attack on Lord Brougham to which I shall
allude later. Except for *Mrs. Caudle's Curtain Lectures,* the *Punch*
series which he half-despised as mere entertainment (and which
ironically is the only one of his works to survive as literature), there
is little good humor and much *saeva indignatio* in his writings.
The gentlemanly Thackeray, who began to write regularly for
Punch in 1844, becomes increasingly uneasy at "pulling in the
same boat with such a savage little Robespierre"; when in 1846
they quarreled openly, Dickens wrote privately to Jerrold support-
ing him.[48] Jerrold's sharpness was much resented even by those
whose feelings toward the poor were as kindly as his own. Fitzgerald, writing to Frederic Tennyson only a few days before the
publication of *The Chimes,* complains:

The London press does nothing but rail at us poor country folks for
our cruelty [to the poor]. I am glad they do so; for there is much to
be set right.... Punch also assumes a tone of virtuous satire, from the
mouth of Mr. Douglas Jerrold! It is easy to sit in arm chairs at a club
in Pall Mall and rail on the stupidity and brutality of those in High
Suffolk! [49]

Reviewing the first number of *Douglas Jerrold's Shilling Magazine*
on 5 January 1845, the *Era* remarks that most of its contents are
"tinged with that tendency which is obvious through all Mr.
Jerrold's writings, to look at the worst side of society, of decrying
the rich and upholding the poor, abusing the aristocracy, and, in
a certain measure, finding fault with the world as it is, and advocating any innovation that may create a change."

The difference between Dickens's geniality and Jerrold's bitterness in their common pursuit of social reform had often been noted
by contemporaries, and the Jerroldian tone of *The Chimes* was
perhaps regarded as a temporary aberration; in 1846 we find a
reviewer of the stage version of *The Battle of Life* declaring that
Dickens

likes to dwell upon and magnify the better qualities of human nature.
He sees everything through a favourable medium, and though he
sketches bad men and base passions, he never leaves off without re-

⁴⁸ See Gordon N. Ray, *Thackeray: The Uses of Adversity, 1811–1846* (London,
1955), pp. 369ff.
⁴⁹ *Letters of Edward Fitzgerald,* ed. J. M. Cohen (London, 1960), p. 53.

forming the former and annihilating the latter. His means of effecting good is the opposite of Douglas Jerrold's, for that writer always attacks the follies of the age, and by severely lashing with cutting satire, the baseness of the world, seeks to effect an amelioration in the condition of his fellow men.[50]

Similarly, Thomas Powell, writing on Jerrold in his *Pictures of the Living Authors of Britain*, notes:

Jerrold flies at his enemy like a tiger, and never lets go while there is life in him; while Dickens contents himself by giving him a sound drubbing. Jerrold is most in earnest, but Dickens is more effective. There is a candour and fair play about him which we miss in Jerrold; the latter will hear nothing in defence of his foe, and consequently punishes him vindictively.[51]

In the same year (1851) that Powell was writing, however, Dickens as author of *The Haunted Man* is again taken to task for being influenced by Jerrold: a reviewer in *The Man in the Moon* regrets that Dickens, "one of the glories of his age," should have been misled by "the gang of malevolent quacks who introduced 'writing with a purpose.' " [52] Dickens's own view of the matter is no doubt reflected in a *Household Words* review of Blanchard Jerrold's biography of his father in which Wilkie Collins, the reviewer, says, "We admire this so-called bitterness as one of the great and valuable qualities of Douglas Jerrold's writings, ... because we can see ... it stems from the uncompromising earnestness and honesty of the author." [53]

In May 1843 Dickens wrote to Jerrold congratulating him on his article, "Elizabeth and Victoria," which had appeared in the first number of Jerrold's *Illuminated Magazine*. The article attacks the myth of the "good old days" and dwells at length on the tortures and cruel punishments which existed in Tudor times. As we have seen, these things are alluded to by Dickens in a cancelled portion of *The Chimes* where the Young England gentleman is

[50] *Weekly Dispatch*, 27 Dec. 1846, p. 620, col. 3.

[51] (London, 1851), p. 175; Powell's book was first published in New York in 1849.

[52] 5:50ff.; the prospectus for *Douglas Jerrold's Shilling Magazine*, reprinted in 1845 as the preface to the first volume, had announced: "It will be our chief object to make every essay—however brief, and however light and familiar its treatment—breathe WITH A PURPOSE."

[53] 5(1852):52. Collins's authorship is established by the copy of the *Household Words* Contributors' Book at the Dickens House. Jerrold died in 1857; the biography was published in 1859.

pictured dreaming. Jerrold points out the greater everyday comfort of even the poorest Victorians compared with Elizabethan peasants. Just so, as we have seen, Mr. Filer (for a moment on the side of the angels) is made to counter the old City Tory's praise of the good old days by remarking that the peasant then had hardly a shirt to his back or a vegetable to put into his mouth. Dickens and Jerrold found themselves in close agreement not only in this but also in most matters relating to the Condition-of-England Question.[54] There is evidence that Dickens was a keen reader of Jerrold, and I have suggested elsewhere that Jerrold's attack on Lord Brougham (*Punch*, 6 April 1844) gave him some ideas for Sir Joseph Bowley in *The Chimes*. It seems likely also that he caught a hint for Alderman Cute from one of Jerrold's many onslaughts on the Middlesex magistrate, Sir Peter Laurie, especially one which appeared in *Punch* on 5 October 1844 when Dickens was at Genoa "staggering on the threshold" of his projected Christmas story. This article, "Peter the Great," was occasioned by the case of Elizabeth Morris who was brought before Laurie charged with attempted suicide;[55] the following paragraph describing the magistrate might well have supplied Dickens with an idea for Alderman Cute:

And so this man turns up his varnished cheek at human despair, and with triumphant looks of cunning and incredulity peers at misery, as some self-imagined wit looks at the tricks of a conjuror, pitying the fools who are gulled by him, and, full of his own wisdom, declaring that he is not at all deceived; not he. He has watched the whole legerdemain, and can tell how every trick is done. Fools may admire, but *he* is not to be juggled.

Compare this with the description of Cute's behavior during Will

---

[54] A striking illustration of the closeness of Jerrold and Dickens in their social thinking at this time is provided by a comparison of Trotty's delusions about the poor being "intruders" as shown in *The Chimes* with the attitude of the peasant whom Jerrold feigns to be the author of letter 46 in his series, "Punch's Complete Letter-writer" (*Punch* 7(1844):249). The peasant, asking a landowner for a small allotment of land, says, "It will, I feel, make quite a man of me. ... As it is, sir—I don't know how it can be—but somehow at times I don't feel a man at all. I seem as if I'd no business in the world; as if I were a sort of toad or slug upon the soil; an interloper on the land, having no right even to make a footmark in it." This was published on 7 Dec. 1844 and Jerrold had heard Dickens read *The Chimes* on Dec. 3. It is possible, therefore, that he was indebted to Dickens for some of the ideas in this letter. If not, the coincidence is very remarkable.

[55] Since 1841 Laurie had been conducting a campaign to "put down" suicide among the poor by inflicting prison sentences on all those brought before him charged with attempting the offense. See my forthcoming essay, "Dickens's Tract for the Times."

Fern's impassioned plea for understanding at the Bowley banquet: "Alderman Cute stuck his thumbs in his waistcoat-pockets and leaning back in his chair, and smiling, winked at a neighbouring chandelier. As much as to say, 'Of course! I told you so. The common cry! Lord bless you, we are up to this sort of thing—myself and human nature' " (132).

We know too that Dickens read and admired Jerrold's vigorously Radical novel (or rather collection of episodes), *The Story of a Feather*, which was serialized in *Punch* from January to December 1843. He writes to Forster in August 1844 that he had been reading it and had "derived much enjoyment therefrom." [56] He derived also, it appears, an idea for one of the "strong" scenes in *The Chimes*.

Jerrold's heroine is a poor girl, a feather dresser called Patty, who lives a toilsome life with her ailing mother in a wretched garret. When the mother dies Patty is surprised by a sympathetic word from a girl neighbor of hers, a prostitute, who, "a hundred times when passing in the lane, by venom words and brassy looks, had taunted and out-stared the simple, gentle feather-dresser." Before Patty can thank her she runs away. Later Patty is in her room making herself a poor mourning garment: "with swoln eyes and anxious, bloodless face, [she] is working alone, . . . mechanically working, her face dead, blank with misery—her fingers only moving." The figure is exactly that of Meg toward the end of the Third Quarter of *The Chimes*: "In any mood, in any grief, in any torture of the mind or body, Meg's work must be done. She sat down to her task, and plied it. Night, midnight. Still she worked" (136). Patty is interrupted by a "low distinct knock," and a woman glides into her room. Meg likewise hears a "gentle knocking" and receives a similar visitor. Both authors interrupt the narrative to exclaim at the haggard appearance of the women who enter. In Patty's case the visitor is Jessy, converted by a shocking coincidence (she had found herself accidentally soliciting her own father in the street) from her "life of horror" and come to beg forgiveness before embarking on a reformed existence. Meg's visitor is Lilian (first called Jessie by Dickens, as the manuscript shows), also a repentant prostitute; she too comes to beg forgiveness for she is about to die of a broken heart. Power is added to Dickens's scene by our knowledge of the previous sisterly relation between Meg and Lilian and by its

---

termination in a death. But the central idea is the same. Both penitents invoke the Magdalen, and both are forgiven and blessed by the pure heroines. Indeed so close are the two scenes that one suspects Dickens changed his character's name from Jessie to Lilian not so much for the sake of "prettiness" but to avoid signposting his (surely conscious) borrowing.[57]

This particular resemblance may not have struck Jerrold himself as he sat listening to Dickens's reading of *The Chimes* at Forster's chambers, but it can hardly be doubted that he and Carlyle—one of his fellow listeners—recognized the influence their work had clearly had on the writing of the story they were hearing.

It is true that other literary influences, notably that of Thomas Hood, may be detected in *The Chimes*. No doubt the picture of Meg's toilsome life in her poverty-stricken attic owes something to the "Song of the Shirt," as the idea of the role played by the bells may owe something to Schiller's "Song of the Bell"—but there can surely be no question that the major and all-pervading influences that are at work are those of Carlyle and Jerrold. And one has only to compare this book with its celebrated predecessor, the *Carol*, superficially so similar, in effect so radically different, to see how profound is the difference that these two writers made to Dickens's work.

---

[57] See Forster, p. 353. It was not until he began to write the Third Quarter (by which time he had its final scene clear in his mind) that Dickens decided to change the girl's name—in other words he retained the name of Jerrold's heroine until he realized that the scene was to be so close to Jerrold's work.

Dickens Rediscovered: Some Lost Writings Retrieved

HARRY STONE

MOST LITERARY EXPERTS—indeed many Dickens experts —are astonished to learn that there is prime Dickens that has never been identified or collected. This astonishment is a sign of disbelief that the canon of so famous an author can still be undetermined. It is undetermined nevertheless, and it promises to remain so for years to come. One area of the canon which has been neglected and from which hitherto unidentified writings by Dickens may be retrieved is the extra Christmas numbers of *Household Words* and *All the Year Round*.[1] Within a year or two of the time that Dickens established the extra Christmas number as a regular feature of *Household Words* (the extra number was sold separately from and in addition to the fifty-two weekly numbers of the magazine), he had settled its basic features. In *Household Words* the extra number contains one and a half and in *All the Year Round* twice the matter of an ordinary issue. For the most part these extra issues consist of a framework story into which several self-contained short stories or an occasional narrative poem are inserted. Dickens always conceived the framework situation, always wrote a major portion of it, and usually contributed one or more of the interpolated tales. He also did all, or in some instances most, of the bridging writing— that is, the introductory or concluding or transition passages which integrate the entire number or which introduce or conclude the various interpolated tales. In the earlier numbers the framework and the linking passages are rather mechanical, but in later examples the framework is often skillfully and elaborately contrived,

---

[1] I have recently collected and edited Dickens's hitherto unidentified and uncollected contributions to *Household Words*. See *Charles Dickens' Uncollected Writings from "Household Words": 1850–1859*, 2 vols. (Bloomington, 1968).

accounting for a substantial part of the issue. Furthermore Dickens's comments make it clear that he set great store by the dramatic situation and labored diligently to see that the inter- polated stories not only fit smoothly into their particular niches but harmonized with the overall situation as well.

His usual practice was to draw up a list of prospective contrib- utors (the list always contained many more names than the story spaces available), send to each person selected a brief scenario or synopsis of the dramatic situation, enumerate any limiting factors, and then stipulate the kinds of characters who would tell the interpolated stories. When the stories came in he would choose those he judged best, edit them with his usual freedom (on occa- sion if he were mightily dissatisfied, he would write an additional story of his own), and then weave the stories carefully into the framework. In the later Christmas numbers the framework tends to become an independent work of art (often written in collabora- tion with Wilkie Collins) and the interpolated stories fewer; in two instances, *The Perils of Certain English Prisoners* (1857) and *No Thoroughfare* (1867), he and Collins wrote the entire number, dispensing with the interpolated stories altogether. By 1867, the year *No Thoroughfare* appeared in *All the Year Round*, the format had been widely imitated, and Dickens had begun to chafe under the burdens involved: the inexorable annual labor, the difficulty of finding a fresh idea each year, and the editorial feats necessary to fit the various parts together. And so with *No Thoroughfare* Dickens abandoned the extra Christmas numbers.

That same year, 1867, in connection with the publication of the American Diamond Edition of his *Works,* Dickens extracted his chief personal contributions to seven of the extra Christmas num- bers and made such alterations as would enable them to stand in- dependently. These extracts, plus similar extracts from other num- bers, usually collected under the generic title *Christmas Stories,* have been reprinted in all subsequent editions of the *Collected Works.* But much was lost in the process of extraction. The pas- sages Dickens cut from his segments when he extracted his con- tributions, as well as the more miscellaneous sections that he wrote for the extra Christmas numbers but chose not to extract and re- print, have dropped out of sight since 1867. These lost writings include the introductory and concluding bridges, the transitions, the interpolations and additions, and a number of long composite sections, sometimes whole chapters.[2]

The retrieval of some of these writings is very simple—one need only compare the original Christmas number version with the *Collected Works* version to see what Dickens cut from his own sections and what he added to them. In the case of seven of the extra Christmas numbers, the holograph of these changes, made by Dickens on the numbers themselves, is in the Berg Collection of the New York Public Library. Other passages, especially the proto-Dickensian bridging and linking passages, are also fairly easy to recognize and retrieve. But Dickens's casual additions and changes elsewhere in the Christmas numbers (in sections primarily by other writers, for example) and his contributions to composite chapters written jointly with others are more difficult to identify. One of the noteworthy instances of the exclusions and resultant losses I have been talking about occurs in *A Message from the Sea,* the extra Christmas number of *All the Year Round* for 1860, noteworthy because in addition to internal evidence there is a variety of external evidence which can be used to help identify the excluded and therefore, to all intents and purposes, lost contributions by Dickens.

Late in the nineteenth century Frederic G. Kitton consulted a marked office set of *All the Year Round,* a set that has since disappeared. In his *The Minor Writings of Charles Dickens* (1900), Kitton used this office set to designate which sections of the linking passages in chapter 3 of *A Message from the Sea,* a chapter not included in editions of the *Collected Works,* are by Dickens.[3] But that is only part of the story. Before Kitton did his work, the extra Christmas numbers of *All the Year Round* were collected in a single volume reprinted from the original stereotype plates. This volume, which in its earliest issue is hard to come by, was published by Dickens himself in December 1868 conjointly at the offices of *All the Year Round* and Chapman and Hall under the title, *The Christmas Numbers of All the Year Round, Conducted by Charles Dickens.*[4] Most copies of this edition contain a contents page, and

---

[2] The lost passages from *Household Words* are identified and reprinted in my edition of the *Uncollected Writings.*

[3] (London), p. 163.

[4] The title varies. Some copies contain the following title page: *The Nine Christmas Numbers of All the Year Round, Conducted by Charles Dickens.* In all copies that I have seen, the spine bears the following legend: *Christmas Stories*

the contents page lists the author or authors of each section of each Christmas number—the only official public identification of these originally anonymous pieces.[5] This contents page, if it be reliable (and it has Dickens's sanction), shows that some sections of *A Message from the Sea* which are solely by Dickens were omitted from the *Collected Works* because they are more germane to the whole number than to Dickens's particular contribution; it also shows that other sections heretofore identified as solely by Dickens, and admitted to the *Collected Works* as such, are by Dickens and a collaborator; finally, it offers evidence that still other sections omitted from the *Collected Works* and assumed therefore not to be by Dickens are by Dickens and a collaborator.

The confusion exemplified here is not limited to *A Message from the Sea*. Other extra Christmas numbers from *All the Year Round* contain writings by Dickens that have not been identified or collected. Many of these lost writings are neither dull nor trivial; their exclusion from the canon had little to do with quality or importance. They more frequently were the victims of such considerations as expediency, carelessness, the loss of records, the decision not to collect composite pieces, or similar factors. But over the years chance became custom, and custom hardened into authority—authority being inclusion in the *Collected Works*. There is much first-rate Dickens waiting to be recovered, but I am here primarily concerned with the uncollected segments from *A Message from the Sea*, first published, as already noted, as the extra Christmas number of *All the Year Round* for 1860.

A Message from the Sea consists of five chapters: chapter 1— "The Village"; chapter 2—"The Money"; chapter 3—"The Club-Night"; chapter 4—"The Seafaring Man"; and chapter 5—"The Restitution." Of these five chapters, only chapters 1, 2, and 5 are reprinted in the *Collected Works*, and they are reprinted as solely by Dickens. Kitton, however, presumably basing his remarks on the aforementioned office set of *All the Year Round*, says that Dickens contributed "nearly all" of chapter 1 (Wilkie Collins con-

---

from *All the Year Round Conducted by Chas. Dickens*. There are variations also in the original cloth bindings and in other matters not affecting the text.

[5] Not all the numbers were published anonymously, however; the last two extra Christmas numbers of *All the Year Round*—*Mugby Junction* (1866) and *No Thoroughfare* (1867)—list the authors on the wrapper and on the first page. I have also seen advertisements dated 1864 which list the contributors to each of the first five extra Christmas numbers of *All the Year Round*. These ads simply list each number and its contributors, however; they do not specify who wrote what.

tributing the remainder), all of chapters 2 and 5, and insertions in chapters 3 and 4. He then goes on to say, somewhat contradictorily, that Wilkie Collins was responsible for the whole of chapter 4 and certain portions of chapter 3, but not the four interpolated stories that are part of chapter 3. In a footnote specifically citing the office set as his authority, Kitton lists the sections of chapter 3—largely linking and bridging sections—which are by Dickens.

The 1868 contents page provides a third version of authorship. It makes the following attributions: chapter 1—Dickens; chapter 2—Dickens and Wilkie Collins; chapter 3—Dickens, Charles Collins, Harriet Parr, H. F. Chorley, and Amelia B. Edwards (Dickens is presumably responsible for the long framework introduction and the linking and bridging sections; the four additional writers are the authors of the four interpolated stories); chapter 4—Wilkie Collins; chapter 5— Dickens and Wilkie Collins. Even in the matter of the interpolated contributions there is a discrepancy, for the contents page attributes the third interpolation, a poem, to H. F. Chorley, while Kitton, parenthetically, attributes the verses to R. Buchanan.

The result is confusing to say the least. Without the original manuscripts and the successive stages of corrected proofs some of these conflicting claims must remain moot. But two observations seem worth making. First, the segments of *A Message from the Sea* enshrined in the *Collected Works* are defective in two ways: they are probably not entirely by Dickens, and they certainly exclude a good deal that is by him. Second, Dickens's intervention in the original writing, in the framework, and in the proofs (his own and others) is so pervasive that any labeling, even in an official contents page or an office set, is likely to be a statement of primary rather than exclusive authorship. There is good reason to believe, for example, that Dickens also had a hand in chapter 4, generally ascribed to Wilkie Collins (Kitton partly supports this view), in the opening of Harriet Parr's interpolated story, and in other segments—but this is another matter, and the question of attributions throughout *A Message from the Sea* is one which must be closely argued in another place, preferably in a critical edition of the complete extra Christmas numbers of *All the Year Round*.

Here it only remains to reprint those portions of *A Message from the Sea* which have not been included in the *Collected Works* and which are in all likelihood substantially or solely by Dickens. In identifying these sections the chief difficulty is with chapter 3, for the 1868 contents page implies that Dickens is responsible for all but the interpolated stories, while Kitton attributes specific linking and bridging sections to Dickens and implies that Collins provided the rest of the framework. In actual fact the central conflict is over the long framework introduction to chapter 3, the contents giving it to Dickens, and Kitton, by omission, giving it to Collins. I reprint it below because it seems on internal stylistic evidence to be at least in part by Dickens—the opening paragraph, to cite one small instance, is probably by him—and because, as I shall demonstrate later, Dickens seems to have been primarily responsible here as elsewhere for certain features of the story: Captain Jorgan, for example (Captain Jorgan was based on his old American friend Captain Morgan),[6] as well as most of the local-color writing. Moreover Dickens regarded the framework, by virtue of his triple role as conceiver, unifier, and "conductor," as his special domain. When he assigned a segment of framework to a collaborator, it was always as a joint enterprise, and then he invariably went over and frequently remade what his collaborator turned in. It seems likely, therefore, that Collins wrote an initial draft of the introduction and that Dickens subsequently went over the draft, rewrote it heavily, and added important sections.

Before reprinting this introduction and the other uncollected passages, I should like to say enough about the plot of *A Message from the Sea* to give the passages a context.

৯৯৯

Very briefly, *A Message from the Sea* tells the story of how Captain Jorgan, an American sea captain, having found a message in a bottle in a remote region of the southern seas, obeys the inscription on the outside and delivers the message unopened to its destination. When he does deliver it, in the village of Steepways, Devonshire, to Alfred Raybrock, the young fisherman brother of Hugh Raybrock, the writer of the message, now presumed dead, the contents prove calamitous. The fragmentary message, based upon evidence that Hugh had come upon while on board ship and later when shipwrecked, casts doubt on the good name of their

---

[6] See Dickens's letter to Morgan [Dec. 1860], *The Letters of Charles Dickens*, ed. Walter Dexter, 3 vols. (Bloomsbury [London], 1938), 3:198.

dead father, who is reputed to have stolen £500. This unwelcome revelation jeopardizes Alfred's inheritance and threatens his forthcoming marriage to Kitty. Alfred and Captain Jorgan tell this news to no one and, much to the consternation of Alfred's family and friends, set forth, without explanation, for the little Cornish village of Lanrean where Alfred's father used to live. There they hope to find some ancient cronies of old Mr. Raybrock who can help prove or disprove the accusations. Arriving by night at Lanrean, they enter its hotel and insinuate themselves into a club meeting of old inhabitants. The club requires that each member tell a story when called upon to do so, and after listening to an interlude of marathon storytelling, Alfred and the Captain retire for the evening and subsequently go on to gather the information needed to explode the charges in the cryptic message. Old Mr. Raybrock's reputation is cleared; Hugh, the long-lost brother, is discovered at the inn; and Alfred returns triumphantly to Steepways to wed his betrothed, to reunite his family (Hugh is restored to his child and to his faithful wife Margaret), and to celebrate with Captain Jorgan and entourage the happy conclusion of their adventures.

Now for the uncollected writings themselves. The first of the uncollected passages, probably by Dickens and Collins in collaboration, consists of the introductory portion of chapter 3, "The Club-Night." This introduction advances the framework and also acts as a prologue to the main feature of the chapter, the four interpolated stories. The passage opens with Alfred Raybrock and Captain Jorgan walking through Cornwall on their way to Lanrean:

CHAPTER III. THE CLUB-NIGHT.

A CORNISH MOOR, when the east wind drives over it, is as cold and rugged a scene as a traveller is likely to find in a year's travel. A Cornish Moor in the dark, is as black a solitude as the traveller is likely to wish himself well out of, in the course of a life's wanderings. A Cornish Moor in a night fog, is a wilderness where the traveller needs to know his way well, or the chances are very strong that his life and his wanderings will soon perplex him no more.

Captain Jorgan and the young fisherman had faced the east and the south-east winds, from the first rising of the sun after their departure from the village of Steepways. Thrice, had the sun risen, and still all day long had the sharp wind blown at them like some malevolent spirit bent on forcing them back. But, Captain Jorgan was too familiar with all the winds that blow, and too much accustomed to circumvent their slightest weaknesses and get the better of them in the long run, to be

beaten by any member of the airy family. Taking the year round, it was
his opinion that it mattered little what wind blew, or how hard it blew;
so, he was as indifferent to the wind on this occasion as a man could be
who frequently observed "that it freshened him up," and who regarded
it in the light of an old acquaintance. One might have supposed from
his way, that there was even a kind of fraternal understanding between
Captain Jorgan and the wind, as between two professed fighters often
opposed to one another. The young fisherman, for his part, was
accustomed within his narrower limits to hold hard weather cheap, and
had his anxious object before him; so, the wind went by him too, little
heeded, and went upon its way to kiss Kitty.

Their varied course had lain by the side of the sea where the brown
rocks cleft it into fountains of spray, and inland where once barren
moors were reclaimed and cultivated, and by lonely villages of poor-
enough cabins with mud walls, and by a town or two with an old church
and a market-place. But, always travelling through a sparely inhabited
country and over a broad expanse, they had come at last upon the true
Cornish Moor within reach of Lanrean. None but gaunt spectres of
miners passed them here, with metallic masks of faces, ghastly with
dust of copper and tin; anon, solitary works on remote hill-tops, and
bare machinery of torturing wheels and cogs and chains, writhing up
hill-sides, were the few scattered hints of human presence in the landscape; during long intervals, the bitter wind, howling and tearing at
them like a fierce wild monster, had them all to itself.

"A sing'lar thing it is," said the captain, looking round at the brown
desert of rank grass and poor moss, "how like this airth is, to the men
that live upon it! Here's a spot of country rich with hidden metals, and
it puts on the worst rags of clothes possible, and crouches and shivers
and makes believe to be so poor that it can't so much as afford a feed
for a beast. Just like a human miser, ain't it?"

"But they find the miser out," returned the young fisherman, pointing to where the earth by the watercourses and along the valleys was
turned up, for miles, in trying for metal.

"Ay, they find him out," said the captain; "but he makes a struggle
of it even then, and holds back all he can. He's a 'cute 'un."

The gloom of evening was already gathering on the dreary scene,
and they were, at the shortest and best, a dozen miles from their destination. But, the captain in his long-skirted blue coat and his boots and his
hat and his square shirt-collar, and without any extra defence against
the weather, walked coolly along with his hands in his pockets: as if he
lived underground somewhere hard by, and had just come up to show
his friend the road.

"I'd have liked to have had a look at this place, too," said the captain,
"when there was a monstrous sweep of water rolling over it, dragging
the powerful great stones along and piling 'em atop of one another,
and depositing the foundations for all manner of superstitions. Bless
you! the old priets, smart mechanical critturs as they were, never piled

up many of these stones. Water's the lever that moved 'em. When you see 'em thick and blunt tewwards one point of the compass, and fined away thin tewwards the opposite point, you may be as good as moral sure that the name of the ancient Druid that fixed 'em was Water."

The captàin referred to some great blocks of stone presenting this characteristic, which were wonderfully balanced and heaped on one another, on a desolate hill. Looking back at these, as they stood out against the lurid glare of the west, just then expiring, they were not unlike enormous antediluvian birds, that had perched there on crags and peaks, and had been petrified there.

"But it's an interesting country," said the captain, "—fact! It's old in the annals of that said old Arch Druid, Water, and it's old in the annals of the said old parson-critturs too. It's a mighty interesting thing to set your boot (as I did this day) on a rough honey-combed old stone, with just nothing you can name but weather visible upon it: which the scholars that go about with hammers, chipping pieces off the universal airth, find to be an inscription, entreating prayers for the soul of some for-ages-bust-up crittur of a governor that over-taxed a people never heard of." Here the captain stopped to slap his leg. "It's a mighty interesting thing to come upon a score or two of stones set up on end in a desert, some short, some tall, some leaning here, some leaning there, and to know that they were pop'larly supposed—and may be still—to be a group of Cornish men that got changed into that geological formation for playing a game upon a Sunday. They wouldn't have it in my country, I reckon, even if they could get it—but it's very interesting."

In this, the captain, though it amused him, was quite sincere. Quite as sincere as when he added, after looking well about him: "That fog-bank coming up as the sun goes down, will spread, and we shall have to feel our way into Lanrean full as much as see it."

All the way along, the young fisherman had spoken at times to the captain, of his interrupted hopes, and of the family good name, and of the restitution that must be made, and of the cherished plans of his heart so near attainment, which must be set aside for it. In his simple faith and honour, he seemed incapable of entertaining the idea that it was within the bounds of possibility to evade the doing of what their inquiries should establish to be right. This was very agreeable to Captain Jorgan, and won his genuine admiration. Wherefore, he now turned the discourse back into that channel, and encouraged his companion to talk of Kitty, and to calculate how many years it would take, without a share in the fishery, to establish a home for her, and to relieve his honest heart by dwelling on its anxieties.

Meanwhile, it fell very dark, and the fog became dense, though the wind howled at them and bit them as savagely as ever. The captain had carefully taken the bearings of Lanrean from the map, and carried his pocket compass with him; the young fisherman, too, possessed that kind of cultivated instinct for shaping a course, which is often found among men of such pursuits. But, although they held a true course in the main, and corrected it when they lost the road by the aid of the compass and a light obtained with great difficulty in the roomy depths of the captain's hat, they could not help losing the road often. On such occasions they would become involved in the difficult ground of the spongy moor, and, after making a laborious loop, would emerge upon the road at some point they had passed before they left it, and thus would have a good deal of work to do twice over. But the young fisherman was not easily lost, and the captain (and his comb) would probably have turned up, with perfect coolness and self-possession, at any appointed spot on the surface of this globe. Consequently, they were no more than retarded in their progress to Lanrean, and arrived in that small place at nine o'clock. By that time, the captain's hat had fallen back over his ears and rested on the nape of his neck; but he still had his hands in his pockets, and showed no other sign of dilapidation.

They had almost run against a low stone house with red-curtained windows, before they knew they had hit upon the little hotel, the King Arthur's Arms. They could just descry through the mist, on the opposite side of the narrow road, other low stone buildings which were its outhouses and stables; and somewhere overhead, its invisible sign was being wrathfully swung by the wind.

"Now, wait a bit," said the captain. "They might be full here, or they might offer us cold quarters. Consequently, the policy is to take an observation, and, when we've found the warmest room, walk right slap into it."

The warmest room was evidently that from which fire and candle streamed reddest and brightest, and from which the sound of voices engaged in some discussion came out into the night. Captain Jorgan having established the bearings of this room, merely said to his young friend, "Follow me!" and was in it, before King Arthur's Arms had any notion that they enfolded a stranger.

"Order, order, order!" cried several voices, as the captain with his hat under his arm, stood within the door he had opened.

"Gentlemen," said the captain, advancing, "I am much beholden to you for the opportunity you give me of addressing you; but will not detain you with any lengthened observations. I have the honour to be a cousin of yours on the Uncle Sam side; this young friend of mine is a nearer relation of yours on the Devonshire side; we are both pretty nigh used up, and much in want of supper. I thank you for your welcome, and I am proud to take you by the hand, sir, and I hope I see you well."

These last words were addressed to a jolly looking chairman with a wooden hammer near him: which, but for the captain's friendly grasp, he would have taken up, and hammered the table with.

"How do you *do*, sir?" said the captain, shaking this chairman's hand with the greatest heartiness, while his new friend ineffectually eyed his hammer of office; "when you come to my country, I shall be proud to return your welcome, sir, and that of this good company."

The captain now took his seat near the fire, and invited his companion to do the like—whom he congratulated aloud, on their having "fallen on their feet."

The company, who might be about a dozen in number, were at a loss what to make of, or do with, the captain. But, one little old man in long flapping shirt collars: who, with only his face and them visible through a cloud of tobacco smoke, looked like a superannuated Cherubim: said sharply,

"This is a Club."

"This is a Club," the captain repeated to his young friend. "Wa'al now, that's curious! Didn't I say, coming along, if we could only light upon a Club?"

The captain's doubling himself up and slapping his leg, finished the chairman. He had been softening towards the captain from the first, and he melted. "Gentlemen King Arthurs," said he, rising, "though it is not the custom to admit strangers, still, as we have broken the rule once to-night,[7] I will exert my authority and break it again. And while the supper of these travellers is cooking;" here his eye fell on the land-lord, who discreetly took the hint and withdrew to see about it; "I will recal you to the subject of the seafaring man."

"D'ye hear!" said the captain, aside to the young fisherman; "that's in our way. Who's the seafaring man, I wonder?"

"I see several old men here," returned the young fisherman, eagerly, for his thoughts were always on his object. "Perhaps one or more of the old men whose names you wrote down in your book, may be here."

"Perhaps," said the captain; "I've got my eye on 'em. But don't force it. Try if it won't come nat'ral."

Thus the two, behind their hands, while they sat warming them at the fire. Simultaneously, the Club beginning to be at its ease again, and resuming the discussion of the seafaring man, the captain winked to his fellow-traveller to let him attend to it.

As it was a kind of conversation not altogether unprecedented in such assemblages, where most of those who spoke at all, spoke all at once, and where half of those could put no beginning to what they had to say, and the other half could put no end, the tendency of the debate was discursive, and not very intelligible. All the captain had made out, down to the time when the separate little table laid for two was covered with a smoking broiled fowl and rashers of bacon, reduced itself to these heads. That, a seafaring man had arrived at The King Arthur's Arms, benighted, an hour or so earlier in the evening. That, the Gentlemen King Arthurs had admitted him, though all un-known, into the sanctuary of their Club. That, they had invited him to make his footing good by telling a story. That, he had, after some pressing, begun a story of adventure and shipwreck: at an interesting point of which he suddenly broke off, and positively refused to finish. That, he had thereupon taken up a candlestick, and gone to bed, and was now the sole occupant of a double-bedded room up-stairs. The question raised on these premises, appeared to be, whether the seafaring

---

[7] By admitting a seafaring traveller—actually Alfred's brother, Hugh Raybrock.

man was not in a state of contumacy and contempt, and ought not to be formally voted and declared in that condition. This deliberation involved the difficulty (suggested by the more jocose and irreverent of the Gentlemen King Arthurs) that it might make no sort of difference to the seafaring man whether he was so voted and declared, or not.

Captain Jorgan and the young fisherman ate their supper and drank their beer, and their knives and forks had ceased to rattle and their glasses had ceased to clink, and still the discussion showed no symptoms of coming to any conclusion. But, when they had left their little supper-table and had returned to their seats by the fire, the Chairman hammered himself into attention, and thus outspake.

"Gentlemen King Arthurs; when the night is so bad without, harmony should prevail within. When the moor is so windy, cold, and bleak, this room should be cheerful, convivial, and entertaining. Gentlemen, at present it is neither the one, nor yet the other, nor yet the other. Gentlemen King Arthurs, I recal you to yourselves. Gentlemen King Arthurs, what are you? Yon are inhabitants—old inhabitants —of the noble village of Lanrean. You are in council assembled. You are a monthly Club through all the winter months, and they are many. It is your perroud perrivilege, on a new member's entrance, or on a member's birthday, to call upon that member to make good his footing by relating to you some transaction or adventure in his life, or in the life of a relation, or in the life of a friend, and then to depute me as your representative to spin a teetotum to pass it round. Gentlemen King Arthurs, your perroud perrivileges shall not suffer in my keeping. N—no! Therefore, as the member whose birthday the present occasion has the honour to be, has gratified you; and as the seafaring man overhead has *not* gratified you; I start you fresh, by spinning the teetotum attached to my office, and calling on the gentleman it falls to, to speak up when his name is declared."

The captain and his young friend looked hard at the teetotum as it whirled rapidly, and harder still when it gradually became intoxicated and began to stagger about the table in an ill-conducted and disorderly manner. Finally, it came into collision with a candlestick and leaped against the pipe of the old gentleman with the flapping shirt collars. Thereupon, the chairman struck the table once with his hammer and said:

"Mr. Parvis!"

"D'ye hear that?" whispered the captain, greatly excited, to the young fisherman. "I'd have laid you a thousand dollars a good half-hour ago, that that old cherubim in the clouds was Arson Parvis!"

The respectable personage in question, after turning up one eye to assist his memory—at which time, he bore a very striking resemblance indeed to the conventional representations of his race as executed in oil by various ancient masters—commenced a narrative, of which the interest centred in a waistcoat. It appeared that the waistcoat was a yellow waistcoat with a green stripe, white sleeves, and a plain brass button. It also appeared that the waistcoat was made to order, by Nicholas Pendold of Penzance, who was thrown off the top of a four-horse coach coming down the hill on the Plymouth road, and, pitching on his head where he was not sensitive, lived two-and-thirty years afterwards, and considered himself the better for the accident—roused up, as it might be. It further appeared that the waistcoat belonged to Mr. Parvis's father, and had once attended him, in company with a pair of gaiters, to the annual feast of miners at St. Just: where the extraordinary circumstance which ever afterwards rendered it a waist-coat famous in story had occurred. But, the celebrity of the waistcoat was not thoroughly accounted for by Mr. Parvis, and had to be to some extent taken on trust by the company, in consequence of that gentle-man's entirely forgetting all about the extraordinary circumstance that had handed it down to fame. Indeed, he was even unable, on a gentle cross-examination instituted for the assistance of his memory, to inform the Gentlemen King Arthurs whether it was a circumstance of a natural or supernatural character. Having thus responded to the teetotum, Mr. Parvis, after looking out from his clouds as if he would like to see the man who would beat that, subsided into himself.

The fraternity were plunged into a blank condition by Mr. Parvis's success, and the chairman was about to try another spin, when young Raybrock—whom Captain Jorgan had with difficulty restrained—rose, and said might he ask Mr. Parvis a question[.]

The Gentlemen King Arthurs holding, with loud cries of "Order!" that he might not, he asked the question as soon as he could possibly make himself heard.

Did the forgotten circumstance relate in any way to money? To a sum of money, such as five hundred pounds? To money supposed by its possessor to be honestly come by, but in reality ill-gotten and stolen?

A general surprise seized upon the club when this remarkable inquiry was preferred; which would have become resentment but for the captain's interposition.

"Strange as it sounds," said he, "and suspicious as it sounds, I pledge myself, gentlemen, that my young friend here has a manly stand-up Cornish reason for his words. Also, I pledge myself that they are inoffen-sive words. He and I are searching for information on a subject which those words generally describe. Such information we may get from the honestest and best of men—may get, or not get, here or anywhere about here. I hope the Honourable Mr. Arson—I ask his pardon—Parvis—will not object to quiet my young friend's mind by saying Yes or No.["]

After some time, the obtuse Mr. Parvis was with great trouble and difficulty induced to roar out "No!" For which concession the captain rose and thanked him.

"Now, listen to the next," whispered the captain to the young fisherman. "There may be more in him than in the other crittur. Don't interrupt him. Hear him out."

The chairman with all due formality spun the teetotum, and it reeled into the brandy-and-water of a strong brown man of sixty or so: John Tredgear: the manager of a neighbouring mine. He immediately began as follows, with a plain business-like air that gradually warmed as he proceeded.

John Tredgear's story, by Charles Collins, continues at this point. At its conclusion occurs the following linking interlude, probably by Dickens, and hitherto uncollected:

"Wa'al, now!" said Captain Jorgan, rising, with his hand upon the sleeve of his fellow-traveller to keep him down; "I congratulate you, sir, upon that adventer; unpleasant at the time, but pleasant to look back upon; as many adventers in many lives are. Mr. Tredgear, you had a feeling for your money on that occasion, and it went hard on being Stolen Money. It was not a sum of five hundred pound, perhaps?"

"I wish it had been half as much," was the reply.

"Thank you, sir. Might I ask the question of you that has been already put? About this place of Lanrean, did you ever hear of any circumstances whatever, that might seem to have a bearing—any how— on that question?"

"Never."

"Thank you again for a straightfor'ard answer," said the captain, apologetically. "You see, we have been referred to Lanrean to make inquiries, and happening in among the inhabitants present, we use the opportunity. In my country, we always *do* use opportunities."

"And you turn them to good account, I believe, and prosper?"

"It's a fact, sir," said the captain, "that we get along. Yes, we get along, sir.—But I stop the teetotum."

It was twirled again, and fell to David Polreath; an iron-grey man; "as old as the hills," the captain whispered to young Raybrock, "and as hard as nails.—And I admire," added the captain, glancing about, "whether Unchrisen Penrewen is here, and which is he!"

David Polreath stroked down the long iron-grey hair that fell massively upon the shoulders of his large-buttoned coat, and spake thus:

David Polreath's story, by Harriet Parr ("Holme Lee"), continues at this point. At its conclusion occurs the following linking interlude, probably by Dickens, again uncollected:

When David Polreath had finished, the chairman gave the teetotum such a swift and sudden twirl, to be beforehand with any interruption, that it twirled among all the glasses and into all corners of the table, and finally, flew off the table and lodged in Captain Jorgan's waistcoat.

"A kind of a judgment!" said the captain, taking it out. "What's to

be done now? *I* know no story, except Down Easters, and *they* didn't
happen to myself, or any one of my acquaintance, and you couldn't
enjoy 'em without going out of your minds first. And perhaps the company ain't prepared to do that?"

The chairman interposed by rising and declaring it to be his
perroud perrivilege to stop preliminary observations.

"Wa'al," said the captain, "I defer to the President—which an't at
all what they do in my country, where they lay into him, head, limbs,
and body." Here he slapped his leg. "But I beg to ask a preliminary
question. Colonel Polreath has read from a diary. Might I read from a
pipe-light?"

The chairman requested explanation.

"The history of the pipe-light," said the captain, "is just this:—that
it's verses, and was made on the voyage home by a passenger I brought
over. And he was a quiet crittur of a middle-aged man with a pleasant
countenance. And he wrote it on the head of a cask. And he was a most
etarnal time about it tew. And he blotted it as if he had wrote it in a
continual squall of ink. And then he took an indigestion, and I phy-
sicked him for want of a better doctor. And then to show his liking
for me he copied it out fair, and gave it to me for a pipe-light. And it
ain't been lighted yet, and that's a fact."

"Let it be read," said the chairman.

"With thanks to Colonel Polreath for setting the example," pursued
the captain, "and with apologies to the Honourable A. Parvis and the
whole of the present company for this passenger's having expressed his
mind in verses—which he may have done along of bein' sea-sick, and he
was very—the pipe-light, unrolled, comes to this:

Captain Jorgan's contribution, a poem by H. F. Chorley (or R.
Buchanan), continues at this point. At its conclusion occurs another
uncollected linking interlude, probably by Dickens:

Mr. Parvis had so greatly disquieted the minds of the Gentlemen
King Arthurs for some minutes, by snoring with strong symptoms of
apoplexy—which, in a mild form, was his normal state of health—that
it was now deemed expedient to wake him and entreat him to allow
himself to be escorted home. Mr. Parvis's reply to this friendly suggestion could not be placed on record without the aid of several dashes,
and is therefore omitted. It was conceived in a spirit of the profoundest
irritation, and executed with vehemence, contempt, scorn, and disgust.
There was nothing for it, but to let the excellent gentleman alone, and
he fell without loss of time into a defiant slumber.

The teetotum being twirled again, so buzzed and bowed in the direction of the young fisherman, that Captain Jorgan advised him to be
bright and prepare for the worst. But, it started off at a tangent, late
in its career, and fell before a well-looking bearded man (one who made

working drawings for machinery, the captain was informed by his next neighbour), who promptly took it up like a challenger's glove.

"Oswald Penrewen!" said the chairman.

"Here's Unchris'en at last!" the captain whispered Alfred Raybrock. "Unchris'en goes ahead, right smart; don't he?"

He did, without one introductory word.

Oswald Penrewen's story, by Amelia B. Edwards, continues at this point followed by a framework interlude which is probably another uncollected Dickens contribution. This passage rounds out and ends chapter 3:

The chairman now announced that the clock declared the teetotum spun out, and that the meeting was dissolved. Yet even then, the young fisherman could not refrain from once more asking his question. This occasioned the Gentlemen King Arthurs, as they got on their hats and great coats, evidently to regard him as a young fisherman who was touched in his head, and some of them even cherished the idea that the captain was his keeper.

As no man dared to awake the mighty Parvis, it was resolved that a heavy member of the society should fall against him as it were by accident, and immediately withdraw to a safe distance. The experiment was so happily accomplished, that Mr. Parvis started to his feet on the best terms with himself, as a light sleeper whose wits never left him, and who could always be broad awake on occasion. Quite an airy jocundity sat upon this respectable man in consequence. And he rallied the briskest member of the fraternity on being "a sleepy-head," with an amount of humour previously supposed to be quite incompatible with his responsible circumstances in life.

Gradually, the society departed into the cold night, and the captain and his young companion were left alone. The captain had so refreshed himself by shaking hands with everybody to an amazing extent, that he was in no hurry to go to bed.

"To-morrow morning," said the captain, "we must find out the lawyer and the clergyman here; they are the people to consult on our business. And I'll be up and out early, and asking questions of everybody I see; thereby propagating at least one of the Institutions of my native country."

As the captain was slapping his leg, the landlord appeared with two small candlesticks.

"Your room," said he, "is at the top of the house. An excellent bed, but you'll hear the wind."

"I've heerd it afore," replied the captain. "Come and make a passage with me, and *you* shall hear it."

"It's considered to blow, here," said the landlord.

"Weather gets its young strength here," replied the captain; "goes

into training for the Atlantic Ocean. Yours are little winds just beginning to feel their way and crawl. Make a voyage with me, and I'll show
you a grown-up one out on business. But you haven't told my friend
where he lies."

"It's the room at the head of the stairs, before you take the second
staircase through the wall," returned the landlord. "You can't mistake
it. It's a double-bedded room, because there's no other."

"The room where the seafaring man is?" said the captain.

"The room where the seafaring man is."

"I hope he mayn't finish telling his story in his sleep," remarked the
captain. "Shall *I* turn into the room where the seafaring man is,
Alfred?"

"No, Captain Jorgan, why should you? There would be little fear of
his waking me, even if he told his whole story out."

"He's in the bed nearest the door," said the landlord. "I've been in to
look at him, once, and he's sound enough. Good night, gentlemen."

The captain immediately shook hands with the landlord in quite
an enthusiastic manner, and having performed that national ceremony,
as if he had had no opportunity of performing it for a long time, accompanied his young friend up-stairs.

"Something tells me," said the captain as they went, "that Miss Kitty
Tregarthen's marriage ain't put off for long, and that we shall light on
what we want."

"I hope so. When, do you think?"

"Wa'al, I couldn't just say when, but soon. Here's your room," said
the captain, softly opening the door and looking in; "and here's the
berth of the seafaring man. I wonder what like he is. He breathes deep;
don't he?"

"Sleeping like a child, to judge from the sound," said the young
fisherman.

"Dreaming of home, maybe," returned the captain. "Can't see him.
Sleeps a deal more wholesomely than Arson Parvis, but a'most as sound;
don't he? Good night, fellow-traveller."

"Good night, Captain Jorgan, and many, many thanks!"

"I'll wait till I 'arn 'em, boy, afore I take 'em," returned the captain,
clapping him cheerfully on the back. "Pleasant dreams of—you know
who!"

When the young fisherman had closed the door, the captain waited a
moment or two, listening for any stir on the part of the unknown
seafaring man. But, none being audible, the captain pursued the way
to his own chamber.

⟢⟣

The writings retrieved in this article exhibit interests and techniques that recur constantly in Dickens's work. As we have seen,
Dickens shaped the overall design of each Christmas number; he

also set his distinctive stamp, though perhaps more intermittently, on recurring aspects of characterization, mood, setting, comment, and humor. In chapter 3 Captain Jorgan continues to act and talk exactly as Dickens delineated him in chapter 1. Blunt, honest, genial, and concerned, speaking with a nautical flavor, walking in a nautical manner, he is an American Captain Cuttle but shrewder and more practical than his English prototype. In addition Captain Jorgan's speech, attitudes, and traits, as exhibited in chapter 3, are benign versions of patterns one can also discern in the American chapters of *Martin Chuzzlewit*. The closeness of this relationship is one sign of Dickens's major participation in chapter 3, for Collins had not visited the United States at this time, and it is inconceivable that Dickens—who rarely deferred in such matters under any circumstances, and who also modeled Captain Jorgan on his own American friend Captain Morgan—would defer his firsthand observations of American traits and of Captain Morgan to Collins's more remote knowledge. But in chapter 3 Captain Jorgan follows *Martin Chuzzlewit* in more particular and more incongruous ways. Though an American, Captain Jorgan's comments on his countrymen are always barbed. In this he is like Mr. Bevan, the "good American" of *Martin Chuzzlewit*. In both instances the characters, rather gratuitously and to the detriment of verisimilitude, intrude Dickens's oft-repeated critical views of American traits into their own casual conversation. Dickens, continuing the pattern he set in *Martin Chuzzlewit* and in chapter 1 of *A Message from the Sea,* cannot forbear having Captain Jorgan remark in chapter 3: "I'll be up and out early, and asking questions of everybody I see; thereby propagating at least one of the Institutions of my native country"; or having him comment: "Wa'al . . . I defer to the President—which an't at all what they do in my country, where they lay into him, head, limbs, and body"; or having him engage in the following exchange:

". . . we use the opportunity. In my country, we always *do* use opportunities."

"And you turn them to good account, I believe, and prosper?"

"It's a fact, sir," said the captain, "that we get along. Yes, we get along, sir."

This is *Martin Chuzzlewit* pure and simple, and it shows how little Dickens had changed in his American views between 1843 and

1860. But Captain Jorgan, despite an occasional Dickensian in-
congruity, is a memorable if minor creation. With his blue coat,
capacious hat, and square shirt-collar, with his bluff speech, half-
nautical and half-American, with his constantly reiterated mannerism of slapping his leg, he is another of those good, uncomplex, yet
carefully differentiated and vividly delineated characters who
abound in Dickens's works.

The landscape, weather, and atmosphere in which Captain Jorgan and Alfred Raybrock tramp over the Cornish moors to Lanrean are also memorable and often very Dickensian. The east wind,
the fog, and the cold that penetrate the opening sections of chapter
3 of *A Message from the Sea* are akin to the east winds and fogs of
Bleak House or, to take less familiar examples, to the wind in chapter 2 of *Martin Chuzzlewit* or the prevailing cold of *The Chimes*.
In part this similitude, not merely in tone and use but in technique, grows out of the recurrence of rhetorical devices that are
virtually a Dickens hallmark. In the opening paragraph of chapter
3 the insistent parallelisms and repetitions are such devices. But
in part the similitude is a matter of idiosyncratic, often outrageous
metaphor. In the second paragraph of chapter 3 the dominating
metaphor suggests boxing. One is reminded of The Game Chicken
and the boxing metaphors of *Dombey and Son*. Captain Jorgan is aware of the wind's "slightest weaknesses," knows how to
"get the better of them," and cannot be "beaten by any member of
the airy family." The conceit continues. Captain Jorgan often observed that the wind "freshened him up"; between him and the
wind there was a "fraternal understanding" as "between two professed fighters often opposed to one another." With the end of the
paragraph, Captain Jorgan as Airy Boxer disappears, but he reappears in that role later in the chapter.

At their best and at their most Dickensian, landscape, weather,
atmosphere, and mood transcend the rhetorical devices which are
their most mechanical feature; then mannerism, repetition, outrageous metaphor are muted or transfigured. In such passages atmosphere and weather are fused to—become a part of—larger considerations: social comment, enlarged perspective, and ultimately,
since we are dealing with a great writer, a unique vision of life
which extends and enhances our own vision of the world. Take, for
example, the following passage from chapter 3:

None but gaunt spectres of miners passed them here, with metallic masks of faces, ghastly with dust of copper and tin; anon, solitary works on remote hill-tops, and bare machinery of torturing wheels and cogs and chains, writhing up hill-sides, were the few scattered hints of human presence in the landscape; during long intervals, the bitter wind, howling and tearing at them like a fierce wild monster, had them all to itself.

We respond to this landscape at once—the specterlike metallic-faced miners, the frightening animistic machinery, the accumulating evocations of hell, the ironic use of the word "human," the relentlessly blowing wind. In hardly more than a stroke we understand what "human presence" can mean on a remote Cornish moor. Moreover the imagination we encounter here is quintessentially Dickensian, compounded as it is of perspectives, juxtapositions, and ironies that we meet over and over again in his writings: the hellish industrial landscapes of *The Old Curiosity Shop* or *Dombey and Son,* for instance, or the savage factory landscapes of *Hard Times.*

We meet that Dickensian imagination elsewhere in these recovered writings. At any moment we are likely to come upon gleams and flashes of Dickensian description, characterization, and observation. Captain Jorgan tramps the moors "with his hands in his pockets: as if he lived underground somewhere hard by, and had just come up to show his friend the road." He speaks like a hybrid offspring of salty Captain Cuttle and a downright American character in *Martin Chuzzlewit.* Here is his description of a poetry-writing passenger: "And he was a quiet crittur of a middle-aged man with a pleasant countenance. And he wrote it [the poem] on the head of a cask. And he was a most etarnal time about it tew. And he blotted it as if he had wrote it in a continual squall of ink." There are other Dickensian observations and vignettes. One old member of the Gentlemen King Arthurs Club, "in long flapping shirt collars . . . with only his face and them visible through a cloud of tobacco smoke, looked like a superannuated Cherubim." [8] There are Dickensian things as well as Dickensian persons. Even a tee-totum can play a memorable role: when the spinning teetotum used

---

[8] "Cherubim" as a singular, though still occurring in dialect and vulgar speech, was rare in educated usage at this time. It is noteworthy, therefore, and perhaps further evidence of Dickens's authorship, that he used this obsolete form elsewhere—e.g., in chap. 31 of the first edition of *Dombey and Son.* "Cherubim" was changed to "cherub" in later editions of *Dombey.*

by the Gentlemen King Arthurs slowed down, "it gradually became intoxicated and began to stagger about the table in an ill-conducted and disorderly manner." Here, as in many other instances, shrewd observation is tinged with Dickensian humor and animism, but there are other varieties of Dickensian humor. "Arson" Parvis tells the tale of a man in a coach accident who, after "pitching on his head where he was not sensitive, lived two-and-thirty years afterwards, and considered himself the better for the accident—roused up, as it might be." This outrageous humor is matched by another common Dickensian mode—the politely phrased, classically balanced, acidly devastating comment: "As it was a kind of conversation not altogether unprecedented in such assemblages, where most of those who spoke at all, spoke all at once, and where half of those could put no beginning to what they had to say, and the other half could put no end, the tendency of the debate was discursive, and not very intelligible."

In the latter example one detects Dickens the parliamentary reporter, after-dinner speaker, and creator of innumerable speechifying bores; one need go no further than his earliest works—"The Parlour Orator" in *Sketches by Boz,* for instance, or the famous opening scenes of the Pickwick Club in *The Pickwick Papers*—to see how persistent the theme is with Dickens. Indeed in chapter 3 of *A Message from the Sea,* in the address of the Chairman to the Gentlemen King Arthurs, there is another delightful example of inane speechmaking to add to this venerable Dickensian genre. The fact is of course that Dickens's chief interests and his special vision shaped everything that he wrote. He centered the next Christmas number of *All the Year Round* (*Tom Tiddler's Ground,* 1861) on a miserly hermit who sows his land with paltry sums of money; three years later he devoted a major strand of his last completed novel (*Our Mutual Friend,* 1864–65) to a putative miser who reads about other misers and about the treasures hidden in dust heaps. In view of Dickens's imagination and predilections, it is not surprising to find that chapter 3 of *A Message from the Sea* (1860) also contains a passage devoted to misers, in this instance an elaborate comparison between a miser and the subterranean treasures of Cornwall:

"A sing'lar thing it is," said the captain, looking round at the brown desert of rank grass and poor moss, "how like this airth is, to the men that live upon it! Here's a spot of country rich with hidden metals, and it puts on the worst rags of clothes possible, and crouches and shivers and makes believe to be so poor that it can't so much as afford a feed for a beast. Just like a human miser, ain't it?"

"But they find the miser out," returned the young fisherman, pointing to where the earth by the watercourses and along the valleys was turned up, for miles, in trying for metal.

"Ay, they find him out," said the captain; "but he makes a struggle of it even then, and holds back all he can. He's a 'cute 'un."

Personifying the land as a crouching, shivering miser is very Dickensian. The comparison itself, the imaginative insight, is new, but the fascination with misers and with grotesque comparisons is old. This was always Dickens's way—innovation combined with iteration. That we rediscover Dickens in these pages—a Dickens both familiar and unfamiliar—provides both the motive and the justification for attempting to define his canon. Everything that he wrote casts light on his total achievement and is, in turn, illumined by it. In that total achievement Captain Jorgan, a "squall of ink," an intoxicated teetotum, a metallic-faced breed of miners, and a crouching, shivering, miserly land have a modest but authentic place.

Index

Rahv, Philip, 46
Raleigh, John, 46, 47, 53
Ray, Gordon N., 200 n.
Richardson, Samuel, 117, 118
Robespierre, Maximilien François
    Marie Isidore De, 200
Rowlandson, Thomas, 135, 136 n.
Ruskin, John, vi, 22, 35, 39, 54

Sandburg, Carl, 53
Santayana, George, 1
    Soliloquies in England, 1
Sartre, Jean-Paul, 170
Schaefer, William D., 85 n.
Schiller, Frederich, 204
Scott, Sir Walter
    Antiquary, The, 68
Seymour, Robert, 129, 135
Smollett, Tobias, 56, 58
Shakespeare, William, vi, 1, 195
    Hamlet, 109
Shaw, George Bernard, v
Solomons, Israel, 136 n.
Steig, Michael, 135 n., 146
Stoehr, Taylor, 62 n.
Stone, Harry, 19 n.
Sullivan, Sir Arthur, 80
Sussman, Herbert L., 23

Taine, Hippolyte, 14
Tennyson, Alfred, 47, 65
    Maud, 65
Tennyson, Frederick, 200
Thackeray, William Makespeace, 51,
    64, 166, 174, 200

Henry Esmond, 59 n.
Thomas, Maurice W., 29 n.
Tillotson, Kathleen, 86 n., 90, 91, 155
    n., 185 n.
Tolstoy, Leo, 1
Trilling, Lionel, 60
Trollope, Anthony, 51

Van Ghent, Dorothy, 97 n.
Verlaine, Paul, 13
Vogler, Richard A., 85 n., 135
Voltaire, François Marie Arouet, 180

Wagenknecht, Edward, 182 n.
Ward, John Trevor, 29 n.
Wark, Robert, 135 n.
Watson, Hon. Mrs. Richard, 43 n.
Webb, Robert Kiefer, 26
Welsh, Alexander, 54
Whitehead, Alfred North, 9–10 n.
Wills, William Henry, 25, 26, 27, 31,
    35, 44
Wilson, Angus, 63, 91, 139 n., 167, 168,
    192
Wilson, Edmund, v, vi, 1, 15, 63
    Wound and the Bow, The, 1
Wittgenstein, Ludwig, 125
Wordsworth, William, 2, 10, 11, 12, 14,
    15, 59
    Lyrical Ballads, 11
Wood, Ellen Price (Mrs. Henry Wood)
    East Lynne, v

Yeats, William Butler, 47, 116